Bleako

Bleakonomics

A Heartwarming Introduction to
Financial Catastrophe, the Jobs Crisis
and Environmental Destruction

Rob Larson

PlutoPress
www.plutobooks.com

First published 2012 by Pluto Press
345 Archway Road, London N6 5AA

www.plutobooks.com

Distributed in the United States of America exclusively by
Palgrave Macmillan, a division of St. Martin's Press LLC,
175 Fifth Avenue, New York, NY 10010

British Library Cataloguing in Publication Data
A catalogue record for this book is available from the British Library

ISBN   978 0 7453 3268 0   Hardback
ISBN   978 0 7453 3267 3   Paperback
ISBN   978 1 8496 4785 4   PDF eBook
ISBN   978 1 8496 4787 8   Kindle eBook
ISBN   978 1 8496 4786 1   EPUB eBook

Library of Congress Cataloging in Publication Data applied for

This book is printed on paper suitable for recycling and made from fully
managed and sustained forest sources. Logging, pulping and manufacturing
processes are expected to conform to the environmental standards of the
country of origin.

10   9   8   7   6   5   4   3   2   1

Designed and produced for Pluto Press by Chase Publishing Services Ltd
Typeset from disk by Stanford DTP Services, Northampton, England
Simultaneously printed digitally by CPI Antony Rowe, Chippenham, UK and
Edwards Bros in the United States of America

Contents

Preface
The Plutonomy Papers

The United States is experiencing its worst economic conditions since the Great Depression. Even Americans in the most prosperous communities know the sight of desperate panhandlers on street corners and off-ramps. The reason for this development was thoughtfully analyzed in 2005 and 2006, when an interesting investment strategy was proposed by analysts for Citigroup, the giant "megabank" and financial services firm. The confidential investment memos, later leaked, were based on an economic phenomenon the strategists called "Plutonomy."[1] The investment strategists coined the term to mean an economy "where economic growth is powered by and largely consumed by the wealthy few." The authors consider plutonomy to have appeared in the United States in the past, for example, in the sharp levels of economic inequality seen in the 1920s, on the eve of the Great Depression.

The bank analysts refer to the good deal of recent research indicating that the majority of the US population has seen its share of national income and wealth fall significantly. The analysts' own conclusion was that these had descended to a sufficiently low level that changes in the average American's spending no longer make much difference for the broader economy: "There are rich consumers, few in number, but disproportionate in the gigantic slice of income and consumption they take. There are the rest, the 'non-rich,' the multitudinous many, but only accounting for surprisingly small bites of the national pie."

The numbers that the bank analysts use to back up their conclusion are no joke: "the top 1% of households in the US, (about 1 million households) accounted for about 20% of overall US income in 2000 ... That's about 1 million households compared with 60 million households, both with similar slices of the income pie!" More importantly, "the top 1% of households also account for 33% of net worth." And in an interesting anticipation of the Occupy Wall Street movement, the report observes that "Clearly, the analysis of the top 1% of US households is paramount."

The bank strategists believe that the sharp rise in incomes for the "uber-rich" and the return of a plutonomic system are in large part the result of the "reduction in corporate and income taxes" over recent decades, along with globalization and productivity growth. However, they expect a "potential social backlash" arising from "the post-bubble angst against celebrity CEOs" and "their bloated, very large share of the economy." Indeed, the perception seems to be that while the US and other countries "apparently tolerate income inequality … the most immediate challenge to Plutonomy comes from the political process."

Of course, being investment analysts, the entire point of the report is that it's not a problem having a tiny elite of rich households holding the reins of our economic system. They insist "We have no moral opinion on whether this income inequality is good or bad, just that it matters a great deal." The real issue brought up in their reports is instead how to make money from this development:

> We think the plutonomy is here, is going to get stronger, its membership swelling from globalized enclaves in the emerging world, we think a 'plutonomy basket' of stocks should continue to do well … Binge on Bling … These toys for the wealthy have pricing power, and staying power. They are … more desirable and demanded the more expensive they are.[2]

In other words, when you're rich enough, sports cars and yachts are for showing off, and higher sticker prices send a stronger message. Thus, Citigroup's staff concludes that this "ultra-high net worth" household consumption has now come to drive the whole system, but again "This is simply a case of mathematics, not morality." However, somewhat later in their report, they do concede that "plutonomists or capitalists … have benefited from trends like globalization and the productivity revolution, disproportionately. However, labor has, relatively speaking, lost out ... Ultimately, the rise in income and wealth inequality to some extent is an economic disenfranchisement of the masses to the benefit of the few." And while most theoretical economists have continued to say that economic growth benefits everyone, because "a rising tide lifts all boats," the Citi analysts mock this concept—they ran an investor conference subtitled "Rising Tides Lifting Yachts."

Meanwhile, the conservative London magazine, the *Economist*, described what plutonomy means for most of us:

> More than half of all workers have experienced a spell of unemployment, taken a cut in pay or hours or been forced to go part-time. The typical unemployed worker has been jobless for nearly six months. Collapsing share and house prices have destroyed a fifth of the wealth of the average household. Nearly six in ten Americans have cancelled or cut back on holidays. About a fifth say their mortgages are underwater. One in four of those between 18 and 29 have moved back in with parents. Fewer than half of all adults expect their children to have a higher standard of living than theirs, and more than a quarter say it will be lower.[3]

Crucially, the large majority of economists failed to anticipate the disastrous financial crisis of 2008, which kicked off the current period of economic decline. In the years of the $8 trillion real estate bubble that led to the crisis and recessions, most professional economists ridiculed the idea that the bubble was unstable and dangerous. While a small minority pooped the party, and will be discussed later (see Chapter 14), the majority of the profession massively failed to anticipate the monumental series of chained disasters that it triggered. If economists failed so badly at this basic test, one might ask what is the point of supporting us. Even the much-maligned weatherman can see hurricanes coming a few days away.

This book attempts to break from this embarrassing tradition and explain how we found ourselves in this mess. The approach is to look at the three main components of today's economic straits: deterioration of the world's natural systems, social conflicts arising from concentrated wealth, and the financial instability seen explosively in our recent market bubbles and crashes.

THE PLAN OF THIS BOOK

This book is laid out in three parts, each one dealing with one of the three major economic crises mentioned above. Part I, "External Damnation," is all about the environmental crisis that the world's scientists are up in arms over, considering how "external" side-effects of our economy are causing huge-scale deterioration of the planet's natural systems. The chapters within the section deal with different aspects of this process, starting with an overview in Chapter 1 and then proceeding in Chapters 2–4 to look at externalities that affect ecological systems on land, sea and air, respectively. Chapter 5 looks at the total scale of this destruction, and Chapter 6 extends the picture to the marketplace of ideas.

Part II, "Will Work For Peanuts," looks at the rough conditions of today's labor market, in the context of growing income and wealth inequality, as demonstrated by the Plutonomy Papers above. Chapters 7 and 8 discuss the importance of concentrated wealth for wielding economic power, through huge movements of wealth from place to place. Chapters 9 and 10 look at the history of the struggle between labor and concentrated wealth in US history and around the world, Chapters 11 and 12 deal with the political manifestation of these conflicts, and Chapter 13 considers how the growth of the plutonomy has reshaped our social fabric.

Finally, Part III, "The Invisible Hand Gives the Finger," considers how deregulation and growing economic inequality led to the 2008 crisis and the chain of bubbles common in today's markets. Chapter 14 deals with the causes of the market bubbles we now experience roughly every ten years. Chapter 15 answers the question of why some of our banks became "too big to fail" in the first place, while Chapter 16 looks at their future. Chapter 17 looks at the Federal Reserve's role in all this, Chapter

18 explores the financialization of food, and Chapter 19 looks at how the economics discipline could be rebuilt in the future.

ACKNOWLEDGEMENTS

This book owes a lot to many people, without whom it would never have been written. Several editors contributed greatly to drafts of several chapters. Lydia Sargent of *Z Magazine* suggested valuable changes to the chapters on class dynamics. Chris Sturr of the under-appreciated magazine *Dollars & Sense* gave useful advice for the chapters on finance. Heather Dent provided valuable commentary on many early drafts. The editors of Pluto Press provided crucial beneficial guidance that improved the book immensely. I'd also like to thank the faculty at the University of Missouri-Kansas City for being ready to break from economic orthodoxy, and my parents for reading to me as a child and keeping books around the house.

Despite these generous contributions, any errors in this book are my responsibility.

Part I

External Damnation:
The Market's Unintended
Impact on the Environment

Introduction to Part I:
"Externalities" in Theory

Capitalism is considered by economists to be the best possible economic system, mostly because of the action of an "invisible hand." First conceived by economist Adam Smith, the invisible hand is a metaphor for the market's ability to generate the best possible outcome. Since consumers are free to choose what goods and services they want to buy, and companies are free to produce what they choose, by freely exchanging products, all can be satisfied. The "invisible hand" creates an optimal situation, since suppliers produce what consumers want to buy, satisfying the customers and the company making the goods or services. In this way, without any oversight, markets will efficiently direct resources to their most efficient and productive use.

However, there are some problems with this sunny portrait of the market economy, and you experience one every time your neighbor's car alarm gets on your nerves. For unregulated markets to perform as described in theory, the prices for goods in the market must include the full costs of their production and consumption. In other words, no costs of making or using a product can fall on anyone or anything else, if the invisible hand is going to create the best result. But, if there are costs that fall on others, outside an economic transaction, then significant inefficiencies can arise. These damages to parties outside a market transaction, or "externalities," can end up assuming a monumental scale, as will be seen in Part I.

The approach of most conventional economists to this issue is to assume that external costs are not very common, and not very important where they do exist. External costs are considered to be rare and far between, and where they do arise, the tendency is to treat them as easily fixed, with vague government policies or extensions of property rights. But all these easy fixes still assume that externalities are rare enough to be dealt with individually.

But the reality is that external costs are extremely common. The nice smell of your neighbor's barbecue is an example of a positive externality, and your insomnia when she buys new sub-woofers would be a negative one. These externalities are treated as rare occurrences in economic theory, but the fact is that external effects of our actions are everywhere. As the *Harvard Business Review* puts it, "Virtually every activity in a company's value chain touches on the communities in which the firm operates, creating either positive or negative social consequences."[1]

A few economists, for example, E.K. Hunt and Ralph d'Arge, do take externalities seriously as a theoretical issue, and the theory that results is a far cry from the efficient invisible hand. They conclude that most economic theory fails to address the fact that

> ... externalities are totally pervasive. Most of the millions of acts of consumption (and production) in which we daily engage involve externalities. In a market economy *any* action of one individual or enterprise which induces pleasure or pain in any other individual or enterprise and is unpriced by a market constitutes an externality ... [such as] the upwind factory that emits large quantities of sulfur oxides and particulate matter inducing rising probabilities of emphysema, lung cancer, and other respiratory diseases to residents downwind.[2]

Indeed, the ability to dump costs on others in a market economy means it can pay to create "bads," rather than goods, since you may be compensated for restraining your production of them.

But besides their commonness and their tendency to create market bads, externalities are aggregative—they add up and interact and change. So an economic system that frequently generates negative external costs and bads will tend to see them pile up and combine into serious problems. The chapters in Part I deal with how this has happened in our economy. Chapter 1, for example, looks at the combined effects of lost natural habitat and how it interacts with rising global temperatures from climate change. Chapter 3 looks at the mutually reinforcing dangers of ocean warming and acidification, Chapter 4 looks at power plant emissions and rain forest burning, and so on.

In the end, it turns out that on this issue alone the market economy can be judged to be fundamentally inefficient because of its snowballing "external" costs. Few attempts have been made to judge how the total value of these costs compares to all the benefits of the market, measured in GDP, the official total value of our economy's production. Some small steps to address this are included in Chapter 5; however, it is a fact that for the vast majority of economists, economic performance does not count market bads, only goods.

1

Come Hell and High Water: Scientists Indict Capitalism

In 2009, the prestigious research journal *Science* published a surprising article called "Looming Global-Scale Failures and Missing Institutions" in which an international team of eminent biologists, climatologists, ecologists, and economists reviewed the long list of current global problems and came to an ominous conclusion: "Energy, food, and water crises; climate disruption; declining fisheries; increasing ocean acidification; emerging diseases; and increasing antibiotic resistance are examples of serious, intertwined global-scale challenges spawned by the accelerating scale of human activity. They are outpacing the development of institutions to deal with them and their many interactive effects."[1]

The frank article is accompanied by an illustration, with arrows showing the many connections between "Global drivers," like rising atmospheric greenhouse gas concentration, increasing per capita resource use and nuclear proliferation on one hand, and "Unwanted outcomes" for the Climate, Ecosystem, Human Health, and the Economy on the other (see Figure 1.1). For dispassionate scientists, these are fighting words. Interestingly, the illustration also shows a silhouetted crowd rising up, and raising a giant pair of scissors, seeming to cut these ties. The article amounts to an indictment of capitalism by the important section of the professional class engaged in the hard sciences, as the tough standards of science push them up against the realities of market externalities and US policy. Their conclusions are highly relevant for an understanding of what's happening to the natural systems we count on.

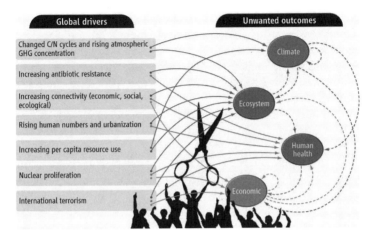

Figure 1.1

ANTICLIMATIC CLIMATE

A central point of the article is the interconnectedness of the various "global-scale failures," and their tendency to combine in unexpected ways. A good example is climate change, which influences several "unwanted outcomes." Consider its effect on biodiversity—the presence in different ecosystems of the rich variety of organisms that naturally occur in different environments. Studies point to the "many benefits" biodiversity provides to environmental systems, including "increased community stability, increased resistance to invasive species, and higher resistance to diseases."[2] But besides these important benefits to the ecosystem, biodiversity also provides enormous economic benefits, including "material goods (for example, food, timber, medicines, and fiber), underpinning functions (flood control, climate regulation, and nutrient cycling), and nonmaterial benefits such as recreation."[3] A good deal of recent research shows biodiversity has continued to decline (see Chapter 5). But some recent studies suggest that its loss due to climate change may be reduced by simple geographic variation. In other words, plant and animal species may be able to partially adapt to a warming regional climate by moving uphill to cooler temperatures, or to greater latitudes where temperatures tend to be lower.

Sounds good, but here the different "global drivers" interact in an unexpected way. The research also suggests that this adaptive ability is itself weakened by the very widespread reduction of available habitat, due to another "global driver," growth of urbanization. Habitat has shrunk to the point that "Over 75% of the Earth's terrestrial biomes now show evidence of alteration as a result of human residence and land use."[4] Their conclusion is that the ability of biodiversity to resist climate-driven decline through migration depends on the character of the developed areas around the remaining habitat fragments—that is, farms are somewhat more conducive to the migration of animal species than paved urban sprawl. Given that urbanization is a classic feature of capitalist development, it's not surprising to find it interacting with another driver, climate change. The article closes by noting ominously that "conservation will require a whole new definition of what is 'natural.'"

While climate change has come to be seen as a controversial issue in the US, among scientists it is considered well-demonstrated. One of many typical articles in the scientific journals summarizes recent research, finding that "Over the past 50 years, human influences have been the dominant detectable influence on climate change ... There is no doubt that the composition of the atmosphere is changing because of human activities, and today greenhouse gases are the largest human influence on global climate ... Anthropogenic climate change is now likely to continue for many centuries."[5] One important dynamic affecting this conclusion is the presence of "feedbacks"—parts of the climate system that are both affected by global heating and reinforce it themselves. Examples include water vapor, which is a greenhouse gas—it contributes to the trapping of energy from the sun, without which life as we know it would not exist on Earth. But as the planet warms due to CO_2 emissions, warmer air can hold more water vapor, reinforcing climate change. Likewise with another feedback mechanism, snow and ice cover. Warming reduces the size of glaciers and snow packs, revealing the darker soils and rocks beneath. Soil has a lower albedo (reflectiveness) than snow, and it absorbs more heat, like a black shirt on a sunny day. This traps more energy, which snow and ice would have reflected back into space. These and other feedbacks aggravate climate change, and make the whole picture somewhat more unpredictable—as the paper concludes, "We are entering the unknown with our climate."

The consequences of this dark prognosis have become everyday news, such as the resolution of a territorial dispute between India and Bangladesh over the tiny New Moore Island. The dispute was settled in 2010, when the isle was submerged under rising waters.[6] Elsewhere, the island groups of Tuvalu and Tokelau in the South Pacific are struggling with a lack of drinkable water, caused in part by the normal La Niña weather pattern, which blows rainfall west of the islands. However, the well water normally relied upon by these islands is now undrinkable, as it has become contaminated with salt water from the rising sea levels.[7]

But of course, despite this ongoing confirmation of the broad scientific agreement on climate change and its human origins, environmentalists have had to make a Herculean effort merely to get the climate issue onto the public radar. This has included overcoming the heavy opposition of industry-funded "climate skeptics," and a politicized media happy to take cheap shots at climate research. The peak of this was the media-manufactured "Climategate" in late 2009, when leaked e-mails from prominent climatologists were presented as refuting the claims of a warming earth and violating scientific propriety. To the extent the hysterical coverage had a point, it was that the scientists had adopted a "circle the wagons" mentality when challenged. Of course, this may itself reflect the fact that, as NASA climate researcher Gavin Schmidt put it, "You can't have a spelling mistake in a paper without it being evidence on the floor of the Senate that the system is corrupt."[8]

This politics-driven excess of caution by some climate scientists was seized upon by the commercial media to prove the untrustworthiness of smarty-pants scientists who want to take away your SUV, and further examples were manufactured to suit:

One was the exclusion of "climate skeptic" work from Inter-governmental Panel on Climate Change (IPCC) papers (which were in fact cited in the end); another was a quote pulled out of context, seeming to indicate that climatologists "can't account for the lack of warming at the moment," but this was in fact a reference to the need for a broader weather observation system, as the surrounding sentences made transparently clear. Further claims made in the feverish denunciations of the global effort to study climate effects were outright falsehoods, especially claims that the scientists were withholding data—which are widely known to be available for study from the US National Oceanic and Atmospheric Administration (NOAA) and the UK Met Office. Of course, surprising or dismaying results from other fields of science are not subject to the hysterical distortions that climatology receives, since their results do not currently conflict with unrestrained consumption under capitalism.

THE DEAD ELEPHANT IN THE ROOM

Another "global driver" described by the scientists is "Increasing connectivity (economic, social, ecological)." These unpredictable interacting effects of our institutions are a key element of the article, represented by the maze of interacting global drives and unwanted outcomes in the illustration. While economic theory encourages us to think of human activity as being basically self-contained, recently awareness of these unexpected connections among different social and natural elements has found an unlikely home, the *Wall Street Journal* (*WSJ*).

In a discussion of the current financial crisis, the *WSJ* concedes that the social costs of economic activity are not always the same as the private costs. Using the example of traveling by train, the passengers on the train are willing to pay based on their saved time and the railroad is willing to provide the service in exchange for a certain return, but outside parties are left out of the decision to buy—such as owners of property around the line that may experience pollution or fire hazard from rail sparks. In economics textbooks, these economic side-effects are called "spillovers" or "externalities," and are usually treated as relatively innocuous nuisances like traffic congestion—fixable with mild reforms.

But the *WSJ* article, in an uncharacteristic move, admits that externalities lie behind some of our biggest problems:

> In banking, the negative spillover can be catastrophic. Many millions of households and firms rely on credit to finance their expenditures. If this credit is suddenly curtailed, spending can fall precipitously throughout the economy. That is what we witnessed at the end of last year ... reforming health care can also be viewed as a counter-spillover policy. Sick people who don't have health insurance often end up using emergency rooms, which imposes a cost on the insured, perhaps as much as $1,000 per person per year ... Global warming presents perhaps the most dramatic example of what can happen if spillovers are ignored.[9]

Startling words from the deregulation-mongers at the *Wall Street Journal*.

We can find more "connectivity" between commerce and ecosystems by noting that international wildlife bodies are being asked by the governments of Zambia and Tanzania to lessen the protection levels of their endangered elephants. Countries can request that the Convention on International Trade in Endangered Species "downlist" their elephant populations if their animals are safe and their endangered classification is being enforced. This downlisting would relax restrictions on sale of elephant ivory, with the largest importers being China, the US, and Japan, primarily for ornamentation. Unfortunately, the countries claiming their elephant populations are secure were implicated in recent ivory poaching busts, such as when "the largest single ivory seizure since the ivory trade ban (6.5 tons in Singapore) in 2002 was shown by DNA analyses to have originated almost entirely from Zambia."[10]

Yet these tons of ivory in the Singapore bust, from thousands of killed elephants, are worth a mere $1 million or so. Small potatoes in world trade, but decent from the point of view of African commerce. This is the nature of externalities in the market economy—with elephant numbers in decline, the future existence of the species is in the balance, but the value of this to the ivory "industry" is zero. This also holds for the many other species that depend on the elephant for their life-cycles, numerous enough for the African elephant to be called a "keystone species:" "Local extirpation of the primary seed disperser of large trees in Central African forests may substantially affect long-term viability of the second most important carbon capture forests in the world." So the African elephant, and the ecosystem it is crucial to, are in existential peril for relatively small amounts, less than 1 percent of the annual tourism revenue of Tanzania alone. But externalities like multiple species' survival aren't accounted for by market transactions, so this "connectivity" driver is again mainly the offspring of capitalist economic forms and their cost "externalizing."

SICK OF PROFIT

Other global problems on the list include two serious global health issues, antibiotic resistance and the swine flu epidemic. Antibiotic resistance refers to the increasing prevalence of bacteria that have evolved resistance to antibiotic compounds, usually in hospitals or health clinics where antibiotics are commonly used. The issue has taken on serious proportions, with numerous genera of bacteria that cause serious infections now "resistant to virtually all of the older antibiotics," as *Science* reports.[11] The role of capitalist forms in contributing to this problem is rarely explored, but the connections are not obscure. Examples from the clinical literature would include a paper published in the *Lancet—Infectious Diseases* journal by a number of Australian epidemiologists, who note that "overcrowding and understaffing in hospitals increase the incidence of HAIs [health-care-acquired infections]."[12] The researchers' survey found that high hospital bed occupancy rates and periods of understaffing of hospital/clinic staff are strongly associated with outbreaks of antibiotic-resistant bacteria and other infections. Not only general cost-cutting, but also other "flexible" labor practices by hospitals play a role, since the movement of hospitals toward "float" or "pool" staff that move from hospital unit to unit with demand, are also correlated with HAIs. The authors specifically note that profit drives this process, as "A common strategy to decrease health-care system costs has been to replace registered nurses with nursing assistants, and to reduce the proportion of full-time staff." In other words, the more health care workers are understaffed, undertrained, and shifted around by institutional demand, the less hand-washing gets done and more resistant microorganisms are spread.

Turning to the swine flu pandemic of 2009–10, the fingerprints of capitalism are present, in the wild divergence in vaccine access. At the peak of the pandemic, health experts bemoaned a tightly limited supply of vaccine donated to developing countries, in the neighborhood of 1 percent of total need—the only consolation was given by Tido von Schoen-Angerer of Doctors Without Borders, who noted that the H1N1 strain was mild by pandemic standards.[13] Yet the very same day, the business press reported an "uproar" as vaccine doses, in a program to treat "high-risk adults," were distributed to several bailed-out Wall Street banks at a time when many New York City hospitals had no doses.[14] The banks, including Goldman Sachs, Citigroup, and Morgan Stanley, had their public criticism cranked up yet another notch. In the end, Morgan Stanley ended up chickening out and sent its doses to city hospitals, after the *Wall Street Journal* called this "another PR headache."

Wall Street may have been relying on connections with major clients for its preferential vaccine access, including pharmaceutical giants like GlaxoSmithKline of the UK. Glaxo has pioneered a new Big Pharma niche as a supplier of vaccines and related equipment to governments, especially crucial as the old profit-center of pharmaceutical manufacturing, drug patents, are expiring. Glaxo was accused of profiteering after an *Evening Standard* article claiming its $10 flu shot cost a mere $1.60 to produce.[15] Glaxo claimed this alleged 80-plus percent profit margin was high of the mark, while its CEO stated "We're not trying to generate here some crazy level of profit—but equally, our shareholders wouldn't want us to do this for anything other than a return."[16]

THE FOG OF BLOWBACK

Another driver of "global failure" decried by the scientists is international terrorism, with the researchers claiming a need for more international cooperation to reduce terrorist violence. These professionals unfortunately leave out the pivotal role of the US in contributing to this problem. The best immediate post-9/11 analysis was in the conservative *Wall Street Journal*, which reported for its elite readership that even prosperous, pro-West Muslims see the September 11th attacks as "a desperate call to America to rethink its support of Israel and, more subliminally, of authoritarian Mideast rulers who deny democracy to ordinary Muslims."[17] The "subliminal" connection to Arab authoritarians is very real—of the 19 9/11 hijackers, there were 15 Saudis, two from the United Arab Emirates, one Egyptian, and one Lebanese. In other words, all but one hijacker came from a country with an American-backed tyrannical government—that's 95 percent of the hijackers coming from US-supported dictatorships (see Chapter 10).

In another article, the conservative newspaper reported that

Anti-Americanism has ... taken root among well-educated middle-class professionals and businesspeople in the Arab and Muslim worlds, born of frustrations much closer to home: the perception that unlimited American power is responsible for propping up hated, oppressive regimes ... Many Arabs and Muslims feel the normal ways societies pick themselves up— developing their economies, renewing their government—aren't available to them again because the US has propped up oppressive regimes.[18]

The *Journal* added that even among elite, US- or UK-educated Arabs and Muslims,

... resentment runs high toward the US and its colonial forebears in Europe for maintaining authoritarian political systems across the Mideast that have resisted all efforts at liberalization ... This sense of betrayal by an America perceived as touting democracy but propagating authoritarian- ism is echoed in all corners of the Muslim world. It is heard in Morocco, Syria and Jordan, where long-ruling strongmen have died in recent years, only to have their sons elevated to power in sumptuous coronations with full American support. It is heard in Algeria, Egypt and Turkey, where secular, American-backed regimes dominated by the military thwart Islamic activists from winning seats in parliament. And it is heard in the oil-rich Persian Gulf countries, where even wealthy businesspeople are growing tired of what they see as a US double standard.

This analysis by the *Journal*'s excellent staff was not limited to post-9/11 soul-searching—in a less-noted article on Donald Rumsfeld, the newspaper noted that

... despite the [Bush] administration's oft-stated pledge to democratize the Middle East, the military's US Central Command ... has a somewhat different emphasis. Its top priority is to help existing government in the region beef up their security to provide a 'protective shield' against al-Qaeda ... In most cases, that means increasing intelligence-sharing with nondemocratic regimes, providing more counterterrorism training and participating in exercises with their militaries. The hope is that once the regimes are more secure, power will slowly devolve to their people.[19]

Amusingly, the *Journal*'s editorial page remains a right-wing ranting ground, since apparently the editors don't read their own journalists' reporting that the military's "focus is more on stability than the democratizing that the administration often cites ... In the near term ... that might involve bolstering the position of nondemocratic regimes." That "near term" goes back 60 or 70 years now.

Finally, turning to the war in Afghanistan, we might draw attention to the "Eikenberry cables," a pair of memoranda from the US ambassador to Afghanistan, to the US State Department, which made headlines when leaked in November 2009. Almost the entirety of the press attention went to Eikenberry's strong skepticism of ultimate success for the Afghanistan escalation, but a real gem of international affairs went unnoticed: "Beyond Karzai himself, there is no political ruling class that provides an overarching national identity that transcends local affiliations and provides reliable partnership."[20] The actual origins of Islamic terrorism, which the scientists reasonably see as another driver of global failure, should now be clear. The US is experiencing what the CIA calls "blowback" from its support for Saudi kings and Egyptian dictators.

The "missing institutions" called for by the scientists could be realized in a revitalized UN and in expansion of related institutions like the World Health Organization. However, the real missing institutions are those that would allow citizens to control their own economies and societies. While public opinion has long called for serious action on climate, stronger regulations to cope with externalities, and a leading UN role in world affairs over US unilateralism, it is institutions of state and capital that decide these issues. To replace this world of elite control with a different vision of a democratic economy, the unusual illustration accompanying the scientists' analysis may be right—the people will have to rise up and cut the strings themselves.

2

Hug Them While They Last:
Costs Beyond the Pump

The first law in American history meant to address the threat of climate change passed the US House of Representatives in June 2009. Unfortunately, the bill went on to die in the Senate, as the slim Democratic majority did not unite behind the measure, but the American Clean Energy and Security Act (ACESA) did secure some praise for the Obama administration. The prominent economist Paul Krugman described it as a "remarkable achievement," while the *New York Times* called it "an important beginning," although both criticized the bill's limitations.[1] Obama himself called it "a historic piece of legislation" that would "finally create a set of incentives that will spark a clean energy transformation in our economy." The legislation creates a "cap-and-trade" regime, where companies that emit large amounts of carbon dioxide must buy permits to do so. This encourages firms to reduce greenhouse output, and, by also allowing firms to trade permits, a market price for climate warming is created. The goal, in other words, is to harness the power of the market to fight the threat of catastrophic climate change, "incentivizing" private investment in the development of alternative energy.

But in reality, the whole problem of human-produced climate change itself shows the inherent limitations of modern capitalism and the market system. The climate menace is an expression of what economists call "market failure" of two major types: the presence of "externalities" and "common goods." To see this vividly, we can consider a striking concrete example—across the world, trees are migrating and dying in ever-greater numbers. It turns out that public policy is missing the forest for the bleached stumps it was turned into.

DEADWOOD RISING

The climate bill passed by only seven votes in the House, the opposition being lead by the GOP and including Representative Paul Broun of Georgia, who claimed that "scientists all over this world say that the idea of human-induced global climate change is one of the greatest hoaxes perpetrated out of the scientific community ... There is no scientific consensus." Yet the actual scientists tell another story.

In January 2009, the journal *Science* published a study of tree death in the western United States. Analyzing old-growth forest stands with trees averaging 450 years old, the scientists found tree mortality to be growing rapidly, and across many criteria. Trees were experiencing a rapid and "synchronous" die-off, among many different species, at different altitudes, at various locations across the American West. Since mortality was increasing in sync across tree categories, other possible explanations were eliminated, leading the scientists to find that "regional warming may be the dominant contributor to the increases in tree mortality rates ... by increasing water deficits and thus drought stress on trees" and by "enhancing the growth and reproduction of insects and pathogens that attack trees."[2]

Elsewhere, the *Proceedings of the National Academy of the Sciences* recently featured research on tree migration in the American West. Controlling for other factors, their findings showed dramatic tree migration upslope—that is, up hills and mountain ranges to higher elevations, due to the warming climate and resulting water stress.[3] A separate Swedish analysis published in the May 2009 *Journal of Ecology* documents scientists' discovery that Scandinavian forest ranges have risen about a meter a year for the past 85 years, in response to climate pressures.[4] And a study of Mexican spruce fossil pollen confirms that rising temperatures will drive tree species into higher mountain regions, but this migration will be limited since "the extent of land currently committed to urban and agricultural use represents a considerable, novel impediment to range shifts of tree populations," and also "implausibly higher migration rates would be necessary for plant populations to match climate shifts in the future."[5] Representative Broun was right about the worldwide character of current climate research, but of course wrong about its conclusions.

With abundant and growing evidence for the effects of greenhouse climate forcing, it's revealing that this subject of scientific inquiry gets very different treatment in public discourse from other areas of science. Research on gene therapy to fight cancer is naturally taken seriously, since it's of great value, most especially to those with money and power. Yet scientific concern about the environmental consequences of our lucrative energy system must be an unholy scientific conspiracy to strangle economic growth. As long as science is coming up with baldness cures and sex performance drugs for obese Americans, no problem, but telling us to rationally invest in new energy forms is sure to be a hoax—even if it comes from the Intergovernmental Panel on Climate Change, the biggest scientific research endeavor in world history.[6] The political market for science is conclusion specific.

But this isn't the only failing market to consider. The very existence of climate change is the result of the market's weaknesses, one of which is the presence of negative externalities.

NATURAL COLLATERAL DAMAGE

Externalities are unintended side-effects of the market economy—impacts of commercial transactions that fall outside the two parties to the transaction. When a consumer buys, for example, gardening tools and materials, a positive externality is experienced by others in the community as the consumer uses the materials to make an attractive garden, which everyone in the community can enjoy and benefit from. On the other hand, if a consumer hires a contractor to cut down the trees on his property in order to park an extra car, the community experiences a negative externality as the scenic beauty, shade, animal habitat and fresh air provided by the trees are lost.

So externalities can be positive or negative, but for the companies that organize the production of goods and services in the capitalist economy, they are to be ignored. Since externalities do not directly affect the responsible parties, profitability is not harmed by them. This principle has lead to some enormous economic impacts—for example, the large-scale outsourcing of US mass production has had massive external effects, including the decline of large urban regions in the US due to depressed demand, the resulting increase in crime, and rising family strain and domestic abuse. These are external side-effects of corporate investment strategies; since they don't directly hurt earnings, American capital has pushed forward in spite of the side-effects.

Climate change is an external effect of burning fossil fuels for energy. When you buy and drive a car, the carbon emissions affect everyone through their contribution to climate forcing. Likewise, when a consumer turns on the lights in a state powered by coal-fired plants, she's unlikely to think of the external climate impacts of burning the coal that keeps the lights on. Yet auto exhaust and coal combustion are the two leading contributors to the elevated levels of carbon dioxide that the allegedly nonexistent scientific consensus says are heating and destabilizing the climate.

This means that rising tree mortality is not only an externality, but a *second-order* externality. If producers and consumers of energy can't be expected to include the costs of climate warming in their affairs, there's not much chance they'll include the effects of climate warming on everything else. This includes the increased variability of the water cycle, and the earlier, heavier melts of mountain snow that leave trees with a longer summer drought and more water stress. Few consumers are thinking of secondary consequences while behind the wheel.

Furthermore, the loss of forest space constitutes a loss of habitat to forest-dwelling species of plants and animals. Even as trees are adapting to warming somewhat by upslope migration, a report in the *American Journal of Botany* confirms that "it might take 13 generations to adapt to climate change, but 13 generations in a tree species is on the order of millennia, whereas pronounced warming will occur on the scale of decades."[7] And in the meantime, the uphill migration of forests puts additional pressure on high-altitude ecosystems, such as the "alpine" habitats where scientists report that "mountain biota, like cold-loving polar species, have fewer options for coping … these islands of tundra are Noah's ark refuges where whole ecosystems, often left over from glacial times, are now stranded amid uncrossable seas of warm lowlands."[8] These animal and tree declines will represent a *third-order* externality of the market. It's hard to see how the market includes these ripple effects in its immediate pricing. In fact, externalities are destroying the great outdoors.

So the dying trees of the American Rockies are evidence of a fundamental problem with the market economy. Most economists defend the market despite its record of environmental devastation, pointing to the market's ability to process information as one of its compelling merits. Markets allegedly communicate information about the scarcity and value of goods by allowing supply and demand to adapt to each other, requiring no bloated public structure to gather information and make production/consumption decisions. Regrettably, what the whole climate phenomenon suggests is that the market does not in fact process and deliver information efficiently. It delivers short-term, limited information about the immediate commercial value of goods to individuals, and nothing about the long-term or external impacts on other people, future generations, or the requirements of natural systems. Rational social planning organized along democratic lines, requiring broad public participation, would be a meaningful alternative.

But bad as it seems, this inability to account for externalities is only part of the failure of markets illustrated by rising tree deaths and altitudes. The other has to do with a category of goods and services that benefit everyone: "common goods."

MONEY GROWN ON TREES

Common goods are those that are naturally available for everyone to enjoy, like the oxygen produced by plants, or sunsets. These natural goods have real value; in fact, our lives depend on them, to say nothing of our civilization. Trees are excellent examples, as they provide many valuable common benefits to humanity—benefits that scientists call "ecosystem services," such as limiting floods through soil retention, or providing shade in place of expensive climate controls, or important windblocks for crops. Not to speak of simple prettiness. Other critical benefits of trees and forests to the broader ecosystem include a major role in the nutrient cycles, and of course the provision of habitat to animals and other plants, giving precious support to biodiversity (see Chapter 5).

Growing plants also absorb carbon dioxide and incorporate it into their tissues, using energy from sunlight. In a world where "cap-and-trade" regimes like ACESA are turning carbon emissions into commodities with dollar values, this "carbon sequestration" becomes a common good. We all benefit from trees and other photosynthetic organisms pulling carbon out of the air, as it limits climate forcing. Climatologists call growing forests "carbon sinks," since they absorb carbon dioxide. But when trees die, they decay and release their carbon back into the atmosphere, acting as "carbon sources." For temperate and tundra forests, the positive climate effects of the carbon sink is reduced by the low albedo of forests—they are darker than plains or crops, which warms the area around them. But since the forests of North America have been gradually recovering after being substantially cleared during settlement of the US and Canada, they are now a significant and valuable carbon sink, pulling carbon out of the atmosphere and thus somewhat reducing climate warming.[9] While this carbon sink will decline as the forests mature and tree growth slows, the service is meaningful and far better than the alternative—when logged, trees and stumps decay, releasing the stored carbon back into the atmosphere.

Notably, while these benefits of trees are important, they are limited in their carbon uptake potential relative to the huge growth in anthropogenic emissions of carbon into the atmosphere. A paper in *Science* examined the possibility of fighting future climate change by planting more trees, thus increasing the carbon sink. The data suggests that the potential increase in carbon uptake would be "not insignificant, but it is small relative to the projected CO_2 concentration ... The main challenges for avoiding excessive climate change are to curb carbon emissions from energy and transport systems and to avoid deforestation. Enhanced carbon storage on land can play a small but important role."[10]

So today's dying and retreating trees represent the transformation of a common good into a common *bad*—a negative development that affects everyone. Just as with the rainforest burned for agriculture, once beautiful and ecologically valuable trees are now self-reinforcing contributors to the overheating of the earth's surface. What this points to is a major market weakness, the snowballing of neglected external impacts of market transactions, which may aggregate into serious problems.

WILTED HOPES

Obama's climate bill itself is emblematic of his administration's "neoliberal" contours (see Chapter 11). While the bill does mandate that carbon emission rights must be purchased, the "cap-and-trade" legislation bent over backwards to avoid actually costing polluters anything. This is clear first in the actual cap, which is quite high relative to that required by the international Kyoto Protocol. The ACESA required reductions of 17 percent in total emissions from 2005 by 2020. Kyoto, which is itself considered by climate scientists to be light in its requirements, demands a 5.2 percent reduction over *1990* levels by 2012. The first indication this bill lacks real teeth is that the "ceiling" to be imposed on greenhouse emissions is a rather high one.

But even more telling is the "auction" issue, a major sticking point during the drafting process. The question is whether the permits that energy companies must hold to emit carbon should be free or auctioned off at some price. While Obama's budget originally planned on several million dollars in emission permit auction revenues, energy lobbyists and congressional conservatives have campaigned mightily against having to pay to emit. In the end, the bill would have given away a full 85 percent of the permits, the practice to continue for an unspecified transition period.[11] Thus the House Republicans and Democrats agreed that it should be some time before polluters pay a dime for the climate impacts of their emissions. In the end, they got their wish since the bill failed to clear the then Democratic Senate.

A final neoliberal element of the bill can be seen in Obama's own reaction to it. While apparently satisfied, there was an element in the House's version of the bill he had hoped the Senate would strip, namely the imposition of tariff taxes on imports from countries that fail to limit or price carbon dioxide emissions.[12] This is especially telling because the proposed tariffs would not take effect until 2020, giving developing countries a full decade to ease into local carbon-reduction schemes. However, the neoliberal orientation of Obama's economic staff is not about to countenance trade barriers that fail to benefit US corporations invested in overseas export platforms.

CLIMATE OF OPINION

The spectrum of debate on the climate bill is as limited as can be expected from the commercial press. The right wing of debate is suggested by Representative Broun above, giving the tenor of the anti-scientific conspiracy theories making the rounds of talk radio. As for the liberal end, we find Paul Krugman and the *New York Times* editorial board partially dissenting from the Democrats' bill on the grounds of its limitations, mainly for giving away the permits without charge. However, there is little mention of the fact that the ceiling being put on emissions is significant higher than the Kyoto target, and far higher than the amount proposed by the scientific community if we are to avoid real climate disruption.

The *Times* editorial also has a line that is an especially charming instance of devotion to power—the bill "would show that the United States is ready to lead and would pressure other countries to follow." As anyone who follows climate policy will know, that's a real howler. The US has yet to so much as ratify Kyoto, although the rest of the developed nations and even

Russia have signed on. The US is ready to lead from behind, once again.

Of course, the *Times* editors and other liberals are right that the bill has some value just for establishing the principle that a price will be attached to carbon emissions. And we might wonder what has allowed this issue to become a national political priority. The answer is provided by the *Wall Street Journal*, which informs us that this issue has satisfied the real-world criterion for political importance: the business elite now has diverging opinions on the subject. As the *Journal* puts it, "Business factions split on the measure. The Edison Electric Institute, which represents investor-owned utilities, backs it. Other companies—particularly those with big investments in alternatives to fossil fuels—praised the vote" while "The US Chamber of Commerce and the National Association of Manufacturers lobbied against passage" along with "Groups that represent airlines, oil producers and mining companies."[13] Likewise, when the bill died in the Senate, the press reported "the outcome was also viewed as a setback by some utility executives who had hoped that Congress would set predictable rules governing carbon pollution."[14]

This development is very similar to health care, which also became a prominent national issue requiring public action. Again, the change is due to the "external" costs of a particular industry piling up to the point that other industries' earnings are impacted. In the case of health care, the preposterously high costs of private insurance and treatment in the US have seriously harmed large segments of US capital, and have even become a factor in driving investment overseas—the auto industry has publicly noted its huge potential savings in merely moving to Canada, where unit health expenses are about one-tenth of the US level.[15] So some factions of capital are moved to demand lower system-wide health costs, inevitably meaning some form of public provision (see Chapter 11).

The same is true for climate change. As its costs have become clearer and larger, more elements of US capital favor regulation and reduction of total emissions, as the *Wall Street Journal* describes. Of course, public opinion is quite past all this and has favored public action for some time, including ratification of international treaties with binding emissions reduction targets.[16] The situation is again similar to health care, where some type of national health program has been popular for many years. But what has moved the subject onto Congress's and the President's agenda hasn't just been public opinion, but also the inability of an industry to continue externalizing its costs relentlessly.

THE STUMP OF LIFE

Many peoples have considered trees to be symbolic of natural orders. Many pre-Columbian cultures revered a sacred tree, especially Mesoamerican cultures like the Aztec, Maya, and Olmec. Thought to represent their creation myths and the breadth of the world, trees are heavily used in these societies' iconography and surely influenced how they treated the trees in their regions. Now the trees in neighboring parts of western Mexico and the US are parched from second-order effects of the market economy. Actually enacting parameters for American cap-and-trade would reduce this, but the issue suggests that the externalizing machine we call capitalism would be best replaced by rational social planning on a participatory, democratic basis. As the dominant right wing cries "Communism" at even the mildest centrist reforms, that replacement seems far off. But the longer we wait, the more our life-nurturing forests will wither in the drought of market irrationality.

3
Hot Water:
Capitalism's "Best Economic Case"

In June 2010, as the eyes of the world were focused on the relentless torrent of BP crude billowing into the Gulf of Mexico, the leading American research journal *Science* released a special issue on the world's "Changing Oceans."[1] Unsurprisingly, the news was dark, but the clear sense of mounting alarm in the scientific community makes the collected articles only more compelling, as they provide the context for the conditions of the world's seas *before* the emerging era of huge spills from deepwater drilling.

Researching the effects of huge spills is still a young field, but clearly the consequences of the oceans' current problems will be felt for generations, diminishing the seas for future citizens. Unborn generations are thus injured by this activity, regardless of not being involved—again, externalities. The ocean scientists' conclusions, while guarded and understated in the manner of the profession, largely back up the positions of the environmental movement and critics of our economic system, a development we would be foolish to be unfamiliar with.

THE BLACK-AND-BLUE SEAS

The "Changing Oceans" special issue kicks off with a summary of recent research on ocean acidification, an additional and less-known side effect of rising CO_2 levels. The ocean's pH has dropped radically, with studies finding a 30 percent increase in surface-level acidity over just 15 years.[2] The normally reserved geochemists aren't holding back: "Aside from the dinosaur-killing asteroid impact, the world has probably never seen the likes of what's brewing in today's oceans. By spewing carbon dioxide from smokestacks and tailpipes at a gigatons-per-year pace, humans are conducting a grand geophysical experiment, not just on climate but on the oceans as well." The scientists go on to compare this development with a previous world extinction event, the Paleocene-Eocene Thermal Maximum, with less total carbon involved but entering the oceans far faster.

The problem is that as oceans acidify even moderately, many ecologically crucial organisms are losing their ability to function. A research survey by Woods Hole Oceanographic Institute chemists found that all species of tropical coral slowed their growth process in conditions of lowered pH. The Great Barrier Reef of Australia, for example, has experienced a 14.2 percent drop in calcification since 1990, indicating the reef's structure is growing more slowly, with no sign of a previous drop of this magnitude. The issue is especially serious because the world's corals are already reeling from "bleaching" in higher global temperatures—a condition more difficult to recover from in acidic conditions. Acidification is also causing some varieties of plankton to form thinner, lighter shells than over the past millennia, as are sea snails and oyster larvae. The significance of this is that these organisms are crucial for the broader ecosystem—oysters and especially coral provide essential habitat for untold thousands of ocean organisms, and plankton and mollusks are at the bases of the marine food web. Any decline in these organisms will likewise spread up the chain and weaken the ocean's other systems.

The scientists go on to consider ship noise, the profoundly loud, low-frequency, underwater din from the world's 100,000 or so large commercial ships. The deep-register noise from global commerce is

> ... swamping low-frequency wavelengths that whales and other sea creatures use to communicate, find mates, and navigate their watery world. Researchers worry that the cacophony is making it even harder for these creatures to overcome the numerous human threats—from toxic pollution to overexploitation—that have already pushed some to the edge of extinction.

Despite the especially disruptive effect of military sonar, scientists have found that regular commercial ship traffic is the main source of this little-known problem, as the rapid growth in world trade has driven low-frequency ocean noise up *32-fold*.[3]

An early research effort monitored noise levels in the Stellwagen Bank National Marine Sanctuary off Massachusetts, chosen because the channel to the busy Boston Harbor passes through it. The propeller noise is low and loud enough to make it challenging for whales to maintain acoustic contact, and reduces the range over which whales can communicate by as much as 90 percent. Whales are raising the pitch of their calls, up to a full octave for the highly endangered Atlantic "right whales," so-called because they were "right" for efficient killing and harvesting by the whaling industry of the eighteenth century. About 400 of the animals remain alive in the North Atlantic today—another species nearly "externalized" out of existence by capitalism.

Reduction of ship noise is therefore essential, and the journal notes that "Engineers say such a reduction is technologically feasible, but the costs—and opposition from some shipping companies—could be formidable." Fixes include technical changes to propellers, "streamlining boxy hulls now optimized for storage, and slowing cruising speeds," although each of these changes would mean forcing shippers to cease externalizing large costs onto the environment.

The Great Pacific Garbage Patch—a Texas-sized ocean eddy saturated with minute plastic particles—is also included in this ocean survey. The science writers characteristically deride the mainstream media's sensationalization of the patch: "Although many media stories conjure up a chunky soup of bottles and tires, it is mostly an unstrained consommé of small bits of floating plastic ... A similar accumulation of plastic particles—which include weathered fishing line, Styrofoam, wrappers, and raw resin pellets—has shown up in the North Atlantic Ocean."[4] Since its discovery by Woods Hole oceanographers in 1972, the problem has apparently escalated, with a 2001 survey voyage finding 334,271 pieces of plastic per square kilometer, coming to an almost unbelievable 6:1 ratio of plastic to zooplankton biomass. The discovery of these floating garbage soups has driven more research, since, as the journal indicates,

> In the past, researchers have mostly focused on larger threats: abandoned fishing nets that trap turtles and seals; plastic bags that block the digestive tracts of turtles; and the toothbrushes and bottle caps that seabirds mistake for food, sometimes starving as a result or dying from a blockage. But toxin-laden microplastics may add another risk to marine life. Benthic worms, mussels, krill, sea cucumbers, and birds will ingest tiny plastic particles.[5]

The centerpiece of the special issue examines recent research on "The Growing Human Footprint on Coastal and Open-Ocean Biogeochemistry." While conventional economic theory encourages treating the economy as if it exists in an empty world that can absorb endless pollution, the scientists are not so optimistic, noting for example that 25–30 percent of humanity's total CO_2 emissions since the beginning of the industrial era are now dissolved in the oceans. Besides acidification, there are serious effects on fundamental biological productivity, since warming surface layers makes them circulate less with cooler, lower waters, thus increasing ocean "stratification." This circulates fewer nutrients, driving the menacing decline of phytoplankton in strong correlation with warming temperatures, especially in the tropics and subtropics.[6]

Also encouraged by vertical stratification of the water column is the problem of hypoxia, extremely low oxygen levels in coastal waters due to excessively high volumes of oxygen-consuming algae and bacteria. These algae feed on the nitrogen-rich waste of human commerce: "Fertilizer runoff and nitrogen deposition from fossil fuels are driving an expansion in the duration, intensity, and extent of coastal hypoxia, leading to marine habitat degradation and in extreme cases, extensive fish and invertebrate mortality." (See Figure 3.1) There are currently over 400 coastal hypoxic zones worldwide, including the massive "Dead Zone" in the Gulf of Mexico.

Among the more heartbreaking aspects of the research survey is the conclusion that while major sources of industrial pollution

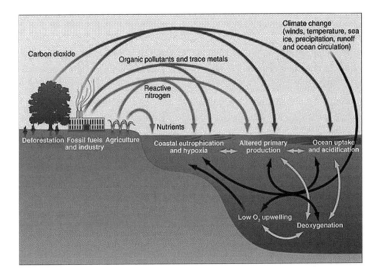

Figure 3.1

are often very visible, less attention goes to "the global spread of industrial pollutants into what otherwise would appear to be pristine environments." This includes organic mercury and persistent organic pollutants like DDT, "found in even the most remote marine locations, transported through the atmosphere in the vapor phase, aerosols, and soot particles [and] by ocean currents." Importantly, the situation is not hopeless, as a chemist contributor describes: "It is encouraging that, after the phase-out of leaded gasoline in North America that began in the mid-1970s, the high levels of anthropogenic lead observed in the North Atlantic declined sharply and are now comparable to those occurring at the beginning of the 20th century."[7] Environmental disruption as a side-effect of capitalism can be turned back, but it would take the equivalent of a lead-gas phase-out for fossil fuels.

Science's spotlight on the oceans concludes with discussion of the acceleration of polar ice-sheet melting, raising median expectations of sea level rise by year 2100 from about 60 centimeters to a full meter.[8] The pace has risen recently, due to the combined effects of quickening inflow of water mass from the ice sheets and also from thermal expansion of the existing ocean as it warms. In addition to the known melting of the ice sheets of Greenland and West Antarctica, it's been discovered that the East Antarctic sheet ice sits much lower on bedrock than thought, with many stretches well below sea level, and therefore subject to far more melting from rising ocean temperatures.[9] Global effects of sea-level rise are expected to be highly uneven, but in dry scientific language, the "socioeconomic effects ... appear to be overwhelmingly negative."

Other entries compare the climate and ecosystem effects of human activity to large meteor strikes, review the potential for interaction and destructive synergy among all the above problems, and warn of the "increased risk of sudden nonlinear transformations." It is into these stressed and degraded waters that major disasters like the *Deepwater Horizon* spill now intrude.

DRILL, MAYBE, DRILL

Despite the glaring spotlight that shone on BP and its *Deepwater Horizon* well from the rig explosion in April 2010 until the final capping in September, mainstream coverage has treated the disaster as an accident due to factors unique to particularities of the well. However, reporting in the business press and scientific journals has documented something more menacing—the spill followed a consistent pattern of cost- and corner-cutting by BP. This reflects a clearly inadequate provision for the great risk that lay outside of BP's investment—the huge danger to the Gulf's battered ecology in the event of a major spill. These costs to the ecosystem, for which businesses typically are not held accountable, fall outside the firm and are therefore "externalities" from the point of view of market exchange.

The pattern is exemplified by BP's admitted decision to ignore the results of a "negative pressure test," in the hours before the well exploded, killing 11 workers and triggering the US's biggest oil spill to date. The test had indicated a "very large abnormality," which ultimately turned out to be a column of high-pressure natural gas erupting up the well, as workers attempted to temporarily seal it. Whether it was the on-board BP managers who made the final call to proceed despite the result, or the Transocean workers who ran most of the oil rig, is still in dispute.[10] Indisputable is the fact that BP was days behind the drilling schedule and over budget, with each additional day of rig operation costing the company $1 million.

But the ignored pressure test is just one example of BP's relentless corner-cutting and hastiness, which of course elevate risk, much of which affects others' livelihoods, the Gulf's ecology, and future generations. The business press, and especially the *Wall Street Journal*, has documented a parade of cost externalizing by one of the world's most powerful corporations. Examples include skipping cement quality tests, important to make sure the seal around the well's pipe was airtight and prevent the release of high-pressure natural gas. Another was skimping on centering devices, which ensure the pipe is fully surrounded by cement—BP's cement contractor, Halliburton, recommended 21 of these, but BP went with 6, despite a warning from Halliburton that the well would face "a SEVERE gas flow problem."[11] The issue of proper cementing was especially relevant, considering BP also made the unusual decision to run a single pipe from the sea floor to the oil reservoir, rather than the standard practice of two pipes nested one within the other, which "provides an extra level of protection, but also requires another long, expensive piece of pipe."

BP's drilling logs also indicate the corporation cut short another important safety procedure called a "bottoms up" test, where the drilling "mud" is cycled through the well, bringing material at the bottom of the well up to the rig for testing. This pivotal procedure allows for detection of natural gas entering the cement, a crucial safety issue, but is also time-consuming. The full test takes 6–12 hours, but the test was done for only 30 minutes the day before the explosion, plausibly to spare BP the $500,000 an additional half-day would have cost in rig rental and expenses. Rig workers reported being instructed to finish other work double-time, "like they were trying to rush everything." Also, the last of the cement pumped into the well was not tested for quality, again despite the particular importance of the cement to the well design. Evidently, cement contractors were aboard the rig to perform these tests, but were told by BP management no test was needed and were flown to shore at 11 a.m.—the only lives known to be saved by BP's systematically risky behavior.

There are other negligent policies that might also have enabled the explosion—an enormous spring was meant to lock down the seal at the top of the well, but BP's reports show no installation. And the final error appears to have been the decision to remove the company's heavy drilling "mud" before injecting a cement plug to cap the well until later extraction of the oil. But the picture is pretty clear—an under-valuing of risk, which is to be expected in markets based on private exchange, with no regard to effects downstream. These early conclusions were ultimately substantiated in a subsequent report by the US Coast Guard and federal regulators, who cited "poor risk management" as a crucial contributor to the disaster.[12] And so the well exploded on April 20, shattering eleven families and sending several million barrels of oil streaming into the Gulf of Mexico.

Notably, the Minerals Management Service, BP's offshore regulator, approved most of the above risky maneuvers, including several hasty changes to the well which were rubber-stamped in a matter of minutes—literally five minutes to approve a tapering pipe, and less than one day to approve the single-pipe design that may have played a major role in the gas eruption.[13] Prior to this, the Interior Department, which includes the MMS, released a report documenting that Louisiana regulators accepted lunches, sports tickets, and other gifts from the oil majors, which are very often their former and future employers.[14] This is a classic instance of "regulatory capture," where the enormous wealth and economic power of major corporations is enough to keep their regulators in the corporations' pocket.

The ultimate statement of this corporate undervaluation of risk due to external costs came from a BP engineer, who wrote in an April report that the one-pipe option was "the best economic case."[15] As long as potential costs to others are omitted.

OIL AND WATER DIDN'T MIX

While the early signals were highly ominous, the full effects of the spill won't be known for years, in part due to BP's efforts to control and impede the research process. In the weeks after the rig explosion, BP caused "a public cry of outrage" over an effort to "buy up" scientists, after BP offered funding to study damage from the spill but "would have banned ... discussing or publishing any data collected on their dime for up to 3 years," as *Science* reports.[16] BP ultimately backed off after massive negative press attention and the refusal of many scientists to participate. In a similar fashion, the National Oceanic and Atmospheric Administration (NOAA) was ultimately forced to relax its tight restrictions on publishing spill data. However, BP was notably slow to disburse the $500 million in research money it promised after the spill; four months afterwards, only $30 million had been distributed, with no stated plan for the rest, which "limits scientists' ability to plan research over several years."[17] Only in September 2011, 18 months after the original blowout, did BP's "Gulf of Mexico Research Initiative" finalize its first long-term grant recipients. While the funding is surely better late than never, the science press has noted "concerns that critical data were being lost as they waited to begin work" and that research subjects like the behavior of underwater oil dispersants had to wait over a year, despite being "a subject many felt would have been better studied during the spill."[18]

Meanwhile, the Obama administration had no problem pressuring NOAA to mislead the public, as its post-spill report was alleged to have found that 75 percent of the oil was "gone," having been burned, evaporated, and dissolved. While this claim received enormous media attention, it was almost immediately leapt upon by the scientific community and ripped to shreds. A review by the University of Georgia found that even assuming favorable conditions, at least 70 percent of the total spill remains in the Gulf, or about 3 million barrels.[19] Another account in *Science* found that NOAA's much-hyped report got the numbers exactly reversed—75 percent of the spill remains, with one-quarter removed/destroyed. Later analyses suggest higher totals for both the volume of oil spilled, revised up to 4.4 million barrels, and for the amount remaining.[20] These findings ultimately led NOAA's senior scientists to repudiate the original feel-good report, and to condemn the White House's stance of low-balling its estimates of spilled oil and for refusing to allow NOAA to make its models public.[21] These volume estimates were rough, of course, both due to the relatively recent occurrence of the spill and the fact that BP clearly prioritized keeping the oil below the surface.

The scientific literature describes BP's use of chemical dispersants as "a story of scientists turning to desperate measures during desperate times." The dispersants—essentially detergents—break up oil flows into microscopic drops for microbes to eat, much like dishwater detergent breaks up oils on dishes.[22] But these chemicals have spotty health records even when used on the surface of oil spills, and an effort by the National Institutes of Health to monitor the health effects on cleanup workers took many months to begin, and had little baseline data.[23] The use of detergents thousands of feet underwater is an experimental exercise in any case. The determination seems to have been that crude oil is so deadly for marine life that oil-plus-chemicals was considered barely worse.

The effect of dispersants and the great pressure at the well leak was to create the now-notorious plumes of oil and gas thousands of feet below the Gulf's surface. The plumes have been proven through isotopic analysis to flow from BP's well rather than natural seeps, and are over 20 miles long, a mile wide and about two-thirds of a mile underwater. While BP's dispersant use has kept the oil from already-battered coastal wetlands, it has sentenced the deepwater Gulf ecology to an unknown fate. And perhaps more compelling for BP, it keeps the oil out of sight of news cameras and makes damage surveying far more challenging.

Throughout the coverage, the hope was raised that native bacteria, evolved to consume oil from natural seeps on the sea floor, would break up most of the spilled crude. Unfortunately, the emerging body of research on microbial consumption of the BP spill paints a disappointing picture. A team of earth and marine scientists found that about 70 percent of the bacterial feeding seems to be on the natural gas compounds in the underwater plumes.[24] Further analysis suggests that bacteria are preferentially consuming the smaller compounds in the crude oil mixture, rather than the bigger, polycyclic aromatic hydrocarbons, which are the most toxic ones.

Finally, more recent research seems to support this conclusion, finding that microbial activity, as measured by the decreased oxygen levels it causes, is breaking down the oil plume itself far more slowly than anticipated. Research voyages have found that the underwater oil plumes "persisted for months without substantial biodegradation," and that the hypoxia generated by the microbes is lower than expected.[25] On the one hand, this is good news, as strong hypoxia is harmful to higher marine life and the Gulf is already struggling with low oxygen levels caused by algae feeding on agricultural runoff from the Mississippi basin. But on the other hand, it also "suggests that the petroleum hydrocarbons did not fuel appreciable microbial respiration on the temporal scales of our study … if the hydrocarbons are indeed susceptible to biodegradation, then it may require many months before microbes significantly attenuate the hydrocarbon plume." In other words, elements of the oil mixture may stick around for some time—a far cry from "75% gone."[26]

The microdroplets of oil and the chemical dispersants are having effects that are just now being examined. Marine geochemists from the University of Southern Florida have found oil in microscopic plankton, at the base of the marine food web, meaning it will tend to bioaccumulate in higher animals eating the plankton and one another. The effects are seriously deleterious for organism health: "Biosensor assays indicate that marine organisms, phytoplankton and bacteria, express a strong toxic response" in waters with petroleum hydrocarbons present.[27] While these findings are new and not yet corroborated by further research, the signs are not encouraging, especially in light of the fact that since the spill, the industry and government regulators have been visibly eager to return to business as usual.

Notably, drilling in the Gulf has escalated since the expiration of the Obama administration's moratorium, and with more complex technology and admittedly higher risks. A former Chevron executive admitted that "Our ability to manage risks hasn't caught up with our ability to explore and produce in deep water," with risks to nature wildly overshadowing risks to corporations from accidents.[28] Rigs are more complex and further from shore, some 20 hours out to sea, ensuring that future explosions and fires will burn longer before action can have an effect. Obviously, hurricanes also remain a perennial peril to these rigs, perhaps reflected in their rather cute names, like Blind Faith and Atlantis.

BP itself has maintained its presence in the Gulf, continuing existing projects like Atlantis and announcing plans for new drilling just days after the release of the regulators' report enumerating its shortcuts and failure to include a real accounting of risks. The corporation is alleging it has cleaned up its act, now using more failsafes than regulators require, although as before it is plausible that BP may use its resources to manage what regulators will demand.[29] And even as BP made its claim of turning a corner, the US Coast Guard announced that an oil sheen coating the surface of the Gulf had been observed by submersible video to be emanating from the underwater wreckage of the Deepwater Horizon drilling rig.[30] Not for nothing does BP invest so heavily in media time and space, from featured YouTube content to prime-time advertisements, positioning its brand as uniquely eco-friendly, oily reality notwithstanding.

It should be borne in mind that the situation is not hopeless. The removal of lead from US gasoline was driven by the introduction of catalytic converters after citizens demanded Environmental Protection Agency (EPA) action, and was followed by decreases in the lead content of the North Atlantic. Likewise, scientists have noted that NOAA's current policy of sharing BP's spill data was driven by loud public demands for openness, and BP probably wouldn't have been so eager to hide the crude underwater if it thought no one cared about the environment. Prospects for radical change lie in the public's desire for a clean environment for their grandkids, who will clearly suffer from corporate America's undervaluing of risk, and who are therefore victimized by capitalism's externalities as much as the fisherman out of work due to contaminated catches and the coral bleached by warming and dissolved by acid.

Capitalism's structural inefficiencies make its "best economic case" into a worst-case scenario for the world.

4
The Brown Peril: Atmospheric Brown Clouds and Asian Neoliberalism

Molecular epidemiologists who focus on environmental links to illness increasingly do much of their work in the developing world, where pollution is so ubiquitous that its complex connections to health can be calibrated even in small study populations.

Scientific American[1]

The ancient Chinese were a scientifically advanced people. The standard reference work describes them as "the most persistent and accurate observers of celestial phenomena anywhere in the world before the Arabs."[2] So respected were astronomers in Han China that they were accommodated within the Imperial Palace. And yet for the typical Chinese of today, a different situation obtains: on many nights in both town and country in the People's Republic, the stars are not visible at all.

This is because of atmospheric brown clouds, or ABCs, huge plumes of air pollution that are visible on the ground as a brownish haze, and from space as thousand-mile-long brown stains on the globe. The clouds are composed of huge quantities of tiny pollutant particles, including soot, smog, and fly ash, jointly referred to as "aerosols." They develop every year from December to April, can reach over a mile thick and stretch from the Arabian to the Yellow Sea. They blot out the sun and stars, shroud the horizon and can be tasted on the tongue.

These clouds have received some publicity after a recent UN Environmental Program report on their composition, environmental impacts, and health ramifications.[3] As the UNEP report is quick to point out, "These pollutants are emitted from

A version of this essay was published in *Capitalism Nature Socialism*, Vol. 21, No. 3, September 2010.

anthropogenic sources, such as fossil fuel combustion, biofuel cooking and biomass burning,"[4] but in fact we can go a step beyond that. In many of their basic aspects, these toxic ABCs are the products of "neoliberal" economic forms, including fiscal reductions in social supports, liberalized trade policies, and foreign direct investment. It's not correct to say neoliberal globalization fails to protect the environment—the active destruction of livelihoods and ecology in neoliberal Asia now has a physical manifestation visible from space.

THE ABCs OF ABCs

The report notes early on that ABCs are observed over many large metropolitan regions, including Europe and eastern North America. However, these northern hemispheric regions have wet winters, when precipitation washes out the suspended aerosols that make up these clouds. So the report's main focus is on the region framed by three "ABC hotspots": East Asia, South-east Asia, and the Indo-Gangetic Plain in South Asia. This suggests that a third of the world's population is seasonally blanketed by toxic, sooty clouds, and the human impacts can increase very quickly.

While greenhouse gases emitted by fossil-fuel burning trap energy in the earth's atmosphere and thus warm it, ABCs have mixed effects. Many elements of these clouds scatter light back into space, thus reducing the rise in global temperature; other elements, such as soot, absorb light and thus warm the atmosphere. But ABCs also cool and dim the earth's surface beneath them—Guangzhou province, for example, now receives 20 percent less light than in the 1970s.[5] In fact, the most recent report of the Intergovernmental Panel on Climate Change concludes that as much as half of the global warming effect of CO_2 has been cancelled out by the cooling effect of the tiny particles in these clouds.[6] Therefore the overall climate effect of ABCs is estimated to be negative—scientists say they "mask" climate effects from greenhouse gases.[7] But this creates a serious obstacle to solving ABC pollution—removing the brown clouds without reducing greenhouse emissions could lead to a further increase in global temperatures of up to 2 degrees Celsius. So this variety of air pollution may be the only thing protecting us from our other types of air pollution.

These massive clouds also have enormous effects on Asia's already-strained water systems, on which millions depend. The soot in the clouds is being deposited on Asia's many glaciers, which makes them darker and warms them. Also, the ABCs heat the upper atmosphere at the glacier's high altitudes. On top of already existing greenhouse warming, these factors have led to a heavy melting of the Hindu Kush-Himalayan glaciers system.

For example, the mammoth Gangroti Glacier feeds 70 percent of the flow of the Ganges River, upon which over 400 million people depend. The Earth Policy Institute notes that if the glacier continues its well-documented retreat, "the Ganges could become a seasonal river, flowing during the rainy season but not during the summer dry season when irrigation water needs are greatest."[8] Likewise, the Yangtze River fertilizes about half of China's rice harvest, and is fed by the Tibet-Qinghai Plateau glaciers. These are retreating tens of meters annually, and could be two-thirds gone by 2060. Note that both of these river basins support a population larger than the entire US.

It might be noted that the question of when the Himalayan glaciers will ultimately vanish was at the heart of one of the few clear errors to be found in the IPCC's voluminous 2007 report. A claim of glacial extinction by 2030 was found not to be based on peer-reviewed research, and the Panel released a statement to that effect, eagerly leapt upon by advocates of responsible science reporting like Fox News and CNN.

In addition to the risks to agriculture from glacial diminishment, the tiny particles in the clouds tend to "suppress" the summer monsoon storms—thus the season has shortened and the storms are more severe. While the rainfall science is at an early stage, in light of the clear impact ABCs have on glacial melting, tampering with the other main water cycle vector in the world's most-populated regions is serious business. In the context of Asia's falling water tables, the combination of receding glaciers and perturbed monsoons "could lead to politically unmanageable food shortages," as the Earth Policy Institute suggests.

The direct health effects of this long-term haze are another story. The UNEP report is highly conservative in predicting particular health impacts, and limits itself to calling for study and noting the individual health impacts of the particular elements that make up the ABCs: cardiovascular disease for fossil fuel emissions, vascular lesions from concentrated aerosol particles, immune responses and cancer from fine smoke.[9]

Disease researchers are making their way to the developing world to collect data on the effects of the pervasive mixed pollutants. *Scientific American* describes Dr. Frederica Perera's investigation of the effects of pollutants on children in the womb. The scientists visit a Chinese town that recently closed a coal-burning power plant, once choked with exhaust but where "passing cars no longer kick up clouds of black soot from the street and families can hang their wash outside to dry for more than a few minutes without their white shirts turning gray." The results were that "children born in 2002, when the power plant was still operating, have smaller heads and score worse on developmental tests than those born in 2005, a year after the plant closed."[10] In this way, ABCs tilt the playing field against the poor even before birth.

MADE IN ASIA—AT GUNPOINT

In light of these perilous developments, the crucial question is exactly how these clouds are created. NASA photos reviewed in *Science* suggest the clouds come not only from "industrial air pollution from fossil fuel combustion … but that emissions from biomass burning (forest fires, agricultural waste burning, and vegetable fuel combustion) were important as well."[11] The pivotal study was the "Indian Ocean Experiment," where scientists found "Anthropogenic sources contributed as much as 80% (±10%) to the aerosol loading" in the region.[12]

But the physical composition of the clouds has become clear only lately. An international team recently determined that the clouds are approximately two-thirds products of biomass combustion, and one-third fossil fuel combustion.[13] This indicates that the Asian haze comes from wood- and dung-burning home stoves and agricultural forest burning as much as from Asia's foreign-owned factories and millions of new motorists. But the social origin of each of these elements deserves some analysis, which comes to show that neoliberal policy and investment patterns are substantially responsible for the haze.

Of the three ABC hotspots the UNEP report describes in Asia, the South-east Asian region's cloud is especially driven by "biomass clearing"—slash-and-burn agriculture, typically for palm oil exports, making short work of the Indonesian rain forest. The *Economist* notes that besides the burnt biomass, the smog "serves as a kind of atmospheric lid to contain all the lead, carbon monoxide, sulphur dioxide and particulates that the industrializing and motorizing countries of the region pump relentlessly into the air." The conservative journal went so far as to suggest these clouds may be "the most pernicious man-made smog in history."[14] The press describes the health fallout: "Dry throats, running noses, sore eyes, asthma seizures ... Malaysia's government has advised people to stay indoors."

Beside the medical care costs from the smoke, the economic losses have been significant and build every year, from closed schools to missed flights to ship collisions. High ozone levels from the enormous fires compounded the health and economic damage on crops.[15] In one memorable episode, as the annual smog forced the ASEAN countries to meet in Indonesia to discuss the problem, the ministers had to hastily move their meeting place to escape the smoke.[16] This led Indonesian dictator President Suharto to make an address wherein he "stunned the region by publicly apologizing for the smoke," as the *Wall Street Journal* reported.[17]

Much of the smog was due to the "structural adjustments" to Indonesia's economy made by the International Monetary Fund in the wake of Asia's 1998–99 financial crisis. The IMF is an institution that organizes "rescue packages" for governments that are drowning in debt. It and its associated institutions, like the World Bank, make these loans only on condition that the receiving government undertake "structural adjustment programs," which usually involve driving up the payments on debt by governments through reduction in services for the poor. Indonesia had enormous debt after years of US-backed dictatorship, and so the IMF forced a cornered Indonesia to accept fiscal austerity in exchange for credit, particularly through reduction or elimination of subsidies for many basic products, including food, fuel, and electricity. The price of kerosene, essential to the poor for cooking fuel, shot up by 25 percent in the blink of an eye. This led to riots across the country, and then what the *Economist* prosaically called "the familiar armory of riot police" being put to use against those out of work.[18] Following months of student agitation on campuses, the US-backed Suharto regime clamped down: "The authorities' unstated fear was that disaffected students might find natural allies in poor districts nearby, many of whose inhabitants, especially the unemployed, have been hit just as hard as the students by the economic disaster." A real nightmare, for readers of the *Economist*. In the end, much of the violence was directed against the entrepreneurial Chinese minority, and the impoverished masses of Indonesia were forced to fall back on biofuels for cooking, contributing to regional soot emissions.

The IMF also demanded trade policy changes in exchange for $43 billion in loans. Notably, Indonesia ended its ban on the export of palm oil on April 1, 1998—leading first to a sharp price spike in this crucial cooking oil, and second to the possibility of profitably exporting palm oil from large plantations. And since another structural tweak the IMF insisted upon was liberalization of investment rules, multinational corporations (MNCs) moved fast to take advantage of the new rules by buying land and clearing space for palm oil plantations. As the *Financial Times* describes it, "the appetite of foreign investors" built on Indonesia's tradition of clearing land, and combined with population pressure, "the arrival of logging and plantation firms have made the situation much worse in recent years."[19] Thus the years of annihilating Borneo's dense rainforest growth are very much based on deregulated, neoliberal economic modes. The corresponding suffering of Indonesia's squeezed population, the imminent extinction of the orangutan and thousands of other species, and the foul ABC created in the process are all externalities.

Another ABC "hot spot" is the Indo-Gangetic plain, the vast area that supports a large part of the hundreds of millions of souls in India, Pakistan, and Bangladesh. This region's haze is especially characterized by biofuel burning—household use of dung or agricultural waste for cooking and warmth. A recent analysis published in *Science* found that while "Soot or black carbon emissions in the south Asian region arise from fuel combustion for transportation, industrial, and residential uses … the combustion of solid biofuels—such as wood, agricultural waste, and dried animal manure in cooking stoves—is the largest source of [soot] emissions in India."[20]

As the *New York Times* has noted,[21] affordability is a principal reason for biofuel use—incomes in the region can't support electricity or gas service. A UN agency refers to similar conditions in rural China, "where most of the farmers do not earn enough to pay for fuel or electricity" and must rely on farm waste like hay.[22]

While India has never entered full IMF receivership, its fiscal crises of the 1990s led to numerous IMF warnings to cut state outlays and privatize public enterprise. The former has been pursued more aggressively, and since 1992 India has repeatedly cut energy subsidies for its impoverished multitudes. While the *Far Eastern Economic Review* considered "India's IMF-supervised economic restructuring" to cause "relatively little pain," the resulting price jumps for energy have surely been a factor moving rural India toward far cheaper, but dirtier, biofuel alternatives,[23] especially since India continued to further reduce its subsidies, through 2008.[24] The IMF and many economists can point to a reduced fiscal shortfall and improved GDP growth since the "reforms." But critics could point to the falling fortunes of India's majority, the sooty cloud that covers their land for the winter, and the 700,000 annual excess deaths found by UNEP in India and China from indoor air pollution exposure.

Turning to the last Asian ABC hotspot, East Asia, we can consider fossil fuel combustion. Burning carbon fuels produces carbon dioxide, the most prominent greenhouse gas, as well as many of the tiny particles that make up the ABCs, including soot, sulfates, and ozone. Asia's carbon emissions skyrocketed in the 1990s and have now surpassed Europe and North America's.[25] This owes to many economic developments in the region, including the rapid growth of automobile use and the use of coal in the home for winter heat. But a crucial and revealing driver of Asia's emissions has been China's export growth explosion.

While China is no neoliberal playground, with extensive government intervention in the economy, its export-led growth boom has required rapid growth in its electrical capacity. China presently burns over two billion tons of coal annually, and has for many years opened an average of one new coal-fired power plant per week.[26] The great pall of China owes to its "electricity companies … building power stations with gay abandon," as the *Economist* puts it.[27]

Several studies have attempted to estimate the proportion of China's carbon emissions that derive from the export sector. A study by the Tyndall Centre suggests about 23 percent of China's emissions are the result of net exports, although this figure "excludes important indirect emissions that originate from inputs used in production of exports."[28]

Another review of the subject applies an input-output model and finds that fully one-third of Chinese emissions result from export production, up from 12 percent in 1987.[29] The authors note that "exports are on average no more or less carbon-intensive than domestic consumption and investment," suggesting MNCs that outsource to the PRC are not leading China toward greater efficiency, but rather taking advantage of the country's cheap wages and coal-driven power. The authors note that the growth rate of emissions from export production is greater than the growth of total emissions, suggesting "the particular importance of exports to China's growth in CO_2 emissions."

We can see the hand of neoliberalism in this origin of ABC aerosols, if we consider that China's export sector is overwhelmingly owned by foreign MNCs. The Tyndall Centre notes that fully 60 percent of China's exports in 2006 were produced by multinational ventures, "accounting for the majority of high-tech and high value-added exports from China," and thus also for the majority of its carbon output.[30]

Capital mobility, a key feature of modern capitalism (see Chapter 8), is thus significantly responsible for the greenhouse emissions element of the ABCs. "A good portion of China's air pollution is simply outsourced smog: industry that has migrated from the U.S. and E.U. to China to help maintain low prices or clean Western skies,"[31] was *Scientific American*'s rendering.

China's new position as leading greenhouse gas emitter owes much to its unique development process, almost a parody of Victorian England. Destitute urban construction workers and rural peasants burn coal to keep warm, automobile use has shot up among the urban affluent, and antiquated coal plants are used to keep the export boom on its feet. The *Far Eastern Economic Review* surveys the circumstance: "As the Western countries (and Japan) got richer, they relegated coal combustion to generation of electricity in large power plants with highly efficient electrostatic precipitators that remove up to 99.99% of all particulates."[32] As citizens become more affluent they can also afford to switch to gas and electric heating, as in the West, but this day is far off in China. Also, while traffic smog is no stranger to the developed nations, it requires sunny conditions for car exhaust to experience photochemical transformation into smog. As the *Review* notes, "This means that the phenomenon is seasonal in Toronto and Paris, but it persists for most of the year in subtropical and many tropical cities with high concentrations of vehicular traffic." Thus the classical, soot-based smog from industry and the more modern, car traffic-derived smog can mingle and accumulate into Asia's ABCs.

The conclusion is that the Asian atmospheric brown cloud is a product of neoliberalism—from Indonesia's SAPs reducing subsidies and bringing in foreign resource-extraction firms, to India's IMF-driven fuel subsidy cuts, to China's MNC-owned export emissions boom. It has been a common argument for many years that corporate globalization takes no account of ecological externalities, but now there is a clear, physical demonstration of this reality. The ABCs are a manifestation of market inefficiency that's visible from airplanes, blocks the sun, and shrouds billions of people.

BLOWBACK IN PARADISE

The effects of these corporate policies have ironically boomeranged on a few of the exporters' tony headquarters. Consider Disney Hong Kong, crammed onto reclaimed land, which had 80 percent of its building costs covered by the city government.[33] Yet according to a report commissioned by investment bankers, even upon opening in 2005 the theme park was doomed to "suffer from constant haze." In spite of Disney's best efforts, including their trademark bland castle within a few hours' flying time of actual ones, the park has fallen far short of its projected 10 million visitors a year. This is probably due to what the report politely describes as "a serious visibility problem"[34] (and perhaps also what the *Times* of London calls its "utterly homogenized" feel).

Of course, besides Hong Kong's own heavy auto exhaust and the ozone-heavy haze from burning rain forests to the south, Hong Kong is adjacent to Guandong Province on the Chinese mainland, a sprawling industrial crucible. The press reports that "While the government tends to disregard public sentiment if it might hinder economic growth, Hong Kong officials are more likely to listen when big business talks. A chorus of criticism is now coming from business organizations," noting that the falling air quality has "obscured the jaw-dropping harbor view from executive suites."[35] However, the *Financial Times* points out that "Although Hong Kong is the victim of pollution from China, Hong Kong businesses are partly to blame, since many of the factories in China are owned and run by Hong Kong companies."[36] The *Times* notes that "Most manufacturing industries have migrated to the Chinese mainland in search of lower costs," since on the mainland "there are no real environmental laws." The folly of the Hong Kong businessman, it turns out, is living downwind of your own export platform. Never put your money where your home is.

Another global-city love-in to fall casualty to the giant brown externalities was the Beijing Games. In a development not seen since the Summer Games in Mexico City in 1968, Olympic athletes chose to commute. Dozens of teams, especially from wealthier countries, went to Japan or South Korea in order to avoid Beijing's foul air and questionable water.[37]

On the very night of the opening ceremony, the air had been hazy with low visibility for almost a week. In spite of China's best efforts for the Games, including removing millions of cars from the streets and even shutting down nearby industry, the air quality was poor even by US standards, although still a "Blue Sky Day" for the Chinese government. China's main problem was described in *Business Week*: "Despite the measures the government has taken in the capital, southern winds threaten Beijing's efforts to clean up by bringing pollutants from hundreds of miles away ... much of the problem comes from the densely populated, industrial regions southeast of Beijing."[38] No matter how effective the power of the state, one city alone can't stay clean in the middle of a regional ABC, and Beijing's air deteriorated soon after the Games were over.[39]

In the end, if the Beijing Games were meant to be China's coming-out party to the developed countries, the clouds were a persistent embarrassment. Athletes canceled competition in Beijing over health concerns like asthma, and some cyclists on the US team had to be scolded by the US Olympic Committee for wearing face masks. They issued an apology as directed— embarrassing the PRC is a prerogative of the government.[40]

THE BROWN PERIL

Reviewing the record, it's clear that neoliberal capitalism is responsible for severe social and environmental disaster in Asia. Whole regions, home to millions of people, face futures of serious water scarcity and degraded health, far from the "optimum efficiency" predicted by the dominant schools of economic theory. But in addition to grinding down society and raping nature, neoliberalism has all but manufactured irony. Consider Disney characters singing "it's a small world after all" to cramped Hong Kong tourists while wrapped in smog from China. But Asian neoliberalism has also ironically fulfilled a long-running American paranoia.

Probably ever since their industrious labor was first harnessed to American capital in the nineteenth century, prejudice against and fear of Asian peoples has been lodged in the American consciousness. Of course, this "Yellow Peril" is in the long American tradition of fearing groups which are being exploited and destroyed, as with the native Americans, African Americans, and the poor generally. The bigotry climaxed with the interning of a hundred thousand individuals of Asian descent during World War II.

This enduring xenophobia has also played a role in coverage of the ABCs. What coverage is present reliably takes poor families to task for their role in originating components of the clouds, especially use of biofuel in the home and in slash-and-burn subsistence agriculture.[41] However, American MNCs are rarely singled out for their own crucial role in exporting polluting industries to Asian export platforms, except in the odd business press article. Similarly, the rising consumption levels of the growing Asian middle classes are almost without exception blamed for rising energy and food prices, inspiring fearful visions of shortage caused by the clamoring Asian professionals.[42] This well-evidenced double standard reflects the class interests of western opinion.

But the hidden irony is that there is now a very real threat to America's West Coast from Asia. But it's not Japanese kamikazes or hordes of Chinese commies storming the waterfront—it's the drift of the brown clouds produced by our own outsourced industry. Scientists have noted that aerosol lifetimes are about one to two weeks, whereas Pacific air currents can transit from East Asia to western North America in about one week.[43] Thus we arrive at the situation where a staggering three-quarters of the soot over the American west coast in springtime is emitted in Asia.[44] Scientists are now investigating whether deposition of soot in California's mountain ranges will accelerate snowpack melt—the Sierra Nevada may face the same fate as the Hindu Kush.

After years of paranoia, America's long-feared Asian threat has arrived, even if in the event it's a Brown Peril. And in the end it was good old American capital mobility and neoliberal policy that have brought it to our shores. Irony loves company.

5
Cause and Side-effect:
Big-picture Externalities

Economists give the market economy a good deal of credit for its "wealth creation." The idea is that by giving entrepreneurs the incentive to invest in their businesses, they create both jobs and the products to buy with the income earned from them. This is usually represented by the growth of economic production, measured in Gross Domestic Product (GDP), which has grown exponentially over the history of capitalism.

However, economists have managed to cook the books on economic history. While the value of products manufactured by businesses are counted toward GDP and economic growth, the damage to the ecosystems that provided the raw materials is not, until the system is exploited to the point of collapse. Also, the wastes emitted and dumped in the production process are certainly not counted against GDP, unless someone is paid to clean them up. The scale of these neglected economic side-effects is not small, and the affects of them on land, sea, and air have been considered in Part I. However, the full scale of the massive destruction standing side-by-side with the proud GDP numbers can only be appreciated by looking at the impact of externalities on life itself.

MASS EXTINCTION #6

In Chapter 1, a number of scientists were quoted referring to the impact of human economic activity as comparable to a meteoric strike. Now their full meaning can be considered, as we turn to what the scientific community is calling "the extinction crisis." An enormous loss of the world's species of animals, plants, fungi, and microorganisms has been underway for centuries, and science is taking it seriously.

In a very carefully argued and documented study published in the respected science journal *Nature*, a team of biologists and paleontologists endeavored to answer the question of whether human economic activity has become so destructive as to constitute a sixth "mass extinction."[1] Mass extinctions are cataclysmic events in the fossil record, in which at least 75–95 percent of the Earth's species went extinct in a short timespan. There have been five such events in the last 450 million years, and have been triggered by various natural phenomena, including abrupt climate cooling and warming, colossal series of volcanic eruptions that dimmed the Sun, and the meteor impact at the end of the Cretaceous era which is believed to have exterminated the dinosaurs.

The biologists "take a conservative approach to assessing the seriousness of the ongoing extinction crisis, by setting a high bar for recognizing mass extinction ... the modern rates [of species extinctions] we computed probably seriously underestimate current [extinction] values." Even so, the picture is dark. Finding that today's species exterminations are happening at an extraordinarily fast rate, even relative to the previous mass extinction events, the scientists' "numbers suggest that we have not yet seen the sixth mass extinction, but that we would jump from one-quarter to halfway towards it if 'threatened' species disappear."

They conclude that while "the recent loss of species is dramatic and serious but does not yet qualify as a mass extinction in the palaeontological sense of the Big Five [extinctions]. In historic times we have actually lost only a few per cent of assessed species (though we have no way of knowing how many species we have lost that had never been described)." However,

> ... there are clear indications that losing species now in the 'critically endangered' category would propel the world to a state of mass extinction that has previously been seen only five times in about 540 million years. Additional losses of species in the 'endangered' and 'vulnerable' categories could accomplish the sixth mass extinction in just a few centuries. It

may be of particular concern that this extinction trajectory would play out under conditions that resemble the 'perfect storm' that coincided with past mass extinctions: multiple, atypical high-intensity ecological stressors, including rapid, unusual climate change and highly elevated atmospheric CO_2 [as well as] habitat fragmentation, pollution, overfishing and overhunting, invasive species and pathogens ... and expanding human biomass ...Without concerted mitigation efforts, such stressors will accelerate in the future and thus intensify extinction, especially given the feedbacks between individual stressors.[2]

Other scientific studies find similar results. A comprehensive review of the subject in *Science* evaluates the biodiversity commitments made by the world in the Convention on Biological Diversity, which were then incorporated into the prestigious United Nations Millennium Development Goals.[3] The goals include making a "significant reduction" in the rate of loss of forest, marine resources, the number of species threatened with extinction, and others. The scientists found that the core of the problem is that the "Pressures" on biodiversity "show increasing trends over recent decades, with increases in aggregate human consumption of the planet's ecological assets, deposition of reactive nitrogen, number of alien species," and the "proportion of fish stocks overharvested" in addition to the impact of climate change. Their conclusion is that "at the global scale it is highly unlikely that the 2010 target has been met. Neither individual or aggregated indicators of the state of biodiversity showed significant reductions in their rates of decline ... all pressure indicators showed increasing trends, with none significantly decelerating."

The smaller picture is only more distressing. Ecologists' recent findings include a concern that Britain has experienced decline or extinction of 71 percent of its butterfly species, 54 percent of its birds, and 28 percent of studied plants.[4] The decline of the butterflies is particularly ominous, as "Experts had assumed that the sheer number of insects would safeguard them against mass extinction ... As insects comprise more than 50% of the planet's species, a large die-off would be bad news for global diversity."

Loss of habitat to human settlement and excessive nitrogen use on agriculture were considered most responsible.

STRANGLING SUSTAINABILITY

As activists have brought awareness of the deterioration of natural systems to wider audiences, "sustainability" has become a prominent concept. Sustainability indicates that a society's use of natural resources and emission of wastes are within limits that nature can regularly meet—in other words, we're not consuming so many resources and polluting so much that the system is weakened over time. Like the concept of "going green" in general, this idea has been stretched and abused in a way typical of our media system (see Chapter 6), but the concept itself is very important.

One of the earliest efforts to draw attention to the idea came from a very valuable book called *Limits To Growth*, put out by MIT scientists in 1972, suggesting that the world held finite resources and that those limits could be overshot—meaning that a civilization that focused on growth could consume an unsustainably large amount of resources and ultimately see those resources collapse, at great peril. The book was largely written off and considered outside the mainstream.

But when the book was re-released in 2004, the great volume of data on climate change, fishery collapse, and oil spills meant it was more favorably received:

> The decline in oil production within important nations, the thinning of stratospheric ozone, the mounting global temperature, the widespread persistence of hunger, the escalating debate over the location of disposal sites for toxic wastes, falling groundwater levels, disappearing species, and receding forests ... All of them illustrate and are consistent with our basic conclusion—that physical growth constraints are an important aspect of the global policy arena in the twenty-first century.

Based on computer models of different possible futures in which resources were used differently, the new study set out to suggest the range of possibilities humanity might encounter. As the researchers conclude, "the more successfully society puts off its limits through economic and technical adaptations, the more likely it is to run into several of them at the same time. In most [simulated computer] runs ... the world system does not totally run out of land or food or resources or pollution absorption capability. What it runs out of is *the ability to cope.*"[5]

The authors note that transitioning our economy to a sustainable pattern would require fundamental changes to its institutions, and also serious changes in how humans relate:

> Individualism and shortsightedness are the greatest problems of the current social systems, we think, and the deepest cause of unsustainability. Love and compassion institutionalized in collective solutions is the better alternative ... The sustainability revolution will have to be, above all, a collective transformation that permits the best of human nature, rather than the worst, to be expressed and nurtured.

The stakes if we should fail to take heed of these warnings are carefully reviewed by Franz Broswimmer, who meticulously analyzes the collapses of many ancient and more recent civilizations, and finds that in addition to the ruin of war and the strain of conflict between different social classes, severe environmental problems play major roles in most of them. To take a representative example:

> Following a common socio-cultural pattern in other stratified civilizations ... Roman society prominently exhibited status- and prestige-driven patterns of conspicuous consumption ... But with the over-expansion of the Roman Empire, problems with regard to the quantity and reliability of food supplies arose. Rome was predominantly a grain-based empire, sustained largely by slave labor. Subject to diverse social-military, ecological, and climatic stresses, the main Roman grain supply areas moved over time from Egypt to Sicily, and then from Sicily to Morocco ... [as overexploitation ruined previously productive land] Growing food imports caused economic crises and contributed to the strains which led to the eventual decline of the Roman Empire ... The outflow of gold to India resulted in a severe economic crisis. Roman emperors could no

longer finance the customary free distribution of food. Unable to pay its soldiers, Rome was no longer capable of stopping the 'barbarian incursions' in the north. Ultimately, the overextended and financially strapped empire collapsed.[6]

Besides showing the scale of catastrophe societies flirt with when they neglect ecology, Broswimmer also makes the important point that environmental destruction is far older than capitalism, being partially responsible for the collapse of many storied classical civilizations. However, capitalism does earn special mention for its laser-like focus on accumulation of personal wealth and the systematic, perpetually-growing exploitation of nature for that purpose: "Many ecological critics would agree that, of all its core features, the systemic growth imperative is perhaps the most destructive dimension of the capitalist ethos."[7]

INSANE AT ANY SPEED

Despite the apocalyptic trend of capitalism against life on the planetary scale, it can be seen even more easily closer to home. During a 1997 court case brought by an American family that had been horribly burned after a very mild rear-end collision, GM was forced under threat of contempt of court to produce an internal memorandum circulated in 1973. Written by Edward Ivey, a GM engineer, at the request of company management, the document mathematically analyzed the costs to GM of deaths in fires resulting from accidents involving cars it manufactured. The document was called "Value Analysis of Auto Fuel Fed Fire Related Fatalities," and has since come to be called "the Ivey memo."

The short document, easily viewed online,[8] was prepared because of the tendency of very light rear-end collisions of certain models of GM cars to result in massive, fast-burning fires ignited in the gas tank. This is because the tank on these models was positioned at the rear of the car, before the bumper, but without a strong reinforcing plate that would prevent minor rear-enders from resulting in a very serious fire. However, adding a protective shield or plate to the back of the vulnerable cars would be expensive, and so Ivey was commissioned to prepare a cost/benefit analysis for GM.

The calculation was chillingly simple. Based on the approximately 500 fatalities a year caused by fuel-fed fires in car collisions, and the fact that each fatality came with a cost of $200,000 to the company in court cases, the product of these figures divided by the 41 million GM cars on the road resulted in a cost to GM of fuel fire fatalities of $2.40 per car. Next, Ivey estimated that if GM added protective plates, it would result in a value of $2.20 per car for GM to prevent this type of fire in accidents. On these grounds, the memo suggests that slightly re-engineering their cars for safety was not cost effective.

GM's attorneys had denied the existence of the Ivey memo, then denied it was circulated among management, and then insisted it was irrelevant to the case. The key to this revealing memo, and its relevance to how externalities disprove "market efficiency," is the second piece of data fed into the first equation: "Each fatality has a value of $200,000." The point isn't that GM's employees are cold-blooded and don't care about human beings; in fact, the memo says in its concluding paragraph that "it is really impossible to put a value on human life." The point is that only the court-awarded average cost of $200,000 affected GM, and this is the value used in the calculation. So while it may be "impossible" to put a value on a person's life, it is quite possible to put a value on their life *to General Motors*. Indeed, the computation ends with "fatalities related to accidents with fuel fed fires are costing General Motors $2.40 per automobile in current operation."

In other words, it's not that there are no other costs. It's just that they are truly, literally, out of the equation. GM pays two hundred grand, the family grieves their dead loved ones and must live with their disfiguring injuries.

The very large majority of economists are happy to point to the benefits of the market, in terms of the value of the goods and services it has organized. These goods and services are indeed valuable, and this seems to be the great historic role of capitalism, to build up the productive capacity of the economy, which is indeed a precious legacy to anyone who values a higher standard of living than a hunter-gatherer lifestyle. However, what economists are willfully ignoring is the silent mountain of ecological destruction and human suffering, which the market system failed to price high enough to make them worth avoiding.

If these negative side-effects can give a corporation mathematical reason to deliberately not intervene to prevent disfiguring trauma, or approach the scale of the geological catastrophes brought about in the past by mountain-sized meteor impacts, they go a long way toward overshadowing the great gains in standard of living brought by capitalism.

The market system has already inflicted extinction on thousands of species. And what goes around comes around.

6

As Not Seen On TV:
The Market and the Media

By now we've seen how markets have failed to put an adequate price on any of the major externalities that are impacting our world, from atmospheric CO_2 to ocean acidity to species extinctions to auto safety. These issues are enormously important and interact with one another, escalating the stress on our natural systems and the economy that depends upon them. But one of the most important negative externalities found in the market economy has nothing to do with ecological deterioration, but rather access to information, including reasonably accurate news and diverse opinions about it.

The commercial media are businesses that dominate our information system, from TV news to newspapers to magazines to online news portals. These media are of course for-profit, and operate in a very concentrated market environment, where the eight largest media conglomerates own the enormous majority of media companies in terms of viewer/readership. For example, in the US, the four largest cable companies serve 62 percent of the market, while the four largest radio broadcast networks hold a similarly enormous share of the market.[1] And cross-ownership is also extensive—General Electric owns a large part of the NBC conglomerate, along with Comcast, the cable firm; Disney/Buena Vista owns CBS's many media outlets; Time-Warner AOL owns CNN and *Time* and *Newsweek*; News Corporation owns Fox News, the *Wall Street Journal*, and many other print outlets, and so on. These media, including the news media that provide information about world events, have a standard business model, based on selling media time and space to advertisers. Companies are willing to pay for ad time to promote products, and this is the main revenue source for commercial media.

But the fundamental reason for the existence of the news media is to support the democratic functioning of society, giving Americans access to the wide range of news, ideas, and opinions without which we couldn't make any constructive use of our political rights. If we don't know what's going on in our country, let alone abroad, it's hard to see how we can arrive at any sensible conclusions.

Unfortunately, the commercial media's business model means reliance on other corporations for the majority of revenue, meaning that offending the marketplace is poison for company income. The media industry has a long record of omitting important news and shaping what is reported, so as to shield from scrutiny their own parent companies, the corporations that make up their own advertising market, or the small class that owns it (see Chapter 7). The state is usually also given special treatment, since the media need access to government figures and spokespeople on reasonably friendly terms. For this reason, bloody or shameful actions overseas often don't make it into the newspaper's back-sections, let alone the TV news channels.

This filtering of often crucial information puts strong limits on society and our political system, to the point that citizens often are completely unaware of events around them, know nothing about corporate or state complicity in disasters, and generally are left with a neutered picture of the world. This hugely negative outcome is another side-effect of the commercial transactions of a major industry—that is, an externality.

WEAPONS-GRADE PLUTONOMY

The Plutonomy Papers (see the Preface) are generally recognized by anyone reading them as significant documents. They were produced by prestigious analysts at Citibank, one of the US's biggest financial companies (see Chapter 15), and a powerful institution with great political clout and surely a good deal of expertise dealing with wealthy clients. The documents make impressive claims, for example, "the top 1% of households account for 33% of net worth," and the economy now depends more on sales of "toys for the wealthy" than the needs of the "non-rich" and their "surprisingly small bites of the national pie."

What was the reaction of the dominant media to this revelation from high-paid strategists for a "megabank," which by the time the Papers were leaked had been bailed out with about $45 billion in TARP and other funds, plus another hundred billion or so in covered losses and other assistance? There were few mentions in the national press, and even more impressively, what media attention was granted to the Papers dealt almost exclusively with the analysts' stock advice—how to make money off the rise of the super-rich over everyone else.

Fittingly, the *Wall Street Journal* led the charge, giving brief mention to the "plutocrats" while placing the report next to several other index funds also based on the consumption tastes of the affluent. No particular attention is paid to the implications of having a tiny elite monopolizing the productivity gains of the American work force. Likewise, no mention was made of the analysts' conclusion that falling high-income tax rates were in good part responsible for the plutonomy, which would place the super-rich's orgy of buying in the realm of politics. The biggest picture drawn in the article is by an official at Germany's biggest stock exchange, who suggested that "From an emotional point of view, these are goods that people want to have but maybe can't afford to buy directly … so they participate through the index."[2]

This pattern was followed by the *Washington Post*'s own George Will, who focused on the "envy" regular people feel toward the rich, and noted that finding investment opportunities that truly cater to the wealthy is getting harder as more mass-produced brands try to rebrand themselves as "luxury."[3] The *New York Times*' sole coverage of the memos, safely tucked away in the business section, confined itself exclusively to investment advice, endeavoring to answer "Where is gold to be dug from the widening mire?"[4] Notably, besides investing in rich consumers, the *Times* suggested buying the stock of firms that focus on the dire straits of the "multitudinous many," like equities of low-budget retraining companies like DeVry, cheap rent-to-own firms, and fast food. Apparently no revelation of ruling-class contempt for the struggling majority is too great to be overshadowed by investment advice.

It should be noted in this connection the media of the business world, being written for investors, executives, and other elites, are often significantly more candid than mass media like Fox and CNN. If you're going to make profitable investments, you need a reasonably accurate picture of the world, making business media a valuable resource for catching what the mainstream media are leaving out—even if they do see plutonomy as just an investment opportunity. But beyond this rather limited business press coverage, I've been able to find essentially no record of any coverage of these memos in any TV news program. The only reference I can discover refers to the memos briefly appearing on Glenn Beck's show on Fox News, suggesting that the plutocrats are all liberal conspirators. In reality, the plutonomy class comes in liberal and conservative flavors, with little impact on their social role.

Incidentally, we might also note that while many news outlets have found plenty of time to mock Occupy Wall Street's demonstrators, few of them felt obliged to mention that their main criticism was evidently vindicated in the memoranda. In the early days of the demonstration, for example, the *New York Times* judged that the participants had an "apparent wish to pantomime progressivism rather than practice it knowledgably" and a "wish to burrow through the space-time continuum and hunker down in 1968." The media generally insisted that the "We are the 99%" rhetoric was meaningless, but the Citi memos note that when discussing US consumption levels "Clearly, the analysis of the top 1% of US households is paramount." Rather than even discuss this interesting corroboration of the main argument of OWS—that the 1 percent dominates society—media treatment has kept to its rhetorical power.[5]

WMD BS

The gentle evasions practiced by media out to avoid offending advertisers, powerful banks, and affluent elements also apply to the state. A classic example of this would be Saddam Hussein's Iraq. While Hussein is universally known to be a dictator and mass murderer, an important part of his bloody history has been conveniently omitted. With the US the dominant power in the Middle East since Britain was weakened in the World Wars, the United States gave enormous support to Saddam Hussein prior to his invasion of Kuwait in 1990. This was in part to support Hussein against Iran during the long war between those countries in the 1980s, which killed over a million people. However, fighting Iran was clearly not the only reason for US support, since it continued after the war ended.

This fact has been almost fully kept out of mainstream US media, but the business press has been somewhat more open about the subject. Notably, the London *Financial Times* reported that "The Bush [41] Administration pushed through a $1 billion loan guarantee to Iraq for farm exports just 10 months before the invasion of Kuwait," and well after the Iran–Iraq War's end. Noting that several administration members were opposed to the move, the *Financial Times* reports:

> The debate over the issue came to climax at a White House meeting on November 8, 1989 when senior officials from the Federal Reserve, US Treasury and Commerce Departments all objected to the $1 billion guarantee to back US farm exports to Iraq. The reasons cited, according to participants at the meeting, included the view that Iraq was no longer creditworthy—it was then in default on its $65 billion of foreign debt—and that Baghdad had already admitted to the US that it had abused the same loan guarantee scheme.[6]

The Under-Secretary of State told the meeting that cutting off the food aid would run "contrary to the president's intentions."

This was not wildly out of character for the US State and Defense Department. As reviewed in Chapter 1, the business press is usually the venue for the most honest reporting on US influence in the Mid-East, including the *Wall Street Journal*'s reporting that usual US practice is support and "intelligence-sharing with nondemocratic regimes, providing more counterterrorism training and participating in exercises with their militaries. The hope is that once the regimes are more secure, power will slowly devolve to their people."[7] Finding any mention of these common practices is difficult outside the media that cater to business, and they certainly don't turn up on broadcast or cable TV news.

With specific regard to US support for Hussein, by far the most significant break in the mainstream media's silence on the subject was in a rather good 2002 *Newsweek* article. Highly unusual for the American press in the early days of the run-up to the Iraq invasion, the piece refers to Donald Rumsfeld's friendly meeting with Hussein in 1983, when he was sent by Reagan as an oil-industry envoy to build friendly relations with one of many US-supported Arab dictators. Years later, when Rumsfeld led the charge to overthrow Hussein and occupy Iraq, he failed to mention the meeting in the countless TV appearances used to build up war enthusiasm. As *Newsweek* observes

> ... the United States backed Saddam's armies with military intelligence, economic aid and covert supplies of munitions ... during the 1980s, America knowingly permitted the Iraq Atomic Energy Commission to import bacterial cultures that might be used to build biological weapons ... According to confidential Commerce Department export-control documents ... the shopping list included a computerized database for Saddam's Interior Ministry (presumably to help keep track of political opponents); helicopters to transport Iraqi officials; television cameras for "video surveillance applications"; chemical-analysis equipment for the Iraq Atomic Energy Commission (IAEC), and, most unsettling, numerous shipments of "bacteria/fungi/protozoa" to the IAEC. According to former officials, the bacteria cultures could be used to make biological weapons, including anthrax ... The United States almost certainly knew from its own satellite imagery that Saddam was using chemical weapons against Iranian troops. When Saddam bombed Kurdish rebels and civilians with a lethal cocktail of mustard gas, sarin, tabun and VX in 1988, the Regan administration first blamed Iran, before acknowledging, under pressure from congressional Democrats, that the culprits were Saddam's own forces.[8]

Other than in this article, *Newsweek* generally followed the mainstream line of accepting more or less uncritically the Bush administration's claims of Hussein's WMD. What was left out, in *Newsweek*'s and most other coverage, was the fact that our government sold them to him.

BOUGHT AND SOLD AND SOLD-OUT

It's worth noting that the thinking behind the use of media to shape people's perceptions is far older than Iraq War propaganda. In fact, the modern use of public relations is an American-British invention, beginning with a number of influential psychologists and publishers who served on the government's Creel Committee. This body's specific job was to whip America's pacifist population into readiness for World War I. Among the figures to emerge from this was Edward Bernays, whose *New York Times* obituary called him "the father of public relations," and who famously lead a large PR campaign to make the color green more fashionable, in order for women to not feel their clothes clashed with the packaging of Lucky Strike cigarettes, his employer.

Bernays wrote in his seminal book *Public Relations* that indeed, after the war, many Creel Committee members "applied (on behalf of business) the publicity methods they had learned during the war."[9] In fact, Bernays wrote a classic article for the *American Journal of Sociology* between the wars, called "Managing Public Opinion: The Why and How," detailing a number of PR campaigns, and summarizing "Public opinion … is the power of the group to sway the larger public in its attitude." Referring to the new discipline he had helped to found, Bernays called it "a new technique—the psychology of public persuasion. Through the application of this new psychology [one] is able to bring about changes in public opinion that will make for the acceptance of new doctrines, beliefs, and habits." Bernays drew a comparison of PR with education, but acknowledged there was "this dissimilarity: Education attempts to be disinterested, while propaganda is frankly partisan."[10]

But of course the most ubiquitous form of corporate communication is advertising, due to the massive amounts of money routinely spent on it by firms across the economy. A good example of the ability of advertising investment to shape behavior is the re-acceptance of "home equity loans" by Americans during the housing bubble of the first decade of the twenty-first century. These loans, taken out against the value of one's home, used to be known as "second mortgages," and were considered a desperate measure, since it put the security of a person's home on the line for cash. As the business press records, "Today these loans have become universally accepted, their image transformed by ubiquitous ad campaigns from banks."[11]

Memorable corporate easy-money slogans from the era include "Live richly" from Citicorp (now Citigroup), and Fleet's "Is your mortgage squeezing your wallet? Squeeze back." In other words, if paying down your mortgage so you can own your house is reducing your spending money, borrow against it *more*. Focusing on the Citi "live richly" campaign, the *New York Times* reported that the campaign "urged people to lighten up about money and helped persuade hundreds of thousands of Citi customers to take out home equity loans—that is, to borrow against their homes."[12] The campaign to change men and women's minds cost Citi alone $1 billion, but over 30 years led to an increase in the value of home equity loans, from about $1 billion to a $1 trillion market. The business section reports without judgment that "None of this would have been possible without a conscious effort by lenders, who have spent billions of dollars in advertising to change the language of home loans and with it Americans' attitudes toward debt." This suggests the raw power of large amounts of money. And the more immediate externality associated with these transactions is also not small: "For the first time since World War II, the portion of home value that Americans own has fallen to less than 50 percent."[13]

Externalities vary in their nature and effects from industry to industry, whether acid rain from manufacturing, or dead zones in world oceans from agricultural runoff. In the commercial media industry, the externality is the loss of news and analysis that might reflect badly on state and corporate power centers. And as bad as the environmental externalities reviewed in this section are, the externality of lost access to information is significantly worse, because it prevents citizens from even knowing about the full range of other problems, let alone taking action on them. Alternative media do exist, including many outlets that gave the above subjects the careful attention they deserve. But due to the concentration of the media marketplace, and the high costs of publicity campaigns to draw attention to remote corners of the Internet, the corporate media may well continue their role as the crucial factor that prevents real social change.

Part II

Will Work For Peanuts:
The Job Market and
the War on Labor

Introduction to Part II:
The Labor Market In Theory

The market economy is considered by economists to provide a fair income for a day's work, regardless of what type of work you do. This is because the dominant "neoclassical" school of economic theory considers incomes to be based on a person's productivity—the amount of goods and services you can make in a day. The higher your productivity, the larger your income will grow, because your higher productivity makes you a more valuable employee. This implies a fair distribution of income to those who most deserve it, and means that workplace hierarchies are essentially meritocracies.

Unfortunately, the reality observed in markets, especially to the extent they've been deregulated in the last 30 years, is rather different. The theory begins to weaken when we consider that markets only have the property of paying you for your productivity if the market has a more or less "competitive" structure. This means that it must not have any large concentrations of power— that is, the ability to shape economic circumstances, such as prices. If power does exist in the market, then the market may not work at all efficiently or reward work with proportionate income. This is indeed the case for many industries, and since a large body of unemployed workers usually exists, workers are typically a leg down in bargaining with large, organized employers for higher wages.

This is especially visible in today's economy, with high unemployment meaning particularly low worker bargaining power, which besides low wages has also meant that employers can extract harder work rates from workers through fear. The *Wall Street Journal*, for example, reports:

> US workers have yet to share much in the productivity and profits they've helped generate during the recovery. From mid-2009 through the end of

2010, output per hour at US nonfarm businesses rose 5.2% as companies
found ways to squeeze more from their existing workers. But the lion's
share of that gain went to shareholders in the form of record profits,
rather than to workers in the form of raises. Hourly wages, adjusted for
inflation, rose only 0.3% ... in other words, companies shared only 6%
of productivity gains with their workers. That compares to 58% since
records began in 1947.[1]

Regrettably, this is the exact opposite of what theory anticipates,
but the pattern is very clear. And indeed, the subject is a very
common one in the more real-world analysis of the business
press, where one often finds articles like the one above, referring
to the dynamics of asymmetric bargaining power and its different
affects on prices, suggesting that for workers, "Unemployment
is high, so they have little bargaining power."

Bargaining power shapes all transactions, however, not just
those between firms and labor. A simple example can be found
in another recent article, this one on the subject of big vs. small
firms and how fast they pay their bills. The *Journal*'s research
found that in the current "credit crunch," with expensive and
unpredictable access to loans, "Large corporations are tightening
the screws on their smaller counterparts as the credit crunch
intensifies companies' efforts to hold on to their cash ... So far,
the biggest and fittest companies are often flexing their financial
muscle, benefiting at the expense of smaller and weaker ones,"
which the *Journal* calls "corporate Darwinism at work."[2] A
former Wells Fargo economist suggests "There's a power struggle
going on ... Big firms can force their terms on suppliers and
customers. And if you're a small business or a small store in a
mall, you have no bargaining power and have to take what's
given, which is not much today." Sounds similar to the condition
of the workforce.

Of course, part of the reason that workers have so much
less bargaining power than in the past is the loss of union
organization. Over the last 30 years, the unions have been
smashed down to the point that they represent only 7 percent of
the US private-sector workforce. And while that hasn't stopped
media from making them out to be big powerful institutions that

manipulate government, it does prevent workers from having the power to stop firms from pushing pay freezes and health plan cost increases down their throats.

Since economic theory is based on the concept that markets are competitive, neither companies nor workers are supposed to be able to muscle up their incomes. However, even neoclassical theory does suggest that large organizations, either companies or labor unions, will have more ability to influence the price of what they sell, either goods or human work. But while economists often make use of this theory to advocate eliminating labor unions, it is almost never applied to corporations of large size.

It turns out that once again, mainstream economic theory is ill-equipped to understand current market events. In Part II, we'll take a look at how recent developments have shaped the economy, starting with the gigantic divergence in wealth between a small rich minority vs. the 90+ percent of Americans in Chapter 7, the tools of outsourcing and finance that allow a small elite to exercise political control in Chapter 8, and see some of the effects of this power on our political world in Chapters 11 and 12.

7

Classroots:
"Run-of-the-mill Class Conflict"

The Occupy Wall Street demonstrations around the world are a clear sign of growing class consciousness, but for some time even conservative observers have been commenting on the growing chasm between the wealth of a small upper class and the majority. An especially impressive landmark was reached in 2008, when a study ranked the top ten world cities with the greatest levels of income inequality. Incredibly, an American city, New York, cracked the top ten, usually dominated by Third World metropolises like Nairobi and Buenos Aires.[1] New York has also joined Abu Dhabi, a playground for rich Arab monarchs and investors, in a new fad among the wealthy: eating gold, as it is used as an ingredient in chocolate cake, champagne, cappuccinos, and sundaes. The *Wall Street Journal* reports that wolfing down the precious metal has become a hip status symbol.[2]

It's not just numbers on paper—the well-heeled are going to town, from $700 cigars to $1,500 facelifts to $10 million personal helicopters. What an average American would make in a hundred years, the rich drop on a chopper to take from Long Island into Manhattan, so as to shop without sitting in New York traffic. Sales of luxury brands struggle today, but are helped by "a sustained increase in the number of wealthy consumers, particularly in countries like Brazil, Russia, India, and China."[3]

Indeed, the number of multimillionaires and billionaires worldwide is now bigger than ever before. A report prepared by financial analysts on the subject was described in the *Financial Times*: "The ranks of the world's rich swelled to eight million during 2007 as the wealthy proved immune to the strains across global economies in the latter half of the year."[4] These "high net worth individuals" are defined as having at least $1 million of investable capital (excluding their primary residence), coming to about 1 percent of the US population, again anticipating the grievances of the Occupy Wall Street movement. The report concludes that the "truly rich" were able to "shrug off the credit crunch."

And no better proof of this can be found than the superyacht. These massive state-of-the-art private islands run into tens of millions of dollars, plus about a tenth of the purchase price in maintenance and fuel cost annually. No mere recession is going to put the yacht brokers out of business, "an elite group who matchmake the super-rich with what is regarded as the ultimate luxury."[5] But it's not all easy being the ruling class, because when your yacht is 300 feet long, "One thing money cannot always buy is space at the marina." The tear-jerking shortage is aggravated by the lack of suitable new harbor locations, which must have "all the infrastructure needed to attract the big boats, including easy access by air, possibly a nearby airstrip that can handle private jets or helicopters and the potential to become a chic destination in its own right," as the elite press laments.[6]

The class symbolism of yachting was also described in a *Fortune* magazine article reporting from the 2009 St. Barts Bucket yacht race, calling the timing of the event "a testament to tone-deafness [and] megawealth ... If you have sufficient millions, it may not really matter if your portfolio plummets. Nor may you particularly care if the proles are offended by your profligacy"[7] Elsewhere, the *Financial Times* reported that "America discovered class war" in the finance crisis, thanks to wealth inequality becoming "a Grand Canyon."[8]

The question is why does such a small class of people have so much wealth to itself, while the rest of the country struggles with chronically elevated unemployment and falling incomes? How can this upper class keep so much of the value the economy produces, while the majority gets less and less? There are a few reasons for this "class war," as the business press calls it.

THIS LAND'S NOT YOUR LAND

At the heart of class conflict is the ownership of productive property—the factories, machinery, offices, and other "physical capital" that can be used to produce goods and services. For class analysis to apply to an economy, the ownership of these means of production (and the wealth they bring) must be concentrated among some social stratum. A good indicator of this ownership is the stock market—stocks are pieces of companies, so the ownership of these pieces means ownership of America's productive resources. The conventional wisdom suggests that today's America is characterized by a broad "owning class" made up of the more than half of American households that own stock. But this is hardly accurate. First, less than half of American households now own stock and, more importantly, the richest 10 percent of US households owned 81 percent of all stock by value. The lower 80 percent of America owns less than 8 percent of US equity.[9] That is a tightly concentrated ownership of America's productive resources, a crucial fact about our "free market" that economists usually prefer to dismiss or ignore.

The concentrated ownership in itself amounts to class conflict, since households lousy with physical and liquid wealth naturally earn higher incomes, even in times of economic distress. The recent economic crisis and deep recession are perfect examples. While news headlines document the phenomenal public pain of this "jobless recovery," *Fortune* magazine described the corporate world's experiences as "the anatomy of a bounce"— the business world had bounced back to major profits again. The reason was a "wondrous surge in productivity" as the major US corporations shed over 3 percent of their total payrolls, driving the remaining employees to greater effort out of fear of joining the mobs of the unemployed.[10] This, of course, reflects what the business world recognizes as "the relative bargaining power of labor and capital," between people who work and people who own (see the Introduction to this Part). Recessions drive workers to harsher competition for precious jobs as layoffs escalate—a circumstance many Tea Party and Occupy Wall Street demonstrators are familiar with.

That's the most basic type of class conflict, which also explains why the stock indices so frequently improve when unemployment goes up—higher unemployment puts employers in a stronger position relative to workers, who are more afraid to join the jobless. This means higher productivity and lower wage growth for workers and, therefore, higher profits, driving the stock indexes up.

The conventional economic view says that because there is no law that says a person on the street can't become rich, we all have an equal chance. But this weak-sauce ideology misses the fact that wealth has been concentrated for generations, and while you may "work your way up," the potential of this is limited when the top 5 percent owns two-thirds of American capital. However, while this absurdly lopsided ownership of the economy is the fundamental basis of class warfare, it is only the beginning of the modern practice.

ORGANIZE FOR SIZE

Second in importance only to concentrated ownership, organization for scale is pivotal to all modern class conflict. Here the conditions of labor and capital are wildly divergent. To the corporate world, it's usually taken for granted that organization and size are all-important, and businesses will usually take any opportunity to grow in scale and market clout, if they can raise the cash for a merger/acquisition. One relevant example from the universe of corporate behavior might include the intense concentration of the freight rail industry after Reaganite deregulation. Rail is often looked to as a valuable low-carbon alternative to auto transport, so it's important to note the impact of "megamergers" in the industry. As *Fortune* describes: "The consolidation boom began after the bankruptcies of legendary lines ... and industry deregulation in 1980. Today each of the Big Four has at least 21,000 miles of track."[11]

But the archetypal example is commercial banking, where the companies have become so enormous that they had to be bailed out lest their bankruptcies sink the broader economy. Here again, as soon as deregulation took hold in the 1980s and 1990s, the banks went on a merger binge, resulting in the "too big to fail" financial institutions of today.

Why are firms so gung-ho for this growth? Part of the answer lies in economies of scale, which are savings companies enjoy when they grow larger and produce more output. Economies of scale give firms a great incentive to enlarge, since this will improve per-unit profitability. These economies may come from many sources, depending on the industry. In manufacturing, they come from "spreading" the big up-front costs of factory space, machinery and equipment over more products. In rail, they arise from the ease of moving freight further distances without changing carriers and thus losing time and money. In banking, they can come from spreading the costs of large computing systems over more and more output (see Chapter 15).

The large size firms strive to attain also may grant some degree of power—the clout of being a large institution with significant business to throw around. Large rail firms can demand lower prices from suppliers and charge clients more because their options are diminished as the market concentrates. Likewise, huge banks can muscle retailers to charge higher fees for debit card use. Economies of scale and market power go a long way to addressing perhaps the major bone of contention between OWS and Tea Party—do markets mean corporate power or efficient competition? The further concentration and corporate growth proceed, the more the market tends toward the former.

On top of the growth of corporations, we should realize that companies are themselves organized into industry groups, which belong to various national business organizations like the US Chamber of Commerce and the Business Roundtable, organizations with massive resources and political pull. The influence and political spending power of these umbrella groups of capital is an order of magnitude beyond what labor as a whole can muster. The conservative *Economist* of London described business organization this way:

> Take a really big international industry such as cars ... Write down all the manufacturers' names (there are more than 20 large ones for cars) along

the fours sides of a square. Now draw lines connecting manufacturers that have joint ventures or alliances with one another, whether in design, research, components, full assembly, distribution or marketing, for one product or for several, anywhere in the world. Pretty soon, the drawing becomes an incomprehensible tangle. Just about everyone seems to be allied with everyone else. And the car industry is not an exception. It is a similar story in computer hardware, computer software, aerospace, drugs, telecommunications, defence and many others … [corporate alliances] have long been a feature of oil exploration and mining, for example, being used when a new well or mine looked too risky for one firm to develop on its own.[12]

Labor's condition is a near-polar opposite of the large-scale organization of the corporate world. By now, only 12.3 percent of American workers are represented by a union, yet *Business Week* reports that the share of American workers saying they want a union in their workplace has been increasing for decades, to nearly half of non-union workers. So if workers are increasingly interested in unionization, why have union numbers tended in the opposite direction for the last 30 years? The magazine's analysis is that

… heightened corporate power has checked union growth … Unionization elections are typically so lopsided today that most unions have all but given up on them. Most employers pull out the stops when labor organizers appear, using everything from mandatory antiunion meetings to staged videos showing alleged union thugs beating workers, backed by streams of leaflets and letters to workers' homes. While most of these tactics are legal, companies also illegally fire union supporters in 25 percent of all elections.[13]

Historically, while corporate capital accumulated and gained quasi-monopoly positions, conspiracy laws forbade workers to organize themselves. US labor history remained unusually blood-soaked well after Europe's (see Chapter 9), yet to this day Americans remain sympathetic to the countervailing strength of worker organization. The commercial press's reliable description of US labor as "powerful" is disingenuous in light of the growth and influence displayed by US business. The business press's description is more realistic: "Clearly, in an economy dominated by corporate giants ... unions must gain scale" in order to "wield market clout" as the firms do. The consistent and wide divergence in state treatment of these two strains of social organization speaks volumes about the power of concentrated wealth.

In Chapter 8, we'll look at the more modern methods of exerting the power originating in concentrated ownership of wealth and organization. They mainly involve different types of "capital mobility"—being able to move large amounts of money or productive property from place to place and country to country. This has become associated with the massive "outsourcing" trend in today's economy, and has evolved into the main way class conflict is waged in the modern world.

However, there are some more direct methods. One memorable instance took place in 2010 when the *New York Times* reported that the largest US banks were shifting their massive political contributions from the Democrats, who they supported in 2008, to the GOP. The *Times* suggested that "Republicans are rushing to capitalize on what they call Wall Street's 'buyer's remorse' with the Democrats."[14] The Democrats have passed an extremely mild finance reform bill that leaves the system almost entirely intact (see Chapter 16), but they have resorted to populist condemnation of the bank CEOs in order to shore up their sagging approval numbers. So the banks are putting some of their weight behind the other party, and their political investments indeed brought more Republicans into Congress in 2010.

This dominance of the political system by concentrated corporate and financial capital also has a rougher side than posh investors' meetings and political dinners. Two years ago, the US reached a ratio of 1 in 100 adults in the prison and jail systems, a rate of incarceration unmatched even in the world's police states.[15] One in nine state workers are employed in "corrections" at enormous cost, guarding a disproportionately large number of blacks, Hispanics, and folks from poorer communities. To the extent that deindustrialization and lower economic growth have created great bodies of unemployed, and social policies no longer provide support, the underclass is increasingly warehoused in the penal system.

Class war is only hell for one side, but with Occupy Wall Street opening middle America's eyes to class conflict, the ruling class might sweat too.

8
Hitting the Class Ceiling: The Modern Practice of Class Confrontation

In today's economy, with more than four unemployed working people for every job opening, it's easy to see hard times in the streets.[1] While some political figures say that the out-of-work have themselves to blame, it's hard to square that with the huge spikes in unemployment during and after recessions—unless we're supposed to believe that hundreds of thousands of Americans are becoming lazy at the same time. In particular, the major recession that began in 2008 has meant gigantic increases in the numbers of unemployed and underemployed workers, who would give anything for a job paying a modest $30,000 a year. But for the other end of the class structure, that's petty cash. Among the modern financial elite, hedge fund traders have become notorious for building absurdly large estates, with floor plans sometimes approaching those of the Taj Mahal. In the homes of the ruling class, that $30,000 gets spent in a single room—on curtains.[2]

FORECLOSING THE HOUSE OF LABOR

The intense and increasing concentration of wealth is the fundamental basis of class conflict (see Chapter 7), but that tight ownership gives rise to the modern practice of capital mobility. Capital mobility refers to the ability of the owners of concentrated wealth to move it from one place to another, depriving areas of capital if the owners don't like what's happening there. This can take two forms: movement of physical capital, such as factories and equipment for producing goods; and movement of money capital, the financial wealth needed to run a business. While these have always been important throughout modern history, they have taken on new significance with the advent of affordable containerized shipping and the telecommunications revolution. Let's look at physical capital mobility first, which often goes by other names, such as "outsourcing" or "globalization."

Consider a recent set of contract negotiations that brought a major defeat to a traditional center of working-class organization. Three major Milwaukee-Chicago area manufacturers—Kohler, Harley-Davidson, and Mercury Marine—have recently locked in permanent two-tiered contracts. Usually seen only temporarily in dire recessions, these contracts mean new hires to the workplace will receive far lower pay and benefits than the other union employees. Essentially, it means large parts of a union's gains are surrendered for the next generation of workers. Labor unions therefore usually resist them strongly.

But the manufacturers eagerly turned to their trump card, capital mobility, threatening to shut down the plant and move production to cheaper job markets, typically with non-union shops. In addition to the wide array of traditional antiunion tools normally used by corporations to discourage worker organization, "Harley-Davidson and Mercury Marine ... publicly declared that they would move factory operations to lower-cost American cities ... if the unions failed to accept the concessions set forth in remarkably similar contracts." The organized workforce had previously refused to accept lower pay and benefits for their younger union brothers and sisters and "voted last fall to reject such terms, but a few days later, they voted again and accepted them. They reversed course after the company announced that its headquarters in nearby Fond du Lac would be closed and operations consolidated in Stillwater. The Stillwater factory is now being closed instead."[3]

Local union leaders openly describe the developments as "a surrender" to employers, but say the union rank-and-file membership democratically approved the contracts since they are convinced that "the companies are prepared to move factories from the Milwaukee area." The union leadership had balked at negotiating so early in advance and in a recession, but "conceded after the company insisted it would otherwise use the intervening months to prepare to move operations elsewhere, perhaps to Kansas City."

This phenomenon of modern outsourcing has transformed the fabric of our society. While many Americans celebrate entrepreneurs, it's worth bearing in mind that it is they who have elected to "offshore" or "outsource" more and more industrial jobs over the last few decades. Even the new World Trade Center, the symbol of US resilience, is being rebuilt with Chinese glass. The glass manufacturing industry has followed the trend of outsourcing production overseas to take advantage of cheaper and more controllable labor, and a lack of environmental standards.[4]

Thus, globalization has become a pivotal weapon for putting the squeeze on the folks turning up at Tea Party and Occupy Wall Street demonstrations. As a media technician told the business press, "It would be hard to outsource my job ... But it is used as an unspoken threat to keep wages down." The general message is summarized by the conservative *Financial Times*: "Globalization may have permanently changed the relative bargaining power of capital and labor in the industrialized world."[5]

This connection was explored in more detail in an extremely valuable study by Kate Bronfenbrenner of Cornell University, who found that offshoring grew enormously in the 2000s, following "a systematic pattern of firm restructuring that is moving jobs from union to non-union facilities within the country, as well as to non-union facilities in other countries," and that the "overwhelming majority" of companies engaged in international outsourcing "were ultimately owned by extremely large, profitable, US-based, publicly-held multinationals."[6] This dynamic creates the "race to the bottom" for the world's working people, showing how the "freedom" of the market degenerates into class struggle. It's really the freedom of the world's elite capital owners to pit the world's workers against one another in a fight for a day's work.

The business press often expresses this understanding, including when the *Wall Street Journal* reported in a headline "Why global investors bet on autocrats, not democrats." Comparing the amount of corporate investment in China relative to India, the *Journal* finds that "Global money managers are coming down solidly in favor of the communists." The reasons are not considered to be mysterious, being simply "the untapped potential of China's roughly 1.1 billion people" and strong infrastructure. These low labor costs are the fundamental reason for the "Made In China" inscription stamped on a huge proportion of our consumer products. China has another advantage in its possession of the ex-colonial Hong Kong, which often acts a gateway for multinationals and investors to plow billions of dollars into the PRC. This position is cherished by the powerful corporate and financial entities of Hong Kong, as the *New York Times* described when reporting on large demonstrations for "universal suffrage" in Hong Kong: "Many business leaders oppose further democracy, contending that the public does not understand the importance and complexity of creating an environment conducive to investment."[7] But the main factor remains that China's destitute workforce and authoritarian controls are more important to elite investors and their concentrated wealth than the lack of democracy. These issues of exploitation and social control drive capital movements across the world economy.

BOND MARKET BONDAGE

In addition to moving hard productive assets, the telecom revolution has enabled such swift movements of money that investors can exercise a good deal of control over a society simply through their degree of willingness to lend. This movement of money, or "capital flow," has swollen to trillions of dollars daily, reaching a peak of about $9 trillion in 2007, a ridiculously high level.[8] The huge expansion in fast-moving capital was driven by bank growth, financial deregulation, and the reduced taxes on the giant wealth of the rich, and provides a pivotal new means of social control.

This force can act in numerous ways, the most central of which being through the bond market. Often governments run budget deficits, where they spend more than they take in through taxes. This is sometimes due to sensible "stimulus" spending by government to counteract the shrinkage of private-sector employment during recessions, keeping total demand high to help shorten or weaken the recession. Today, deficits are more commonly caused by drastically reducing taxes on high-income households, done in order to create jobs that seldom materialize. But in order to run any deficit, governments must borrow, and like all large institutions they borrow by issuing bonds, which are promises to pay back the purchase price with interest. So an investor purchasing a government bond is essentially lending money to the state. Additionally, bond market investors are highly concentrated—according to the Federal Reserve, while the huge majority of US households do not hold significant wealth in the form of bonds, bond ownership is concentrated in the top 10 percent of households, and their median holding is $250,000.[9] This allows for serious limitations on what government can do, even in the face of public demand.

Take the now-notorious case of Greece as an example. Greece is presently suffering from a "sovereign debt crisis," where its large budget deficits have run up enough total debt that paying the interest on it is putting a serious burden on the country. While this is a serious issue, the concentrated ownership of Greece's debt in the bond market has meant that certain fixes for the state deficit are considered, like "austerity" (higher taxes and cuts to social programs, schools, and pensions), but not others, such as significantly hiking taxes on the Greek rich and their massive assets. Indeed, the generally pro-austerity package *New York Times* reported critics' view that "the country has failed to adequately crack down on tax evasion among the wealthiest segments of society."[10]

Indeed, the paper elsewhere reports that

> ... the people potentially in the best position to help shore up the nation's finances are mainly keeping their heads down ... among the wealthiest Greeks—whether shipping magnates, whose tax-free status is enshrined in the constitution, or the so-called oligarchs who have accumulated vast wealth via their dominance of the economy like oil, gas, media, banking and even cement ... they have done what Greeks from the richest to those of modest means have traditionally done: pay as little as they can in the

way of taxes. [And although] The moneyed elite in Greece have always been secretive in nature, especially when it comes to their fortunes ... Last year alone, an estimated 8 billion euros ($10.2 billion) in collectible taxes were in arrears—nearly half of the country's budget deficit ... But as children go hungry in Greek schools because their parents have no money with which to feed them, and the streets of Athens become home to growing numbers of desperate, jobless people, pressure is mounting on the country's rich to do what the state can no longer do: write checks.[11]

After Greece seemed headed for a default (a declaration of inability to repay a debt, parallel to personal bankruptcy), a bailout was organized by the large economies of the Euro zone, primarily France and Germany. But the austerity cutbacks demanded in exchange for the Europe-IMF rescue package are intense: 30 percent pay cuts to public-sector workers, new property taxes, value-added taxes, privatization of the public water company, new taxes on the self-employed, and more measures that the press calls "the dismantling of a middle-class welfare state in real time—with nothing to replace it." Indeed, as consumer buying power has been squeezed by the need to pay foreign creditors, Greece's economy actually shrank 7.5 percent in the last quarter of 2011, meaning its crucial debt measurement of debt relative to economic size, actually *rose* to about 150 percent.[12]

But with the French and German government having bought up the Greek bonds formerly held by French and German banks, European governments prove their preference of protecting rich bond investors and sticking it to the Greek on the street. Especially because these finance crises have a way of causing widespread panic among investors, a process called "contagion" (see Chapter 14), and already seen to be happening with the debt of other European countries, like Spain and Italy.[13] A permanent Euro bailout fund was agreed to in spring 2012 partially for this reason.[14]

Unsurprisingly, these austerity measures are routinely described as "unpopular" or "deeply unpopular," and severe riots and countrywide strikes have broken out in opposition to the punishing terms dictated by foreign lenders (see below). This underlying intense unpopularity has led to the surprising rise of the anti-neoliberal SYRIZA, the Coalition of the Radical Left, in the Greek elections of 2007 and 2012. As the Greek economy deteriorates under five successive waves of austerity, to the point that a fifth of storefronts in Athens were empty in 2012, Greek politics has entered an era of unpredictability.[15]

This dynamic of social control by a concentrated bond market is not limited to small economies like Greece. It can be seen just as clearly in the case of the world's biggest economy, the US. A good example is Pimco, a particularly large bond dealer that *Fortune* magazine described as so large that it "has become essential to the functioning of the credit markets," a size derived in large part from "shrewd bets on government intervention"—that is, guessing when the government will consider a company too big and important to be allowed to go bankrupt.[16] Pimco has become a "partner" of the government, as its CEO says, and in fact it runs the Federal Reserve's quarter-trillion-dollar "commercial paper" program, which "keeps short-term loans flowing to corporate America" during the credit crisis and aftermath.

Pimco is only one player in the bond market, but its size makes it an especially clear example of how the bond market can push even governments around. When the government moved to take over the mortgage companies Fannie Mae and Freddie Mac, Pimco wanted the companies' shareholders to take the hit, not the bondholders who had lent them money. Financial observers say that Pimco gave the government an "ultimatum"—since only Pimco had enough liquid capital to absorb the hail of bonds the government issued in the crisis while buying bad assets from huge banks, Washington "can't afford to let him walk away." So Fannie and Freddie's shareholders lost their investments, but the bondholders were repaid, one of numerous episodes in which the company confronted the state, and the state "blinked."

These examples illustrate the power of highly mobile capital. University of New Mexico law professor Timothy Canova has extensively studied this phenomenon and found that

> … the liberalization of international capital flows has created a world in which the sovereignty of any one nation is surrendered to the forces

of private financial speculation. Capital is capable of staging a general political strike against the policies of any nation state, including the United States, by simply voting against that country's currency and bonds in the private marketplace ... even Federal Reserve Board policy is subject to the veto-power of the international capital markets.[17]

This means class war.

STRIKE vs. STRIKE

Despite the fantastic power of concentrated financial wealth to put the US government "over a barrel" as *Fortune* put it, regular people can fight back and win victories against capital, but it takes organization. With organization, workers can take on scale and gradually build up some power that actually responds to their own needs. Skeptics on this point need to consider the record of stomped-upon peoples of the world who are building up their own organization and countervailing power, even now.

Take China, which isn't exactly the worker's paradise it once claimed to be. Wages there are a small fraction of those in the developed world, and Chinese work-safety standards are so weak that an incredible 137,000 workers are killed on the job every year, the equivalent of 45 9/11s annually, so that Wal-Mart products can remain cheap. And while this has made the People's Republic a corporate investment magnet, *Business Week* suggests China's people "are no longer the docile hero workers of the Communist era, or the eager, exploitable legions who made China a manufacturing powerhouse."[18] The reason for this momentous change is a "de facto labor movement" which in several cases has successfully pushed up wages for bottom-of-the-ladder workers, thanks to organization.

But of course, *Business Week* recognizes that investors will not take these improving living standards lying down. "If this labor movement is sustained, foreign investors will have to consider their China strategy in a whole new light," and indeed companies more sensitive to labor costs are pulling up stakes: "China's attraction for sweatshop investors will diminish," and "low-end" manufacturing is already seen by an investing consultant to be "moving to other countries like Vietnam, India, and Pakistan." Capital mobility doesn't cotton to rising wages.

No country more clearly represents the tension between democracy and world capital mobility than Greece. While coalitions of creditors including the IMF and the European Central Bank insist on ramming waves of cutbacks in public services down the people's throats, the people of Greece haven't taken it lying down. They launched a long series of general strikes, where the organized part of the overall workforce ceased to work, expressing people's power as the producers of society's wealth. So many general strikes met the government's austerity drive that the *New York Times* remarked that it "feels like a ritual ... everyone from trash collectors, teachers, retired army officers, lawyers and even judges walked off the job to protest the government-imposed wage cuts and tax increases that they say [are] driving the debt-ridden country into penury."[19]

It's understood that without the demonstrations, the deep austerity measures would have been even worse. Even as the austerity law was signed in November 2011, the press reported "what was different ... was the scale of the protest—tens of thousands of people—and the range of the demonstrators." The fight continued—even as the Greek Parliament passed a new austerity measure, workers in the power union refused to cooperate with an element of the law that would mean cut-off of electrical service for failure to pay the new taxes.

These dynamics can be seen in the United States as well, such as in public-sector unions' fight for collective bargaining (see Chapter 10). But as valuable as the Madison uprising was, Occupy Wall Street is the American movement that's most directly addressed the issue of concentrated wealth and the power of capital mobility. Many media figures have mocked its "We are the 99%" rhetoric for suggesting that the richest 1% is especially powerful or otherwise somehow different from the rest of society. But of course we saw that this is the opinion of many in the richest levels of society, such as in the Plutonomy Papers (see the Preface) which specifically state that "Clearly, the analysis of the top 1% of US households is paramount." OWS is the only organized movement that has successfully drawn attention to class power, and by focusing on Wall Street, it has also directed attention to the use of that power to remake society and extract political favors and rescues.

And despite general media hostility, the OWS demonstrations have been vast and worldwide. Support for the movement, from those too busy to get to protest actions, came quickly when the movement began: "Donations topped half a million dollars weeks ago, and their storehouse, blocks away from the park in Lower Manhattan, is stuffed with nonperishables, blankets and other supplies sent from cities around the world."[20] The movement was as worldwide as its support, with the media forced to report "a wave of protests swept across Asia, the Americas and Europe," including demonstrations in New York, Chicago, Washington, London, Sydney Australia, Tokyo, Spain, Hong Kong, Toronto, and Los Angeles.[21]

For these reasons, unlike the often openly firearm-wielding Tea Party demonstrations, OWS has been targeted for a fair amount of repression. Government repression has been easy to see, especially in the violent crackdowns that have attempted to evict the Occupations from (often public) land in cities across the US and world. Most notable here was the November 15 pre-dawn raid on the original New York City OWS camp in Zuccotti Park, which the press described admiringly as "military-style," with blinding lights and hundreds of riot-gear-armed police officers.[22] The precision reflected careful planning, which officials have admitted was coordinated in conference calls with other cities looking to get rid of their own embarrassing Occupations.

Notably, the sanitation issue highlighted by Mayor Bloomberg as the reason for the "military-style" action was debunked by his own media empire. Bloomberg business news reported earlier in the month that while "Televisions commentators have jibed at the protestors for ... their supposed filth ... The ground is mostly free of litter ... Members of a sanitation crew wander, brooms in hand and mopping the stone ground." Another "half-dozen" demonstrators spent time after meals "composting leftovers and washing dishes."[23]

Besides being driven out of their encampment, OWS demonstrators were tailed by law enforcement after the fact, with protestors waking up in a church that had sheltered them to find they were being counted by plainclothes police detectives. The NYPD spokesman insisted they had merely come to use the bathroom, and Reverend Karpen stated that they had indeed asked this of the doorkeepers. However, as the press summarized his account:

> Instead, both men entered the sanctuary, one remaining near the door while the other advanced down the aisle, apparently counting the demonstrators in the pews ... A demonstrator then confronted the men and asked them to write down their names and badge numbers ... Mr. Karpen wound up escorting the protesters out a back door because, he said, there was an unknown woman photographing people leaving the church's main entry.[24]

But in addition to the very visible government repression, corporate repression has already begun to emerge against OWS. An impressive planning document for this process was leaked after the coordinated OWS evictions, produced by the prominent and well-connected lobbying firm Clark Lytle Geduldig and Cranford. The document proposed that the American Bankers Association develop a full anti-OWS media plan. The memorandum warns not to "dismiss OWS as a ragtag group of protestors," but rather to "show they have the same cynical motivations as a political opponent" which "will undermine their credibility in a profound way ... The research will also identify opportunities to construct fact-based negative narratives of the OWS for high impact media placement."[25] Also, the lobbying company proposed to "identify extreme language and ideas that put its most ardent supporters at odds with mainstream Americans," despite earlier findings showing broad public support for OWS and its celebration of the 99%. As for Clark Lytle Geduldig & Cranford's motivation for conducting this work for the ABA, there is little mystery; they price the smear campaign at $850,000, about what an average working member of the 99% would make in 17 years.

HOLINESS FROM THE CHEAP SEATS

While the ruling class is routinely building personal homes the size of the Taj Mahal, it's also overhauling historical treasures to better accommodate the jet-set lifestyle. Consider the center of the Islamic faith, Mecca, where the Grand Mosque is being incorporated into what the *New York Times* calls a "gargantuan shopping mall" complete with "Numerous luxury high-rises and hotels" and "a kitsch rendition of London's Big Ben."[26] The abrupt construction boom in Mecca caters to the world's super-wealthy and reflects a new desire of the Saudi royal family "to profit from some of the most valuable real estate in the world." While the traditional Hajj pilgrimage is among the most holy Islamic tenets, the "Vegas-like aura" of the new developments has brought "highly visible class lines" to the Kaaba: "Like the luxury boxes that encircle most sports stadiums, the apartments will allow the wealthy to peer directly down at the main event from the comfort of their suites without having to mix with the ordinary rabble below … The issue is not just run-of-the-mill class conflict."

Indeed, the practice of class conflict has constantly evolved through the modern period, from the enclosure movements in eighteenth- and nineteenth-century England that threw the rural majority into the cramped crucible of the Industrial Revolution, to the tony twenty-first-century bond bourses that route capital around the world and batter stubborn efforts for worker organization. With major world religions becoming the sport of the ruling class, movements like the Arab Spring, Occupy Wall Street, and the Greek general strikes will have to join up globally. The fear of employers moving factories could subside if plants in the next state or nation were also organized, forming a power center rooted in the population rather than the state and capital. At least then the class war would be a fair fight.

9
Fight and Flight:
Economic Conflict, Past and Present

One of the most striking aspects of the history of the American labor movement is the tendency for it to be repressed violently. Labor movements everywhere, being the organization of people pitted against the organization of capital, have usually had to endure the power of money expressed through force. But in the United States this persisted significantly longer than elsewhere, for example, Europe, and in some episodes took on an extraordinary scale. However, today labor is disciplined far less through physical violence than through the simple capital mobility discussed in Chapter 8, combined with the political power considered in more detail in Chapter 11. Comparing the two is instructive as to how organizations struggle with one another, as well as to how class control has evolved over the last century.

LABOR PAINS

Possibly the defining episode of American class conflict was "The Great Upheaval" of July 1877. It followed the great economic crash of 1873, including its major spike in joblessness, and a decline of industrial wages by over a quarter. The strike began when West Virginia railroad workers were informed they were receiving their second pay cut in eight months, after which they refused to work on freight shipping. The mayor's police, moving to break the strike, were enormously outnumbered by the strike-sympathizing town population. As the strike soon spread to Maryland, Pennsylvania, Illinois, and Missouri, the B&O Railroad enlisted West Virginia Governor Mathews to order in the state militia. However, the militia failed after strikers prevented the guardsmen from rolling the railcars, resulting in an exchange of casualties. This strike's success kicked off the Great Upheaval, as the strike spread widely across the giant freight operator's lines, and across different professions. This was at a time when rail was a crucial industry itself, and essential for the functioning of the broader industrial economy. Passenger trains rolled during the strike, but no freight, even as Governor Mathews moved under B&O pressure to bring in more militiamen without sympathy with the strikers, only to find none as the state population grew more radicalized.

The eminent historian Eric Foner records that

> …the labor upheaval suggested how profoundly American class relations had been reshaped during the Civil War and Reconstruction … At the same time, the Great Strike revealed the political power and class consciousness of the urban middle and upper classes, which joined with municipal authorities and veteran's organizations to form 'citizen militias' to do battle with strikers. St. Louis's Committee of Public Safety organized a huge private army, commanded by one Union and one Confederate general, and effectively suppressed the city's general strike.[1]

When the strike reached as far as upstate New York, police in Syracuse made use of "crowd prevention tactics" and "kept close surveillance of the situation and immediately threatened the arrest of 'loud' individuals found on street corners," according to strike historians. In these tense climates, the First Amendment meant little to civil and private authorities.[2] Despite unconstitutional restraints on speech and assembly, the strike largely succeeded in shutting down important rail traffic for some time in very large parts of the US.

Ultimately, the companies succeeded in bringing in the US Army, despite its already being engaged in putting down Native American rebellions and enforcing Reconstruction in the South after the Civil War. However, by rushing the soldiers from city to city, the War Department was able to gradually break down the demonstrators and bring in replacement workers. The strike brought about a very high level of civil conflict on the heels of the

Civil War, with street fights breaking out in many cities between partially organized defenders of the strikes and the augmented police, backed by troops and even police specially deputized by the companies themselves. General Hancock, in command of the troops used to crush the strike, called the Upheaval an "insurrection," and in the end wrote in his diary that it had been "put down by *force*."[3]

General Hancock's attitude is typical of the violence- and force-based approach to repressing labor organization of the nineteenth and early twentieth century in the United States. The violence was not just governmental, as through this period employers relied on companies like the Pinkerton Detective Agency to infiltrate early worker organizations and to discourage workers from joining the violence. In the notable Homestead, Pennsylvania strike, a far more organized labor action than the huge 1877 uprising, organized steelworkers asked for a modest wage increase, since the steel industry was prospering; management responded with a 22 percent decrease, and then locked the workers out of the plant. Management placed ads as far away as the East Coast and Europe for replacement workers, to be brought in to break the union. The workers attempted to surround the plant with pickets to keep the strikebreakers out, but when Pinkerton agents landed on the plant grounds by barge, a firefight broke out, killing several on both sides. Ultimately Governor Pattison, having received major campaign help from the Carnegie empire that owned the plant, brought in the state militia. This allowed the import of strikebreakers, and the union was defeated.

STRIKING THE SAME PLACE TWICE

Another impressive episode took place in Minneapolis in 1933, where the workforce had been kept disorganized, in part through a group called the "Citizens Alliance," made up of employers. As usual, employers are free to organize together, just not working people. A group of radical truckers set out to organize the workers in their industry, and by the following year had formed an organization with over 6,000 members. The CA, although its own organization was well-established, refused to recognize the group of workers, and so for recognition and a pay raise the organized workers went on strike. But the CA, having lost the battle of ideas, went to city government to use violence to break the strike.

On Monday, May 21, a major battle between strikers, and police and special deputies, took place in the central market area. At a crucial point, 600 pickets, concealed the previous evening in nearby AFL headquarters, emerged and routed the police and deputies in hand-to-hand combat. More than 30 cops went to the hospital. No pickets were arrested.

On Tuesday, May 22, the battle began again. About 20,000 strikers, sympathizers, and spectators assembled in the central market area, and a local radio station broadcast live from the site. Again, no trucks were moved. Two special deputies were killed, including C. Arthur Lyman, a leader of the Citizens Alliance.

After failing (unusually) to crush the union even with state violence, the CA caved and signed an agreement that conceded most of the workers' needs. However, in the following weeks it became clear the companies had no plan to honor the agreement, as several hundred vocal union members were fired for union activity, in open violation of the agreement. So the union local went on strike again, with the *Minneapolis Labor Review* reporting that "Trucking was again effectively closed down until Friday, July 20, when police armed with shotguns loaded with deer slugs opened fire at point-blank range on unarmed pickets at the corner of 3rd Street and 6th Avenue North in the Minneapolis warehouse district. Sixty-seven workers were shot."

After this terrifying episode, martial law was imposed and arbitration ultimately sided with the community, giving the strikers most of what they had set out for years earlier. The governor set up a public commission to review the events, and it concluded that "Police took direct aim at the pickets and fired to kill. Physical safety of the police was at no time endangered. No weapons were in possession of the pickets." As is common in US labor history, rights and decent living standards for workers were won, but that happy ending came at a significant cost in blood and violence.[4]

One of the darkest pictures of US labor violence is the Ludlow Massacre of 1914. A huge strike of 11,000 workers walked off the job at Colorado Fuel & Iron, a part of the colossal Rockefeller industrial empire. CFI management refused to even meet with the strikers' representatives over the main strike issues, pay and employment terms. The strike dragged on for months, with the miners camped in the bitter cold while the state militia was used to bring in "scabs," replacement workers to undermine the strikers, with extra muscle added by corporate guards. Confrontations simmered until April 20, when militiamen and CFI guards actually machine-gunned the strikers' camp, knowing men, women, and children had been living there for months. The camp was set ablaze, starting a raging fire. Workers from surrounding areas armed themselves and came to back up the strikers, and ultimately the fighting stopped only when federal troops arrived. By that time fully 66 strikers and family members were dead. However, the killing of dozens of striking workers did not bring a fit of conscience to CFI or the Rockefeller family, and by the following December, after 15 months of striking and many deaths, the beaten strikers went back to work.

A subsequent inquiry, part of the Commission on Industrial Relations set up by Congress in 1912, found that the main cause of the strike was the refusal of the owners of the mine, ultimately the fabulously wealthy John D. Rockefeller, to accept a conference with the strikers' designated leaders:

> During all the seven tragic and bitter months that preceded Ludlow, Mr. Rockefeller wrote letter after letter in enthusiastic praise of men whose acts, during this period, had precipitated a reign of terror and bloodshed. It was only when the Ludlow massacre filled the press of the nation with editorial denunciation, when mourners in black silently paraded in front of his New York office, when cartoons in the conservative press pilloried him and his father before an angry public, that at last complacency gives way to concern in his letters and telegrams to Denver ... The Colorado strike was a revolt by whole communities against arbitrary, economic, political, and social domination by the Colorado Fuel and Iron Company.[5]

The difference between the treatment of organizations of business—such as corporations and industry associations—and the treatment of organizations of labor—such as unions and their strike actions—is rather dramatic. A more fundamental difference can also be seen in the pace and nature of legal recognition of these organizations. While corporate personhood was won by the end of the nineteenth century, in a number of Supreme Court rulings, culminating in 1886 in *Santa Clara County* vs. *Southern Pacific Railroad*, working people didn't have the legal right to form organizations of their own until the National Labor Relations Act of 1935, which was bitterly opposed by many in both political parties, and later undermined by additional legislation like the Taft-Hartley Act. The relative ease of corporate organization, and its relatively uncontroversial character compared to labor organization, suggests the different levels of power of the ruling and working classes.

MONEY WALKS

Of course, rather than potentially embarrassing mass violence, today's social conflict is usually carried out through the capital mobility enabled by modern technology and a global market economy (see Chapter 8). As discussed earlier, this movement of money and productive capacity around the world, whipsawing one labor force against another, has become a central means of social control. A relevant dimension to bring up here is the depth to which this practice has come to reshape our entire idea of corporate success, seen clearly in the government bailout of the US car industry.

When GM's flagging sales and high costs led it to crisis in 2009, the government extended a large loan program to the company and moved it through an orderly bankruptcy and reorganizational process. This left the government effectively in charge of the firm (along with the smaller Chrysler), and to a significant extent capable of making its decisions. While the whole process was highly contentious, GM's final government-approved plan was premised on lowered costs through, once again, outsourcing more production through capital mobility. The *Washington Post* reported "the number of cars that GM sells in the United States and builds in Mexico, China and South Korea will roughly double. The proportion of GM cars sold domestically and manufactured in those low-wage countries will rise from 15 percent to 23 percent over the next five years."[6] Likewise, the rescue of Chrysler entailed organizing a merger with Italian automaker Fiat, although here a pledge was obtained to keep at least some production of mostly smaller models in the US. This is an impressive turning point, where even the elected government takes capital mobility and outsourcing of production to the world's poorest places to be the best economic recovery plan one can hope for. Needless to say, the auto bailout has been at least as unpopular with the public as the bank bailout.

Still, the change is dramatic, and actually shows some progress. A hundred years back, raw violence could be unleashed on the workforce if it challenged management's right to cut pay during good times for the company. The violence arose mainly through the influence of employers with the state, from local cops and militias up to US Army troops, but also included corporate-organized militias and thugs. But today, the ability to play one workforce against another has proved to be quite effective as a means of keeping downward pressure on American incomes and has had huge effects on the American society (see Chapter 13). But also, ideology and propaganda have come to play a large role in our society (see Chapter 6), and a complementary practice has developed of trying to turn people against the unions they can organize. As we'll see in the next chapter, this project has had some limited success, but has struggled against organized working people around the world.

10
Mideast Meets Midwest:
Labor Uprisings of 2011

2011 was a tumultuous year. The Arab Spring broke out in February, as Arab peoples began to rise up and sit-in against cruel, long-standing dictators. A few months later in the United States, Republican governors moved to strip public-sector union workers of the right to bargain collectively as an organized workforce, only to be met by surprisingly great numbers of demonstrators in Madison and other Midwestern capitals, resulting in close calls and some rejections. And by year's end, Occupy Wall Street, the worldwide movement to make a central issue of the concentration of wealth at the top of American and world society, was able to break through an early media shut-out to change the entire national debate and put money at the center of it.

Having discussed OWS somewhat in Chapter 8, this chapter will look at a few of the Arab movements that erupted in 2011, followed by a consideration of the labor action wave in the United States.

OUR MAN MUBARAK

We've already taken a look at some business reporting about the support of the US government for authoritarian and tyrannical regimes in the Middle East, such as Saddam Hussein (see Chapters 1 and 6). Another essential case is Saudi Arabia, the nation with the world's second-greatest proven oil reserves and regularly described as a medieval and theocratic regime. The Saudi royal family, particularly the king and various princes, exercises total power with no pesky elected officials to bring up what the Arab

on the street would like to see done with the massive oil wealth
of the country. The United States and United Kingdom struck up
very supportive relations with the Saudis as World War II wound
down, which continue today despite the autocratic and violent
methods the royal family has used to maintain its power. Other
Persian Gulf states, such as Kuwait or Qatar, are also mostly ruled
by hereditary monarchies. Indeed, US businesses have for some
time been raking in fantastic amounts of money by selling these
otherwise poor countries not just regular military equipment, but
also weapons to put down a rioting population. Veteran Middle
East correspondent Robert Fisk for the *Independent*:

> In 1998 and 1999 alone, Gulf Arab military spending came to $92 billion.
> Since 1997, the Emirates alone had signed contracts worth more than
> $11 billion, adding 112 aircraft to their arsenal, comprising 80 F-16s
> from Lockheed Martin and 32 French Mirage 2000-9s. The figures are
> staggering, revolting. Between 1991 and 1993, the United States Military
> Training Mission was administering more than $31 billion in Saudi arms
> procurements from Washington and $27 billion in new US acquisitions.
> The Saudi air force already possessed 72 American F-15 fighter-bombers,
> 114 British Tornadoes, 80 F-5s and 167 Boeing F-15s.[1]

Egypt is another apt example. While not possessing anything
like the energy reserves of the Gulf states, Egypt is crucial in the
MidEast for its strong military and cultural prominence. For 30
years, President Hosni Mubarak exercised dictatorial powers
over Egypt's political system and effectively banned opposition
parties and media. Going further, in 1999 his government
outlawed all independent non-governmental organizations.
Mubarak has also frequently employed one of the classic tools
of the dictator, the cartoonishly faked election, including a
laughable 97.9% of the popular vote in 1999, up from 96.3%
in 1993. This is typical of dictators—we might recall Saddam
Hussein's 99.96% vote in 1993.[2]

However, while most media have not explored these events,
the US State and Defense departments have been heavily
aiding Mubarak's regime. Egypt, with its obviously fraudulent
elections, receives a massive $1.3 billion each year in US military

aid, more than any other country except Israel, in addition to a significant economic aid package. An example of this cozy relationship could be seen when, even as Muburak's tenure was ending under the sustained massive demonstrations of the Arab Spring focused in Tahrir Square, the *New York Times* reported that the Obama administration "was struggling to balance its ties to Mr. Mubarak, its most stalwart ally in the Arab world, with its fear of ending up on the wrong side of history" by opposing the public uprising against a dictator.[3] Indeed, many have noted that while US government statements on Mubarak ranged from mild demands for elections from Condoleeza Rice on a visit to Cairo, to mild praise from Obama when he visited the city in 2009:

> In the end, neither speech may have made much of a difference. The chaos unfolding in Egypt is laying bare a stark fact … In the Arab world, American words may not matter, because American deeds, whatever the words, have been pretty consistent. Ever since that March morning 32 years ago, when Anwar el-Sadat reached out to clasp hands with Menachem Begin on the North Lawn of the White House after signing the Camp David peace treaty with Israel, the United States government has viewed the Egyptian government, no matter how flawed or undemocratic, as America's closest ally in the Arab world.[4]

In other words, analysts have come to understand that governments say whatever provides the most cover, and will support dictators if it fits a regional strategic calculation.

Some of the most candid coverage of the rebellion against Mubarak's dictatorship came from the business press, as often happens. *Fortune* magazine recently published a characteristically informative review of the world arms trade, "America's Hottest Export: Weapons."[5] The article reports that the US has sold huge volumes of military-grade weapons to the countries of the Middle East, rising to an amazing $103 billion-worth in 2010, a rate tripling since 2000, to the point that the region "is teeming with American-made arms."

A sidebar, "Their Uprisings, Our Weapons," notes that "When the first protests hit Cairo in late January, the American government took great pains to position itself as a neutral bystander. American weapons, on the other hand, were in the thick of the turmoil. Television stations streamed footage of General Dynamics-made M1A1 Abrams battle tanks rolling through the crowds," which became one of the enduring images of the military's attempts to intimidate and repress the rebellion. Selling arms to Mubarak's dictatorship also meant that "Egyptian police have reportedly used American-made tear gas against protestors. Lockheed Martin's F-16 fighter jets flew low passes over the streets." Additionally, Yemeni president and dictator Ali Abdullah Saleh, who has faced tens of thousands of people demonstrating for his removal, has received massive American aid to hold on to power. As *Fortune* relates, "Poverty-stricken Yemen can't afford to buy large weapons packages on its own, but that hasn't stopped it from procuring US arms. The DoD gave the country about $150 million in military assistance last year, and the US military recently put in a request to give it more."

This pattern of supporting dictators, from the Saudis to Saddam to Mubarak to Saleh, is pretty clear. As seen above, public statements always favor democracy and freedom, but stability is where the actual policy lies, as this is what sustains regular economic conditions for the extraction of the energy resources of the Middle East. Cruel dictators, energy exploitation of the region, and neoliberal economic policies were what led to the Arab Spring of 2011. Indeed, even as Libya's Muammar el-Qaddafi was overthrown and killed in an episode of the Arab Spring that was suitable to the US and the NATO alliance, companies were already looking to make deals around its lucrative energy sector and related fields.[6]

REVOLT LIKE AN EGYPTIAN

The Egyptian revolution, itself the centerpiece of the Arab Spring, came at the cost of hundreds dead, mostly from the security forces and their American weapons. Driven by hatred of the regime and its repressive emergency laws restricting speech and assembly, and the economic problems originating in the IMF takeover of the economy in the 1990s, the demonstrators took over public spaces, and used traditional labor/activist tactics such as sit-ins, demonstrations, and marches. But labor strikes, driven in part by IMF austerity programs and a resulting "economic apartheid,"[7] played a major role in putting pressure on the regime. The *Middle East Report* summarized the revolution's early accomplishments:

> The popular revolution of January-February has thus far produced a structural change in the governing coalition of Egypt without producing regime change per se ... The military, though it has been the prime beneficiary of the regime's aid packages from Washington, was an institution in decline, as it was increasingly forced to compete for resources [with other parts of Mubarak's machine]. The fact is that the military, once it determined that Mubarak could not survive ... staged shows of support for the crowds, going so far as to turn the turrets of tanks toward the presidential palace as revolutionaries gathered outside the building ... Yet its decision not to disperse the crowds presented the military with a political problem after Mubarak's departure. Having posed as the people's champion for 18 days ... it was left holding Mubarak's bag of widely hated policies.[8]

Since the revolution early in 2011, the military had been engaged in this delicate maneuvering, trying to maintain its traditional power and US aid while accommodating the energized population. The Supreme Council of the Armed Forces at first said it would hand over power to a civilian government by September, then reneged and said it would hold power until after the November elections, then until after a new constitution could be drafted and ratified. In November, the military brought out a new set of ground rules for the new constitution, which included a permanent license to intervene in political decisions and authority over parliament.[9]

This dance continued until November 19, when the police attempted to evict a camp of demonstrators opposed to the military's power grabs, who had taken occupied Tahrir Square, the center of the revolution. Thousands of Egyptians rushed to the plaza and reoccupied it in defiance of the security forces, seeming to reignite the revolution. The security forces made repeated attempts to clear Tahrir Square and to break up the crowds surrounding other buildings associated with repression, especially the Interior Ministry. However, each time they had to back down in the face of massive numbers of demonstrators, while still insisting that the military forces never initiated any violence but only defended themselves against the demonstrators. This includes claims that the military never entered Tahrir Square, even after hundreds of riot gear-wearing personnel had swept through it days before.[10]

These confrontations have led so far to a major coalition of the political parties, secular groups, and radical factions in "a coalition ... seizing on a revival of mass protests that echoes February's revolution, united around a plan calling for an interim government to take power from the ruling military," as the *Wall Street Journal* reported.[11] The coalition, dominated by Islamist parties, came out on top in the 2011 elections, far ahead of the remains of Mubarak's political machine. The elected MPs are meant to draft the new Egyptian constitution; however, the military has only partially honored its promises to repeal its draconian emergency laws.[12] The fast-changing dynamic in Egypt has far to go, but it proves that even the poor subjects of long-serving dictators can bring about changes in society.

FRAMING THE PUBLIC

Back in the far-wealthier US, the election of 2010 saw strong Republican gains on both national and state levels, as many Americans felt (somewhat reasonably) that the Democrats elected in 2008 had done little to improve their economic position (see Chapter 11). Unfortunately, this protest vote brought in several conservative governors who used the states' government deficits—growing due to the recession kicked off by the finance crisis of 2008—to take the opportunity to again try to break up unions, in this case public-sector ones. Most notable among these governors was Scott Walker of Wisconsin.

Walker proposed increasing the payment public workers made on their health plans and pensions, coming to a significant 7 percent cut in take-home pay for most workers. These changes were in line with deficit reduction, as paying people less meant savings for the state. But in addition, Walker set out to "weaken most public-sector unions by sharply curtailing their collective bargaining rights, limiting talks to the subject of basic wages," as the press described it.[13] This of course has no impact on the deficit, but has an enormous impact on power relations, as it strips the workers of their hard-won ability to bargain as a unit to get decent terms.

Notably, no budget-balancing pressure is enough to remove corporations' legal personhood, as that collective social organization serves the wealthiest echelons of our society. But unions just represent teachers and cops and professors and firefighters and clerks, and so can be targeted by political leadership. Indeed, many of the governors elected along with Walker have proposed bringing "right to work" legislation into their states from the South and West, where they are common. These laws prevent unions from obliging union members to pay dues in order to fund their collective representation. This would be similar to a law preventing banks from obliging mortgage recipients to make payments on their loans. Of course, this type of law would never be proposed. But RTW laws significantly weaken unions in states where they're enacted, and their alleged dividends in unleashed economic growth and new jobs have consistently failed to materialize.

Interestingly, Walker and the other GOP governors have played on the public's suppressed class consciousness, blaming public-sector employees for the economic hell created by the ruling class: "We can no longer live in a society where the public employees are the haves and taxpayers who foot the bills are the have-nots."[14] Indiana Governor Mitch Daniels called public employees the "new privileged class in America," an impressive feat for incomes typically in the $40,000 area, and a far cry from the $344,000 made annually by the richest 1% that the Citigroup analysts consider to be the real "haves." These scapegoating moves strongly suggest an elite recognition of the enduring class consciousness of Americans, which they evidently hope to twist to justify their own elite policies.

It's important to observe that the scapegoating of people who work for the government has been only partially effective. While the media have kept public workers in the foreground, treating them as the best-paid part of society, Americans are not quite so gullible. This was seen in a major *New York Times* poll that found Americans opposed to weakening the collective bargaining power of government workers, by a strong margin of two-to-one: "Americans oppose weakening the bargaining rights of public employee unions by a margin of nearly two to one: 60 percent to 33 percent. While a slim majority of Republicans favored taking away some bargaining rights, they were outnumbered by large majorities of Democrats and independents who said they opposed weakening them."[15] That's especially impressive in light of the strong media support for public-sector union breaking. Also notable was that public opinion was pretty far removed from the governors' not just on collective bargaining, but also on how to fix state budget deficits:

> Those surveyed also said they opposed, 56 percent to 37 percent, cutting the pay or benefits of public employees to reduce deficits ... A majority of respondents who have no union members living in their households opposed both cuts in pay or benefits and taking away the collective bargaining rights of public employees ... Tax increases were not as unpopular among those surveyed as they are among many governors, who have vowed to avoid them. Asked how they would choose to reduce their state's deficits, those polled preferred tax increases over benefit cuts for state workers by nearly two to one.

The figures might have been even stronger if the possibility of taxing richer households was brought up, rather than general tax increases for everyone. We might remember that the authors of the Plutonomy Papers (see the Preface) thought the main part of the increase in incomes for the richest 1 or 2 percent of households was because of reductions in the effective tax rates of their giant incomes and wealth.

Comparing the American and Arab theaters of class struggle, one striking divergence is in the means of repression. In the Arab states, violent intimidation is always a presence. Sit-ins are met with aggressive reprisals, the clearing-out of public areas, and many deaths. In the US, violence is certainly to be seen as police and security staff pepper-spray sitting-in demonstrators; however, this is nothing like the mass arrests and dozens of killings faced in Egypt or Bahrain. Rather, as seen above, the main method of repression in the US is twisting peoples' frame of reference, with regard to which institutions are powerful in our society. As imaginatively described by Daniels and others above, the powerful organizations, indeed with "monopoly power," are labor unions that represent teachers and firefighters and clerks; worldwide corporate empires, which are frequently seen to wield real monopoly power, are conspicuously absent.

Another major difference is in the level of public participation. The Egyptian revolution has seen literally millions of men and women in the streets, engaging in sit-ins, occupations, demonstrations, and education/outreach, refusing for weeks to give in to violent repression as well as mostly hostile media. In Wisconsin, Ohio, and elsewhere thousands turned up on short notice and withstood bullying and media misrepresentation. Granted, the issue for the Egyptians—a violent 30-year dictator—was greater than for the Americans—breaking down one of the few remaining forms of public organization. However, the greater level of awareness and public participation that Occupy Wall Street is encouraging may help bring American activism to the next level, alongside our Arab brothers and sisters.

Of course, the last contrast is that the Tahrir Square uprising succeeded after 18 days in bringing down Mubarak (although the struggle with the military goes on), while the Madison uprisings mostly failed to prevent the bills from passage, although Ohio's was later overturned in a voter referendum. But the seeds of OWS were laid, and broader world connections may have been forged, on both sides of the picket line. The Miami Police Department has become prominent for its tough demonstration-management tactics, and its use of surprising levels of violence. In late 2011, Miami's chief of police, who for most of the past decade has been in the post, recently announced his move to Bahrain, to train security forces for the monarchy after its recent use of torture and mass violence against demonstrators.[16] On the other hand, in the midst of the Madison demonstrations, Kamal Abbas, general coordinator of an independent Egyptian union federation, announced the movement's support for Madison, and promised "We want you to know that we stand on your side. Stand firm and don't waiver. Don't give up on your rights. Victory always belongs to the people who stand firm and demand their just rights."[17]

Whether standing together, sitting-in, or occupying, 2011 was a hell of a year.

11
Shortchange You Can Believe In: The Obama Administration and Neoliberalism

In September 2009, the high-profile meeting of the G-20 organization of the developed countries took place in Pittsburgh, Pennsylvania. It was accompanied by three to four thousand demonstrators and a roughly equal number of heavily armed riot police.[1] There might not have been any demonstrations at all, as the city tried to ban protests during the meeting, but backed down in the face of an ACLU lawsuit. Asked for his response to the demonstrations, US President Obama suggested that

> ... many of the protests are just directed generically at capitalism ... Ironically, if they had been paying attention to what was taking place inside the summit itself, what they would have heard was a strong recognition ... that it is important to make sure that the market is working for ordinary people; that government has a role in regulating the market ... so I would recommend those who are out there protesting, if they're actually interested in knowing what was taking place here, to read the communiqué that was issued.[2]

The summit communiqué contains a number of policy recommendations. Reading it reveals that the real "irony" is that our historic first black president's administration has failed to even propose, let alone accomplish, the serious change promised in 2008. The document sheds a lot of light on the current "neoliberal" policy moment, including the economic crisis, the reappearance of the IMF, and global climate change.

The bank bailout is a prime example. The $700 billion bailout program was monumentally unpopular, to the point that Congress was forced (at first) to deviate from its usual role of banking industry rubber-stamper and instead reject rescuing the biggest banks. But the Obama Administration continued the program, "injecting capital" into banks near failure, with some small-business window dressing.[3] Of course, the "too big to fail" banks that received the majority of the bailout money were those large enough to be politically connected—confirmed when the *New York Times* reported that banks were far more likely to get a public rescue if an executive had sat on the board of a Federal Reserve Bank, had some relationship with a finance committee member, or had spent heavily on lobbying.[4]

This suggests that the large banks have used their deep pockets to gain political influence—in other words, they have invested in shaping government policy that affects them. It could also be noted in this connection that the enormous banks were not required to make any loans with the public's bailout money—banks have not increased lending, and so the credit crisis has continued. This is because the US was unique among the developed nations bailing out their banks in 2008, in not requiring the rescued banks to make any loans that would relieve the credit crisis.[5] Another indication of this investment in politics is the failure to seriously reform the banking practices that got the banks in so much trouble in the first place. The G-20 meeting also endorsed the very limited reforms of international banking rules proposed by the Basel Committee on Banking Supervision (see Chapter 16).[6]

These modest regulations are somewhat valuable, but they clearly leave in place the basis of the banking crisis, including large volumes of speculative capital, securitization of debt, and the expectation by large banks of a public safety net. While Obama promised change, and still maintains a partially adversarial public posture toward the banks, the megabanks clearly have a strong hold on finance policy. In fact, with voters demanding serious change after the Bush years and the terrifying finance crisis of 2008, Obama's historic nonwhite candidacy was probably part of the reason for the heavy support for his candidacy from finance, as Paul Street and others have observed.[7] This suggests that the investment theory of party competition has passed yet another test—despite strong expectations and public announcements to the effect that the banks would be dealt with harshly, their key profit activities have been left mostly unmolested. The Democrats' "Change" brand has wilted in the face of large volumes of political investment, leaving the weak-sauce reforms described in the Pittsburgh document to which Obama patronizingly referred.

RECOURSES FOR BUYER'S REMORSE

Obama's commitment to previous economic policies can be easily seen in his relationship with business. In November 2010, Obama made a major trip to India, signing arms and commercial deals. Traveling with him were CEOs of several major US corporations, including Honeywell, PepsiCo, and McGraw-Hill. Among the agreements reached were relaxation of dual-use restrictions on trade with India and ending bans on arms-capable material, mostly imposed after India's first nuclear detonation. Obama went on to headline a meeting of the US-India Business Council and met privately with the CEOs, carrying forward what the *Wall Street Journal* called his "new role: salesman-in-chief for American business."[8] This was seen as a turn for the Obama administration, ending a "war of words" that had soured relations. Even before the 2010 election, *Bloomberg BusinessWeek* had reported that "the White House wants to make amends and will make its relationship with business a priority" although "by many objective measures, most businesses are thriving and should have little to complain about. Corporate profits rose to a record $1.38 trillion" in the second quarter of 2010, five months before the poll.[9]

But the mid-term election did crystallize the situation, with one business analyst suggesting you "can't shut business out anymore or they're going to take you down." Despite backing Obama's campaign in 2008, the investment community experienced what is often and openly referred to in the business press as "buyer's remorse" about a Democratic Washington. Business organizations, particularly the Chamber of Commerce, reacted aggressively to Obama's audience-dependent anti-business rhetoric, as well as fears of taxation and new environmental regulation. Unleashed by the Roberts Supreme Court decisions (see Chapter 12), corporate donors poured a massive flow of campaign dollars into mostly Republican campaigns. The corporate world dealt with "buyer's remorse" by heavily escalating the buying, just on the other side of the aisle.

And how had the administration "shut out" business in the first place? *Business Week*, in reporting on corporate reactions to Obama's early days, points first to "Obama's populist campaign rhetoric, which often became stridently anti-corporate in tone." Further, when the so-called finance "reform" bill was passed, "only a handful of bank CEOs were invited to the elaborate signing ceremony."[10] More significantly, JP Morgan Chase CEO Jamie Dimon famously presented a chart to a White House meeting showing that Obama's administration had the lowest proportion of staff with business experience in 50 years.

Yet the fears of rampant Democratic regulation and taxes were clearly overblown. While finance did face quite modest re-regulation, this was almost inevitable under any administration after the 2008 finance crisis demonstrated the failure of deregulation. And the business community was generally happy with Obama's insurer-friendly health reform discussed below; the bill, unpopular with the public after hysterical news coverage, "met with enthusiasm from US corporations struggling to pay for soaring employee health-care costs."[11] Further, Obama backed down several times on ending overseas tax shelters after heavy Republican opposition, and even cracked when the GOP held an extension of unemployment benefits hostage to extension of the Bush upper-class tax cuts—just before Christmas. It is a true testament to economic power that after the 2008 financial crisis, the Deepwater Horizon disaster, and the tsunami of mortgage fraud by the great banks, all within two years, the business community is outraged when government figures issue hostile rhetoric or threaten mild re-regulation.

We can only hope that Dimon will consider his expectation of heavier corporate staffing of the state to be fulfilled now that William Daley, a former senior executive at Dimon's banking megalith, has joined the administration as chief of staff. Evidently, Obama's other corporate advisors weren't quite enough, despite including ex-financiers like Larry Summers and Citigroup advisor Robert Rubin's protégé Christina Romer.

Of course, the Obama administration's political fortunes have depended on more than the concentrated wealth available to the owning elite and its institutions. Many hard-working American activists summoned enormous effort to boost underserved constituencies, in order to get a centrist Democrat back in the White House. Likewise, along with the continuing job market stagnation and the swings in corporate fancy, heavy working-class disappointment in the Democrats is generally accepted as a principle cause of the 2010 landslide.

STRUCTURAL SUFFERING

Obama's preference for policy continuity over change can also be seen in the Democrat leadership's revitalization of the International Monetary Fund as a means of managing the economic crisis. The IMF, as previously discussed (see Chapter 4) is a world lending institution that organizes loan programs to strapped countries in exchange for government policy changes that typically punish the poor majorities of the Third World countries in receipt of the loans. For this reason, the IMF is well-known in activist circles for its central role in maintaining international "neocolonialism"—keeping the poor countries of the global South in a servile role to the North, in a similar pattern to the colonial era. The main means of doing so have been the structural adjustment programs, or "SAPs," which were a major focus of world popular movements prior to 9/11. These involved heavy cutbacks in public services, tax and interest rate hikes, and privatization of public institutions—all moves which inflict social pain on the peoples of the nations involved but allowed their governments to efficiently pay back debt.

These SAPs become rather infamous for "the strikes, riots and mass job cuts that the ... orthodox reforms provoked," as the conservative *Financial Times* put it.[12] When Brazil sought an emergency refinancing of its debt in 1998, a debt incurred mostly from the 1980s era of US-backed military dictatorship, the IMF insisted that credit could come only with a highly severe SAP. The package consisted of tax increases, fuel subsidy reductions, and public service cutbacks that even the *Wall Street Journal* recognized "would mean a period of severe austerity for Brazilians."[13] The announcement of the IMF-dictated "tough times" was put off "until after a round of gubernatorial elections," since it was considered obvious that the public was seriously opposed.

This long history of antidemocratic "depressioneering" in the global South is considered quite legit by today's investors and the G-20. Few noticed that the Pittsburgh G-20 meeting, including its pledge to reinvigorate the IMF, came on the heels of the tenth anniversary of the acceptance of a typically draconian IMF SAP by Ecuador. It included sharply regressive tax hikes, a dramatic lowering of the minimum-taxable income, and cuts to gas subsidies for the poor majority. The passage was again difficult due to the "recalcitrant Ecuadorian Congress" and its minimally democratic character.[14] Citigroup advised the Ecuadorian executive on the process, but of course when Citigroup was itself bailed out a decade later it accepted nothing like this imposition of harsh conditions against its will.

Even the recognized godfather of conservative economics, Milton Friedman, insists that IMF bailouts "are hurting the countries they are lending to, and benefiting the foreigners who lent to them. The United States does give foreign aid. But ... it only goes through countries like Thailand to Bankers Trust."[15] Brand "Change" falls to political investment yet again.

However, in the intervening decade, the IMF has fallen on harsher times itself: "As with the US military during the Vietnam War, people inside the IMF are bewildered, resentful and frustrated, and don't feel like suffering in silence any longer," as the *Wall Street Journal* tearfully related, on account of the angry turn-of-the-century movement that prevented them from enjoying their meetings.[16] As some countries like Argentina sought successfully to "rid themselves" of the IMF, its importance to the global capitalist system declined along with its clout.

More recently, a further complication emerged, for, as the business press puts it: "During past crises, the fund demanded tough cuts in budget deficits, privatization of industries and liberalization of markets. In light of the response of the US and western Europe to the current crisis, such conditions are clearly not tenable now. The IMF has to soften its stance."[17] In other words, since expansionary Keynesian fiscal and monetary policy are the basic tools for returning a market economy to growth, as shown by the use of them by the G-20 nations when *they* found themselves in trouble, the IMF must moderate its depressionary demands on debtor nations, if only to save face. When Iceland was headed for insolvency in 2008, it went so far as to appeal to Russia for capital before turning to the IMF.

THE RETURN OF THE FUND

However, the Pittsburgh summit did commit to revitalizing the Fund, partly to deal with the risk of collapse of small countries, its traditional neoliberal function, but also to coordinate some multilateral policy responses. Ironically, one is "reducing the economic disruption from sudden swings in capital flows." Of course, the IMF was in part chartered to regulate capital flows, before becoming a leading force to expand their power. But in an ahistorical culture like ours, this type of incongruity is rarely recognized.

But this new mandate for the IMF requires significant capital, and to augment their own strained resources the rich nations have finally agreed to a small reapportionment of the IMF quota system. In a moment of great munificence, the developed nations condescended to increase the global South's share of the IMF voting quota by "at least five percent," insisting however that the present IMF quota formula be the basis from which to work. The uncharacteristically generous move can be explained by the new need to collect capital for the organization, with the Asian currency stockpiles and the oil export surpluses being prime sources, if a few quota percent will bring them around.

Again, Obama's leadership is anything but a significant break from the past. Keeping the IMF in place to dictate depression to the world's majority is hardly the change the world hoped for when the Democrats took office. On the other hand, the IMF has long had the reputation of being the "credit community's enforcer," and its new role in stabilizing world finance is also in line with the demands of world capital.

Another key thrust of the G-20 statement that the protestors "ironically" missed dealt with carrying forward the stalled fight for global free trade. Meetings of the developed nations routinely call for continuation of the Doha Round of free trade talks, but the call was more imperative in 2009 due to the steep fall in global commerce, by over 10 percent from 2008. However, the declaration was thought to be a formality since the going for trade liberalization had recently turned rough.

The core reason is simple enough: "Multilateral trade liberalization has largely benefited the developed economies of the North. They have opened their markets when it was convenient and maintained trade barriers when it was not— in agriculture, above all, but also in certain manufacturing industries."[18] This "has exposed the North's hypocrisy," which would not normally be a big deal, since the fundamental power relations have historically favored the North to the point that it could dictate terms of trade.

This has begun to change of late, as the major states of the global South have partially freed themselves from US-backed dictators and IMF SAPs, and as popular "anti-globalization" movements in civil society north and south make demands for a greater public role. Even the leader of America's free trade process, US Trade Representative Ron Kirk, admitted that "people are afraid" of further trade deals, in spite of low Wal-Mart prices, because "the pain of trade is very real."[19] The economics is simple: low prices don't make up for lost employment and lower wages, nor do they ultimately even benefit the countries in which firms choose to invest: I got a job in a corporate sweatshop and all I got was enough money to buy $1/16^{th}$ of this lousy t-shirt.

Shocking as this may sound to the ear of an orthodox economist, the point is common coin in the business press:

"Conventional wisdom is that the big challenge to trade comes from embittered workers, many of whom didn't enjoy much of the gain from trade in the good times. They see imports and immigrants as a threat to their livelihoods, and press elected politicians to protect them."[20]

The Battle of Seattle, where thousands of protesters confronted the World Trade Organisation's Ministerial Conference in 1999, was a manifestation of the late arrival of this consciousness in the North. The collapse of the Doha Round, meant to further loosen trade and investment regulations and barriers, was a manifestation of the far greater strength of this movement in the South. This was the background of the trade liberalization failure at the WTO Conference in Cancun in 2003, as the major states of the South struggle to cope with surges of subsidized imports into their countries under the neoliberal regime.

The upshot again is the continuation of quite unpopular policies by Obama, as long as the policies benefit the great corporations and banks, and this is surely the design of the IMF SAPs and the Doha Round, requiring poor countries to do without what the rich countries insist on having.

COPENHAGEN COP-OUT

The 2009 Copenhagen summit, the direct successor to the Pittsburgh summit, was a perfect instance of the Obama Democrats' commitment to unpopular business as usual. The US and China, both investment playgrounds, blocked anything more than lip-service to binding emission reductions, and their reasons are easy to understand. As the *Wall Street Journal* wrote, Obama is a "Washington liberal" but a "Copenhagen conservative," busy "supporting the least-aggressive steps, advancing the conservative position of opposition to strict world-wide limits on emissions that ask much more of developed nations than of poorer countries ... the leader of the 'haves' in their dispute with the 'have-nots.'"[21] The energy industry, of course, kicked in $4.8 million into the Democrats' 2008 campaign.[22]

China's move also makes some sense in the light of what's seen to be the core of the issue—the hot fact that the developed nations are responsible for the gigantic majority of total historical greenhouse emissions, and therefore might be seen to bear the major share of the responsibility, having benefited economically from the emitting industries. The EU was livid in the aftermath; with China and the US agreeing only to token future goals, the director general of the lobbying group BusinessEurope Philippe de Buck threatened that European corporations would move operations to world regions with less emission regulation.[23] If there is no progress on binding global emissions limits, the EU could impose tariff duties on goods made in economies with no carbon taxation, a prescription for a great trade war with unpredictable consequences.

This is because even the US only briefly moved toward a very modest greenhouse emissions taxing regime itself, before backing away (see Chapter 2). As recently as 1997, the US Senate voted unanimously to recommend the US not sign the Kyoto Protocol, yet the American Clean Energy and Security Act and its cap-and-trade emissions regime nearly became law. The difference, of course, is not that several respected geologists and climatologists recently published a paper in *Science* describing how Arctic ice core and tree ring records indicate that 1999–2008 decade "was the warmest of the past 200 decades."[24] Terrifying scientific findings don't scare policy makers unless they affect their power and privilege. Climate change is now an issue because large-scale capital has split, and public awareness and organized support for emissions reform have grown.

Obama hardly deserves credit for this development, as it reflects the recognition by large-scale capital that the changing investment climate now requires federal spending to finance a major change in the industry. The break in the normally monolithic energy sector and the hard work by environmental organizers are the necessary conditions for this political maneuvering.

CHANGE YOU CAN'T BELIEVE IN

Finally, the Pittsburgh Summit communiqué contains a reference to "investing in people," for example, through provision of health care. And indeed, health care reform was the cornerstone of Obama's early domestic policy. With nearly 17 percent of Americans lacking health insurance, some fundamental change to the system is required, and is in fact popular with Americans. However, the health reform bill, the Affordable Care and Patient Protection Act, or "Obamacare" as it came to be derisively known, was far from a solution to the health crisis.

By far the most efficient option for health care delivery is the "single-payer" policy, where a national or state/provincial government acts as a single payer of health care expenses, rather than private insurers, although these remain available. A crucial study of this subject was conducted in 1999 by two Harvard Medical School doctors, who found that the average private American insurance company had overhead expenses of 11.7 percent, more than three times that of publicly run Medicare (3.6 percent), and *nine times* more than Canada's single payer system (1.3 percent).[25] The report notes that in 1969, health costs in the US and Canada were similar, but American costs have been on a steep upswing since: "This growth coincided with the expansion of managed care and market-based competition, which fostered the adoption of complex accounting and auditing practices long standard in the business world." Critics will insist that this is due to the lower quality of care in Canada, although this is difficult to square with the average Canadian life expectancy being a good two years longer than the US, especially in light of their similar diets and car-centered lifestyles.

Public health insurance of this type broadly enjoys significant support among the US public, with the generally conservative *Business Week* magazine reporting a survey which found that "67% of Americans think it's a good idea to guarantee health care for all US citizens, as Canada and Britain do, with just 27% dissenting."[26] However, during the legislative battle over health reform in 2009, the insurance industry invested heavily in leading Americans to associate single-payer health care with a "government takeover," with the problems of the long-standing corporate takeover omitted. Indeed, the same business magazine reported that even as the public debate began, "much more of the battle than most people realize is already over. The likely victors are insurance giants such as UnitedHealth Group, Aetna, and WellPoint. The carriers have succeeded in redefining the terms of the reform debate to such a degree that no matter what specifics emerge ... the insurance industry will emerge more profitable." And it was rather profitable to start with.[27]

Taking UnitedHealth as an example of insurer involvement in the political debate, *Business Week* relates its background, including a "decade-long series of acquisitions has made the company a coast-to-coast Leviathan enmeshed in the lives of 70 million Americans," and that "The company has repeatedly hit smaller employers and consumers with double-digit rate hikes in recent years, far greater than the overall rate of inflation." Finding that "The industry has already accomplished its main goal of at least curbing, and maybe blocking altogether, any new publicly administered insurance program that could grab market share from the corporations that dominate the business," UnitedHealth "has also achieved a secondary aim of constraining the new benefits that will become available to tens of millions of people who are currently uninsured. That will make the new customers more lucrative to the industry." For these reasons, in addition to the full court press to shape public opinion, "big insurance companies have quietly focused on ... shaping the views of moderate Democrats." The "Blue Dog" conservative Democrats indeed were crucial to removing the public option and other sensible proposals from the final bill. In light of the final shape of Obama's main domestic policy achievement, no wonder the journal concludes "insurance CEOs ought to be smiling."

Maybe the clearest picture of Obama comes from a little-noticed New Mexico "town hall" meeting in early 2009. Asked by an audience member why the efficiency of single payer was out of the question of health care reform, and why private insurers were given so much say in the issue, Obama replied that he would favor single payer if he was "starting a system from scratch," but "we're not starting from scratch ... We don't want a huge disruption as we go into health care reform where suddenly we're trying to completely reinvent one-sixth of the economy."[28] In other words, the most reasonable health care solutions are off the table because change is disruptive. Maybe a defensible view, but not by someone who gained high office specifically on the platform of change itself.

Together, the main elements of the current neoliberal policy consensus, embodied in the G-20 communiqué, suggest that it takes a heroic amount of faith to buy Obama's "change we can believe in." On the other hand, Thomas Ferguson's investment theory of party competition has held up quite well in the face of the centrist neoliberal policy moment. While Obama's victory was quite historic, the policy improvement is very modest. The reason, of course, is the pivotal economic power held by concentrated capital, preventing any real reform of the out-of-control finance sector or appropriately serious action on climate. As Obama orates, money talks, and the administration's public approval ratings have remained low.[29] This may also reflect other policy elements not referred to in Pittsburgh, most importantly the ongoing war in Afghanistan and the spreading use of drone-based assassinations. Here not only is there continuity of policy, but often continuity of office holders—keeping the Bush war secretary who didn't resign in disgrace, doesn't exactly scream fundamental change.

Finally, it should be noted that the Obama Administration is being confronted with a budget-balancing hysteria similar to that which met the Clinton Administration. The situation is quite similar to Clinton's years, actually—a previous Republican administration (Reagan-Bush 1 then, now Bush 2) ran up monumental budget deficits in those areas which in the US are considered most legitimate—cranking up military spending and hacking taxes on the richest households. Then the succeeding Democrats are obliged to cut down the deficit run up by the GOP, not by cutting imperial intervention or retaxing the billionaires, but by slicing back at the withered remains of the US social services.

It was Clinton who decapitated AFDC (Aid to Families with Dependent Children), the main welfare program for poor families with children, in order to shrink budget deficits run up by Reagan's wars and upper-class tax chopping. Likewise, absent a powerful countervailing public movement in defense of public services, it is Obama who is overseeing the new great wave of austerity measures in the US, perhaps focused in severe cutbacks in funding for state services. This has been anticipated by a number of analysts on the left, notably Doug Henwood of the *Left Business Observer*.[30] What this suggests is a bipartisan rotating door in state policy, where the right fanatically pursues its regressive tax goals and imperial designs, and the center-right Democrats put the pain on the population in order to pursue a centrist budget-balancing agenda. The modern political system has developed into a good cop-bad cop capitalism management team.

The overall economic policy that results from this system is often called "neoliberalism"—the bipartisan commitment to an economic policy of deregulation, diminished social services, globalization of trade, and privatization (see Chapter 4). It has been essentially an agreed-upon economic policy core between the two US political parties, with their own spins on it. These cruel economic policies originate from the 1970s, when worldwide capital experienced an era of "squeezed" profits, due to rising labor costs and the energy crises, that led to business pushing for, and politics accepting, neoliberal policy moves.[31] And it's been downhill ever since.

In the end, Obama said the anti-G-20 protestors were "ironic" because the issues they made such an impolite fuss over are already addressed in the Summit communiqué. But each of the communiqué's high points is a continuation of the neoliberal status quo which the demonstrators condemned and which Obama implied he would alter. The Democrats can promise all the change they want, but with an economy run by all-powerful corporate networks you can't put your money where your mouth is, if you want to stay in office. Unless a popular movement arises to demand the change they believed in, the historic black man in the White House won't be changing a hell of a lot.

Irony loves company.

12
The Subprime Court:
The Corporate Lock on the Roberts Court

It's well-known that the US Supreme Court tilts to the right. Bush's nominees, Justice Alito and Chief Justice Roberts, lead a conservative five-justice bloc, where reproductive health rights have been cut back and the Office of Faith-Based Initiatives has been approved to go on receiving very real public money.[1] No surprises from the Old Men In Black there.

But what's less known is the court's new major function, which is acting as an institution of corporate power. Since Bush's appointments, the court has begun hearing far more business cases, and in case after case has "pushed the law in a direction favored by business," as the *Wall Street Journal* reports.[2] For example, the US Chamber of Commerce, America's most powerful business lobby, took a position on 15 cases before the court in 2007, and its side won in all but two.[3]

That makes sense, since Roberts previously represented and filed briefs on behalf of the Chamber and other prominent business organizations like the National Association of Manufacturers and other corporate clients.[4] The *Financial Times* refers to Roberts and Alito as "pretty much the dream candidates of economic conservatism," calling Justice Roberts himself "a white-shoe corporate lawyer" and noting "Justice Alito often sided with employers in his prior life as a judge."[5]

The result is thoughtfully reviewed in *Business Week*, describing the views of Robin Conrad of the Chamber of Commerce's litigation arm: "The judicial branch offers an alternative forum where business can seek changes it has failed to win from other branches of government. In the 1990s, the chamber and other business groups made this a vital part of their tort reform strategy, pouring money into local judicial campaigns to reshape state supreme courts ... [now] the approach is playing out on a national level."[6] But "tort reform"—where barriers are raised to discourage lawsuits against companies—is only one part of what business expects from the court, in what will probably be decades of "business-friendly" decisions.

Consider banking regulation, which has been in decline for 30 years, and which the banks are today trying to reshape (see Chapter 16). Our highest court ruled in 2007 that national bank subsidiaries that extend mortgage loans, a major part of our current straits, can't be regulated by state governments.[7] Impressive, since mortgages and home equity loans were among the financial assets that were repackaged into the derivatives that ended up bringing down the banks. The subprime legacy doesn't seem to faze the court.

Additionally, the court ruled almost unanimously that banks, being "regulated" by the Securities and Exchange Commission, cannot be sued by investors—making them "generally immune from antitrust liability" as the *International Herald Tribune* describes.[8] Companies face antitrust liability when they become large and powerful, so this decision looks great in our current environment of banking near-collapses. Because if there's anything our "too big to fail" banks need, it's to get even bigger.

The Supremes also decided that citizens have no right to legally challenge the tax breaks used by most of the US states to "lure investment and jobs away from competing localities," as the *Financial Times* reports. "Forty-six of the 50 states offer some form of investment tax credit. Big companies, many of them carmakers, get billions of dollars each year from states and cities in what critics call an 'escalating arms race' of tax incentives."[9] This is a big deal, since this type of tax concession is how firms drive the "race to the bottom" among states and countries—either you lower my taxes or I'll build my plant somewhere that does (see Chapter 8). So for the Roberts Court, if the states want to oversee banks' shady mortgage-issuing, no dice. But if they're cutting taxes on GM or Toyota so they'll condescend to build a plant, no problem.

BULK-BUYING ELECTIONS

Business involvement in elections has been a recurring subject for the court, especially with regard to the McCain-Feingold campaign finance bill, which limited certain specific types of campaign spending. The dismantling of McCain-Feingold began with a 2007 ruling that overturned a significant part of the law, finding that corporations, as well as unions and interest groups, can run "issue ads" immediately before elections.[10] The intention of the law had been to prevent a pre-election flood of campaign advertising, thinly disguised as advocating for a political issue, paid for by companies and other groups. The law was restricted to the period just prior to elections or primaries, and only to ads which were funded by corporations, unions, or other groups from their own general treasuries—a very limited restriction on how companies could use their massive financial advantages in an election environment.[11]

The 2007 ruling set a very high standard for these sham "issue ads" to be found in violation of McCain-Feingold. The ads have to expressly urge a position on a candidate, or be subject to "no reasonable interpretation other than as an appeal to vote for or against a specific candidate," to be found illegal.[12] In other words, they won't be, as described by Richard Hasen, Law Professor at Loyola Law School Los Angeles, in a paper on the court's new ad-friendly stance. Noting that the "burden of proof is on the government to prove the advertisement is not subject to exemption" and that the decision expressly forbids considering the context of the election in interpreting the ad, he finds that most campaign ads of the issue-oriented variety "will comfortably fall on the permitted side of the line."[13] In fact, "Very few ads broadcast close to an election" directly push for a candidate, but "almost always mention a legislative issue, even if they are also attacking a candidate." In other words, the floods of corporate and other campaign ads in battleground states in 2008, 2010, and 2012 owe a lot to our highest court.

But the great turn came in January 2010, when the court struck down several of the remaining limits on the use of concentrated money in political campaigns. Split along its usual lines, the court threw out two precedents allowing limitations on corporate spending shortly prior to an election, in what became the now-notorious "Citizens United" case, the Supreme Court's decision on the legality of a film about Hillary Clinton from the primary season.[14] The idea of these spending restrictions was to reduce the power of money to constantly push a position or candidate in the final days of a campaign, trying to win races by sheer weight of money.

In the decision, the court overturned the heart of the already-reduced McCain-Feingold campaign finance law, with regard to the prohibition of corporate advertising in the final weeks before election day. But the court also struck down several federal and state laws going back decades, which barred business and labor bodies from funding political activity from their general treasuries, requiring they instead make contributions via political action committees (PACs) or other special funds. Since ads that purported to focus merely on a political issue rather than a candidate were exempt from this rule, McCain-Feingold closed that gap at the end of campaigns, until the court ruling struck down them all. Justice Kennedy, writing for the conservative majority, suggested that corporate investment in campaigns represented "political speech" and that "corporations may possess valuable expertise, leaving them the best equipped to point out errors or fallacies in speech of all sorts." And uniquely capable of the spending required to keep their "expertise" in front of television viewers and radio listeners.

Notably, media coverage of the ruling always clung to the phrase "corporations and unions" when describing whose electoral funding would be unleashed. This of course is a joke, as business regularly outspends organized labor on election funding, by an average advantage of *15 to 1*.[15] This makes the constant media equation of the two forms of economic organization highly misleading, and indeed in business coverage like the *Journal*, while the standard "corporations and unions" formula is used at first, the further one reads into an article the less one sees the word "unions," perhaps implicitly recognizing their small-potatoes role.

Another less-noticed provision of McCain-Feingold, the "Millionaire Rule," raised the ceiling on individual campaign contributions for candidates facing a self-financed opponent, whose vast personal resources tilt the playing field in their favor.[16] The court overturned this provision as well, finding that this was unfair for imposing more restrictions on one party in an election than another, although this obviously doesn't address the advantage held by rich candidates who can self-finance. In fact, the Rule itself was a response to a previous Supreme Court ruling overturning restrictions on wealthy candidates using their own cash to gain office. An outside observer might call all this a clear argument for publicly funded elections.

The Supreme Court's money-friendly rulings are not limited to regular political races. Turning to elected judges, the court in another ruling found "an elected judge may rule on a case where one party spent $3 million to help get him elected," as the *Wall Street Journal* reports.[17] The question was whether this violates the constitutional rights of due process and impartial trials. Notably, conservative Justice Scalia held that due process was not violated because the judge's conflict of interest was "vague." Three million bucks sounds pretty specific to me, but I'm no lawyer.

But I am an economist, and I'll tell you that you can thank the court for some higher consumer goods prices as well. By 5–4, the Court overturned a 1911 Supreme Court ruling outlawing "minimum-price agreements" (MPAs), where a manufacturer requires that retailers not mark down the prices of its products. The business press describes the corporate rationale for legalizing this practice: "minimum resale price agreements, although raising prices within brands, could be good for consumers as price competition between brands would be stimulated ... the loss of competition on price would be more than made up for by the way a price floor would allow retailers to compete on service rather than on price alone."[18] The *Wall Street Journal* describes them as "a means to enhance a brand's image and for retailers to make enough profit on their merchandise to provide better customer service," but they "have run into legal trouble in the past when federal officials found they resulted in higher prices for consumers."[19]

This is essentially what economists call "price fixing," where firms work together to increase mark-ups on products, and thus the price paid by consumers. In spite of the companies' argument that the MPAs will encourage price competition between brands, the *Journal* observes that similar video games "Guitar Hero World Tour" and "Rock Band 2" were sold at the same mandatory retail price. And not a low one either: $189. The court's opinion here is that when firms increase prices on us, the extra money will go into improving the product or customer service. Of course, it's just possible that the higher mark-ups will fatten the manufacturer's profitability, instead. But at least the firm's image is enhanced, in that you have to fork over more cash.

BLUE SUITS

But the Roberts Court's trademark has been its limitation of damages in corporate lawsuits and its moves to prevent firms from being taken to court at all. The court reduced the punitive damage settlement against Exxon for the 1989 Valdez oil spill by 80 percent, from $2.5 billion to $500 million.[20] It also reversed a jury decision against cigarette manufacturer Philip Morris, which awarded $79 million to the widow of an Oregon smoker, on the grounds that the jury might have based that number on a desire to punish the corporation for harming other smokers (juries are silly that way).[21] The court now seems eager to further reduce the limited extent to which companies can be held liable through lawsuits for costs they impose on others, or "externalize."

The press describes the court as "closing the courtroom door," preventing lawsuits against corporations, very often from the firms' own investors. The court has found that class-action lawsuits alleging fraud must be brought in federal courts, where they're effectively barred;[22] that investors can't sue Wall Street banks over their losses from the cozy IPO (initial public offering) agreements from the 1990s stock mania;[23] and that they face tighter standards for bringing suit for antitrust conspiracy.

This series of decisions greatly reduced corporations' liability to investor suits, leading Robin Conrad of the US Chamber of Commerce's legal arm to declare the Roberts Court in 2007 "our best Supreme Court ever."[24]

By far the most prominent of these lawsuit-limiting actions was the dismissal of the massive class-action suit against Wal-Mart, filed by 1.6 million of its woman employees, alleging the retail giant consistently paid woman workers less than men doing comparable jobs. While lower courts held that the massive class of plaintiffs were sufficiently coherent to count as a legal class, being injured by the same policies, the court's majority found Wal-Mart's promotional practices to not be specific enough to justify the categorization of the women as a class. As the business media summarized the court's opinion, "statistics showing pay and promotion differences prove nothing by themselves."[25] This means the case against Wal-Mart can never go to court, as the company took the preemptive strategy of challenging the class itself.

But beyond tightening the standards for recognizing a class of people out to recover damages from corporations, the court has also recognized new hurdles to class actions, through changes to business-consumer contracts. The main case, reported on in 2011, involved plaintiffs who tried to sue AT&T for charging $30 in sales tax on phones described in advertising as free. AT&T pointed to a clause in the phone contracts, stipulating that customers must resolve disputes though private arbitration rather than through any class-based proceeding.[26] California's state courts ruled that these contractual surrenderings of the right to sue were void under federal law; however, the Supreme Court overrode that decision, with conservative Justice Scalia's majority opinion indicating that class actions were at odds with the speed of arbitration. Notably, the Roberts Court pattern of overturning its own recent decisions manifested itself again, as a 2005 opinion by the court found that class actions may be the only real form of justice when companies "deliberately cheat large numbers of consumers out of individually small amounts of money."

These aren't ambulance-chaser lawsuits—the Roberts Court is essentially insulating corporations from suits from their owners and customers, although such suits are often the only recourse when firms "externalize" their costs in loose regulatory environments. Closing off that possibility of redress for victims of corporate destruction will save big firms millions and billions of dollars, hence Conrad's grateful attitude. Interestingly, while many of these business cases have been won by the court's five-justice conservative bloc, on these issues of limiting court damages the court has been more unanimous—even the other, "liberal" justices would see firms insulated from accountability for their behavior.

COURTING CHANGE

But there have been some cracks in the corporate lock on the court. One interesting example is the court's treatment of employee discrimination cases. Businesses, of course, would like to see these restricted, and in the first such case the court heard— the now-famous *Ledbetter* case—the court ruled against the plaintiff, Lilly Ledbetter. Ledbetter, a supervisor at a Goodyear plant, learned that her employer had paid every male in a similar position more than her, to the tune of about a thousand bucks more per month. But the court threw out her case since she failed to meet a strict 180-day deadline in filing suit. This tightened statute of limitations meant that very few such cases could be filed. But this became a prominent national issue, after which the court changed its tune. As the press describes, *Ledbetter* led to "loud protests ... But since then, the court has consistently sided with employees who have alleged discrimination, and ruled ... to allow lawsuits to go forward."[27] This suggests that even the august Supreme Court can be made to feel the heat of public opinion, which is encouraging.

Another development suggesting incomplete commercial dominance of the Roberts Court is the recent decision on drug labeling. After having recently found that manufacturers of medical devices are shielded from lawsuits by their government-approved safety labels, the court found drug manufacturers aren't, and that suits against them could go forward.[28] This reversal for corporate power before the court has led some observers to conclude that the court's reputation as a business plaything was premature and that "something of a reevaluation of the court is underway."[29] But it should first be noted that Bush's conservative appointees in fact dissented from this decision, along with Justice Scalia. So the question is what happened to the other two "conservatives," Thomas and Kennedy?

The answer lies in the doctrine of federal "preemption," where government regulation prevents state lawsuits. Preemption has only recently been extended to drugs from medical devices, mainly in a late policy of the Bush administration.[30] Apparently that took obedience to corporate power too far for a few conservatives, but over the long series of business rulings reviewed here, it's a drop in the water, especially since the Roberts Court went on to rule that generic drug manufacturers can't be sued for damages as name-brand firms can, on the grounds that generic labels must copy those of brand-name manufacturers.[31]

In 2012, the Court is expected to rule on the Obama administration's health care bill, the Affordable Care and Patient Protection Act, or "Obamacare." The contention arises from the main provision of the bill, the insurance mandate that obliges citizens to carry health insurance, as motorists are required to carry car insurance (see Chapter 11). While the outcome is unclear, conservative judges have previously taken different positions on the law.[32] The law is of course highly favored by the insurance industry, which as previously discussed was delighted to get tens of millions of new paying customers.

Finally, a number of cases before the court deal with the legality of lawsuits launched against US corporations by foreign citizens. Among such cases before the court is an action brought by Nigerians alleging that Royal Dutch Shell helped the Nigerian government torture and terrorize the people of the oil-rich Ogoni region in the 1990s.[33] The court may well uphold the lower court's decision on the Shell case, which found the corporations are not subject to the law. This would illuminate the nature of corporate "personhood," since although they are "persons" for the purpose of claiming free speech rights for their gigantic campaign spending, they are *not* persons before laws that might expose them to damages for crimes overseas. But it's still heartening that the court seems to have backed off in the face of wide outcry after the *Ledbetter* decision, which suggests that the aroused public can still exert pressure, even on a firm instrument of capital like the Roberts Court.

Granted, the Supreme Court has always been an inherently conservative institution, sympathetic to the wealthy and powerful, from whose ranks the justices have historically been drawn. But the escalation of the number of business cases on the docket suggests that Corporate America has tightened its grip. As the *Economist* has noted, Bush's only lasting success in his "domestic legacy" probably lies in "shifting the Supreme Court significantly to the right."[34] And in keeping with the pattern of the Bush administration, the court's public approval rating is falling as it lines up with corporate demands on case after case.[35] But not everyone is dissatisfied, as the Chamber of Commerce's Robin Conrad remarked of the chamber's new practice of always filing briefs with the court regarding business cases, "There has been a return on investment, not to sound too crass."[36]

Over the coming decades of corporate dominance of the highest court in the land, it will take a more thoughtful, organized, and active version of the response to the *Ledbetter* case to make the court even approach the desires of American citizens, rather than the wet dreams of the Chamber of Commerce. Torts in the courts need feet in the streets.

13
Keeping Down with the Joneses: American Survival Strategies

American paychecks have been headed south for two generations now. Since 1973, US inflation-adjusted take-home pay has been flat or declining, as have health insurance coverage and vacation time.[1] There are several reasons for this—the outsourcing of good-paying blue-collar jobs (see Chapter 8) and the decline in US union representation (see Chapter 7) are two central ones. But causes aside, the effects of the decline in US wages and benefits have been serious business, as Americans have had to improvise ways to cope with falling pay. In fact, our society has been reshaped by the desperate measures taken by working people in the face of our weak-sauce incomes.

9 TO 5 TO 9

One possible strategy for dealing with lower-paying jobs is to work more of them. Over recent decades, holding multiple jobs has persisted, and today figures from the Bureau of Labor Statistics show over a third of multiple jobholders do so out of economic need—to cover bills, pay off debt, or to otherwise increase incomes;[2] this means millions of households are headed by people working two or more jobs to make ends meet. Picking up extra shifts in a spare job has been the most natural reaction to wage stagnation, although not the only one.

However, this coping strategy comes with its own costs—an extra job or two can cut deeply into personal schedules, leaving workers with a diminished quality of life and higher stress. Also, time constraints dictate that additional jobs will probably be part time, and the *Wall Street Journal* refers to certain flaws of part-time employment: "Part-time jobs typically pay 10% to 20% less per hour than comparable full-time work. Often they offer no health or retirement benefits and little job security."[3]

Apart from working multiple jobs, American workers are notorious for working the longest hours in the industrialized world. Back in 1996, the average American worker surpassed the famously industrious Japanese, and we now work about 30 percent more hours each year than the typical European.[4] The US is almost totally alone among the developed nations in not requiring a minimum amount of vacation time for employees. However, the weekly hours worked by the average American over the last 35 years have barely increased, which suggests that work hours have stayed constant over this period of falling wages.[5] To understand this apparent contradiction, we need to recognize the huge increase in the workforce role of women in this era.

As more women have entered the workforce, they have tended to pull down average hours worked, since women are more likely to work part-time hours owing to the expectation of family commitments. So the steady average hours over the last several decades actually suggest more work hours by the average male and female worker. But it's this huge growth in women's labor-force participation, from just a third in 1948 to three-quarters in 2006,[6] that has had some of the most important effects on our social fabric.

The economic independence of women is a major social achievement, expanding women's freedom and opening avenues to self-fulfillment and productivity. On the other hand, its real-world development in the United States has been conditioned as a survival strategy by working families, to make up for flat or falling breadwinner incomes. The result is a steady increase in total hours worked by two-parent households since the mid-1970s, rising by about a quarter over this period.

These twin strategies, of families working more hours and fielding multiple breadwinners, have several affects. The main impact, of course, is on quality time with the family—compared to 30 years ago, modern parents have over 20 hours less per week to spend with the kids.[7] Four full hours a weekday of development and parenting lost, so that mom can try to make up for dad's light paycheck. With over two-thirds of two-adult households fielding multiple breadwinners, this translates into a very broad reduction in parental time with youth.[8] It's worth a moment's thought on how this may be contributing to our constellation of social problems, including drug abuse and school violence. After school shootings, pundits can be counted on to loudly demand "Where were the parents?" of the massacre's perpetrators. These days, they're probably pulling a shift somewhere.

Perhaps it's recognition of this reality that leads to the well-publicized opinion surveys where large proportions of working mothers say they'd prefer to work part time. Of course, the "traditional values" faction loves to jump on these survey results as showing the unhappy harvest sewn by feminism. But the reality is more pragmatic, as the press observes: "Only 24 percent of working mothers now work part time. The reason so few do isn't complicated: most women can't afford to. Part-time work doesn't pay."[9] Moms may not like their kids being raised by TV, but the hard-knock realities of declining wages and benefits demand survival strategies.

The results are serious in the economically tense environment. "Women are really caught between expectations that they should both behave like 'serious' employees and work long hours, and behave as 'serious' mothers and devote more and more time to their children," says labor economist Robert Drago. "If you go back to the 1960s, the hours of managerial and professional men were shorter, and the extracurricular demands of children on parents were much lower. Something has to give."

And often enough, it's workers giving in to exhaustion. The stress from working multiple jobs, often with irregular hours and little job security, and enjoying relatively little time with the spouse or kids, takes its toll off the clock. Juliet Schor, in her classic book on America's work patterns, *The Overworked American*, suggested that perhaps "work itself has been eroding the ability to benefit from leisure time. Perhaps people are just too tired after work to engage in active leisure ... Today, the most popular ways to spend an evening are all low-energy choices: television, resting, relaxing, and reading."[10]

The worst-case scenario is described by the *Harvard Business Review* in a discussion of professional-class workloads:

> As households and families are starved of time, they become progressively less appealing, and both men and women begin to avoid going home. Returning to a house or an apartment with an empty refrigerator and a neglected teenager might prove to be a little bleak at the end of a long working day—so why not look in on that networking event or put that presentation through one more draft?[11]

In other words, corporate America's downward pressure on worker incomes these past 35 years has not just harmed the workers, and the *Review* finds long hours harming everything from family cohesion to workers' sex lives. The ability of families to function is meaningfully eroded by keeping the folks at work and the kids at home with the electronic babysitter.

MINING THE GOLDEN YEARS

Another strategy for dealing with tanking wages is delaying retirement. The Bureau of Labor Statistics finds that while the workforce participation of individuals 55 and older declined for many years after World War II, seniors have recently reversed this exit from the workforce. Bucking the previous national trend, working seniors are on the rise, and by now well over a third are back to work.[12] But older workers are subject to some other considerations of corporate and social policy.

Since 2000, the increase in the normal retirement age for Social Security benefits and the removal of the earnings test have probably prolonged seniors' time in the work force. Besides these neoliberal social policies, crucial changes to corporate retirement plans have also influenced seniors' work decisions. In recent decades, businesses have moved toward defined-contribution pension plans, which put more burden and investment risk on the employee, with the 401(k) being the most common of these.

Previously the defined-benefit plan had been dominant, putting more responsibility on the employer to guarantee sufficient retirement assets. The former therefore are more variable and often seen to be less preferable for workers. Since the 1980s, the proportion of US workers covered by a defined-contribution plan vs. a defined-benefit plan has shifted from 1:1 to 2:1. This probably also encourages longer worklives as older workers add to retirement assets to offset the higher risk of these plans.

Of course, the autumn years could be a time meant for those who have made their contribution to the economy, to relax and reflect, and play with grandkids and the like. Not in our Republic: our wizened seniors get to invest their golden years as Greeters at Wal-Mart. This also adds to familial strain, as child care that might have come from elders must be paid for on the market, with Gramps on second shift bagging groceries.

CREDIT WHERE IT'S OVERDUE

A final means of augmenting inadequate wages is consumer credit, and by now its results are pretty clear. With their wages and benefits on the wane, American consumers have gone on a real credit binge. This is usually portrayed in the media as plastic-happy American shoppers making frivolous purchases, which puts a lot of the blame for the financial crisis on their heads. But even the *Wall Street Journal* observes that the huge growth of consumer debt is "a way for average households to make up for sluggish growth in income over the past several decades," a short-term fix for the corporate community's downward pressure on wages. As they put it, "For Americans who aren't getting a big boost from workplace raises, easy credit offers a way to get ahead, at least for the moment" which is important both because "wage growth is sluggish" and also because Americans are "seduced by TV shows like 'The O.C.' and 'Desperate Housewives,' which take upper-class life for granted, and [are] bombarded with advertisements for expensive automobiles and big-screen TVs." [13]

In a recent report on American consumers, economists Dirk Krueger and Fabrizio Perri found that "despite the surge in income inequality in the US, consumption inequality has increased only moderately," with massive borrowing by American consumers making up the difference.[14] Besides plastic, much of this borrowing came from the wildly inflated home values that allowed American consumers to borrow against their high home prices. Of course, the bubble allowing this strategy has since passed, leaving American workers tightly squeezed by the resulting credit crisis and recession.

In the end, the side-effects of these survival strategies have left the US in rough shape. The *New York Times* discusses a small Indiana town in which the old strip-mining jobs, with their strong pay, have disappeared, leaving the citizens to the slim means of survival described above. The paper of record finds that "few people [have] time to get involved in the community anymore" in part because "As men's wages have declined, more women have taken jobs to make ends meet."[15] The description that follows is as depressing as it is common in the American heartland: kids running amok without adequate babysitting while both parents work, rising rates of divorce and child abuse as family time collapses, and laid-off workers turning to "the drug business," since methamphetamine manufacture is one of the few surviving means of making a living. As in many other American towns, the result is "a condition in which everyone is a breadwinner and the whole town loses."

It turns out that the whole character of the country has been warped by the downward pressure on worker incomes of the last 35 years. From empty downtowns to TV-raised kids to the drug trade, a lot of our social condition comes from America's families desperately trying to keep bread on the table, and to keep the table from the repo man. But with economists now predicting that American average incomes won't return to their 2000 level until 2021, working people need to get out in the streets and drag their share out of the corporate community.[16] Otherwise our wages will lose buying power until we can't make rent. So one way or another, we'll see each other in the streets.

Part III

The Invisible Hand Gives the Finger: The Crisis-prone Finance Market

Introduction to Part III:
Credit Markets in Theory

Economists view finance markets as especially important, because of their role providing credit to other firms, to help finance growth in the economy. Commercial banks collect relatively small deposits from regular folks, and pool them into loans for consumers making large purchases like houses. Likewise, investment banks raise credit for companies by helping them sell their stock, helping firm expansion. This greases the wheels of economic growth, and indeed, because they can make binding agreements over the same moneys to two parties simultaneously (such as depositors and loan recipients), they also play a role in increasing the money supply.

But the more formal picture of how credit markets operate takes this picture a step further, with the Efficient-Market Hypothesis, a darling of theoretical economists which in various forms suggests that markets take into account all available information and represent it in the price the market determines. EMH is an outgrowth of the economic assumption of rational expectations, which proposes that people's expectations of the future, while not necessarily correct, show only random error—that is, they are not biased in any particular direction. The implication of EMH is that deregulation of financial markets will bring efficiency gains, since these markets can use all available information, unlike bureaucratic governments, and can't develop irrational trends.

Unfortunately, this is often not the case. Market expectations are often biased in a given direction, depending on conditions. When a market trends upward for some time, market participants have clearly shown a capacity for upward price biases, contributing to what Alan Greenspan called "irrational exuberance" amid the market "bubbles" discussed in Chapter

14. When these bubbles pop, a dark pessimism overtakes credit markets and they display a very pronounced downward bias.

And indeed, as EMH does not appear to hold in reality, we've had several disastrous and escalating financial crises, about one per decade, since the turn to financial deregulation in the 1970s, '80s, and '90s. In any hard scientific discipline, this clear correlation would be considered experimental data, and would call for significant reconstruction of the discipline. However, despite the enormous human and economic cost of the $8 trillion housing bubble, only small adjustments have been made to neoclassical theory, mainly by keeping to its weaker versions of EMH, but still keeping rational expectations to which it is closely linked. While economists obviously vary significantly in their adherence to these ideas, there has clearly been nothing like the large change in the discipline that would be proportionate to history's massive refutation of rational investor behavior and unbiased markets.

But some economists deserve credit for being out in front of these developments. Most notable are John Eatwell and Lance Taylor, of Cambridge and the New School respectively, who wrote in 2000:

> "Systemic risk" is to financial markets what dirty smoke is to the environment. In reckoning cost of production, the factory owner fails to take into account the cost his smoking chimney imposes on the community. The dirty smoke is an *externality*. Its production has an impact on the welfare of society, but that impact is external, it is not priced through the market ... In the same way, financial firms do not price into their activities the costs their losses might impose on society as a whole. Yet those costs are a familiar consequence of financial failures. Not only do many financial dealings resemble the cliché house of cards, but one house going up in flames can spark a financial firestorm as loss of confidence sweeps away the entire street ... markets reflect the private calculation of risk, and so tend to under-price the risk faced by society as a whole. The consequence is that from the point of view of society, investors take excessive risks.[1]

Most economists, however, continued to propound removal of financial regulations until the next crisis, in 2008.

But beside the issue of undervaluing risk, as with most expectations of market efficiency a competitive market structure is taken for granted, where many firms compete on a level playing field. However, this is very often not the case as firms have strong scale economies obliging them to grow large and powerful, as described in Chapter 15. Particulars of the real estate and other bubbles will be looked at in Chapter 14, along with the industry's efforts to control their own re-regulation in Chapter 16, and the Federal Reserve's role in this picture in Chapter 17.

Once again, market performance expectations of efficient use of resources are undermined, in this case by "external" costs to system stability, the drive for firms to grow large, and the power they obtain once they do. In light of the catastrophic results of moving closer to raw, unregulated capitalism, from monumental bank crashes to disastrously high unemployment, Chapter 19 considers what fundamental changes we could undertake in the future to make our economic system more democratic, stable, and sustainable.

14
Pop Goes the Economy: The Origin of Financial Bubbles

In the first section of this book, a number of side-effects of market activity were considered. Driving cars powered by combustion of gasoline imposes a series of connected impacts on forests and the organisms that depend on them; dumping wastes in the oceans creates massive floating islands of garbage, and so on. What unites these disasters as "externalities" is that they do not directly impact the company or consumer responsible for them. But as the Introduction suggests, these "external" impacts of market-based commerce are not limited to environmental deterioration.

BRUTALLY BEATING THE SYSTEM

For an example of how externalities of this type play out in practice, consider the numerous hedge funds engaged in "short-selling" in the run-up to the 2008 crisis. Selling short is the practice of effectively betting in the financial markets against the prospects of some company. The short-seller borrows a financial asset, such as a company's stock, for a borrowing fee. The short-seller then sells the asset at the current market price. If the price of the asset then has gone down, the seller will spend less money replacing the borrowed asset than received on the sale. Provided the difference is greater than the borrowing fee, the seller makes a profit on the transaction and is therefore betting against the success of a company or other entity.

As various large financial firms such as Lehman Brothers weakened due to losses in their "subprime" mortgage-backed securities, hedge funds and other firms started short-selling those companies' stock, meaning they were betting that firms like Lehman would lose more money. While making a very sturdy profit for the risk-taking short-sellers, the bets encourage a self-fulfilling prophecy as the knowledge among investors that large wagers are being placed against firms makes them more likely to sell, driving down the share price that the short-sellers profit from. This falling share price itself makes it harder for the firms to maintain their credit line or attract new investment, at a time of existing weakness. As the business pages reported in the opening moments of the 2008 crisis, "While Lehman's shares have declined as investors lost confidence in its ability to repair its balance sheet … short-selling played a role in the erosion. A rapid plunge in the shares … ultimately created the conditions that brought the 158-year old firm to its knees on Sunday."[1]

The huge importance of these destabilizing side-effects of short-selling in such a context is that a number of the shorted firms are "too big to fail," after a series of state and federal deregulatory policy changes in recent decades (see Chapter 15). If a firm is large enough and tightly connected to other similarly large institutions, then shorting its stock directly undermines the stability of the market environment. Eatwell and Taylor suggest that "markets reflect the private calculation of risk, and so tend to under-price the risk faced by society as a whole. The consequence is that from the point of view of society, investors take excessive risks."[2]

Elsewhere, the *Financial Times* reports that companies' mismanagement of risk "echoes a fundamental problem about banking … the social cost of a systemic disaster is greater than the private cost to the individual bank. In the end, it is the task of regulators, not investors, to address this externality."[3] For a bank of any size, the stability of the system is someone else's problem, and while investors may not want to see the system collapse, "their fiduciary obligations prevent them from taking a broader, systemic view." The result is that risk is chronically underpriced in the financial markets.

Again, the too-big-to-fail stature of a few "megabanks" puts the issue in sharper focus. As the business press reports, "Private-sector companies and individual bankers have been making huge profits in the bubble. Their risk appetite has been enhanced by previous bailouts and ... by the government's implicit guarantee. Yet their market pricing does not reflect the potential cost to the system of their own collapse."[4] The business world analysts recognize that "[t]his inability to handle externalities" has worsened the financial crisis at every stage. The head of a short-selling company that significantly contributed to bringing down Lehman Brothers said "We would not win if Lehman went down and took the whole financial system with it ... An actual collapse of Lehman—that would not be a good thing." Three months later, the firm applied for bankruptcy protection.

In fact, the market's failure to value external costs and benefits helped lead the banks to hold so much subprime debt in the first place. Law professor and corporate governance expert Janis Sarra explains that before debt was packaged into derivatives, the banks created a "positive externality" for investors: "corporate stakeholders ... could be confident that the bank was engaged in a measure of monitoring and oversight of the firm's solvency," so bank loans created a standard of trust for investors.[5] But since banks now package and sell off loans:

> The exponential growth in use of credit derivatives has shifted the externalities in a way that may contribute to market destabilization ... originating lenders may be less willing to expend the time and resources to undertake due diligence in undertaking credit arrangements, as risk is laid off through derivatives under the originate and distribute model ... previous positive externalities are lost and new negative externalities are created, creating more systemic risks across the market.

IF IT AIN'T BROKE, BREAK IT

Of course, all this takes for granted the freedom of firms to effectively gamble with huge sums of (often borrowed) money, and to use it for such destabilizing ends. Carmen Reinhart and Kenneth Rogoff, authors of arguably the most comprehensive analysis of the historical record of economic crises, surveyed the data and found a "striking correlation between freer capital mobility and the incidence of banking crises ... *Periods of high international capital mobility have repeatedly produced international banking crises, not only famously, as they did in the 1990s, but historically.*[6] Upcoming chapters discuss a few relevant episodes of finance deregulation and illustrate their affects on market performance.

Indeed, in the wake of the deregulation of the US financial system in the 1980s and '90s, the economy has experienced about one major bubble each decade. A bubble is a sustained, out-of-control escalation in the price of some asset. In the 1990s, a bubble in high-tech company stocks dominated the economic scene for the latter half of the decade, and the decade after that experienced a monumental bubble based in "speculation" in housing and real estate. Speculation is the practice of buying an asset in order to sell it later for more, as in the practice of "flipping" real estate, and it can give rise to bubbles if it reaches a sufficient scale.

But consistent with the deregulatory turn of financial policy in recent decades, regulators have been resistant to recognize or act upon bubbles. Alan Greenspan, then head of the Federal Reserve, told Congress that housing was too costly and untradeable to be at the center of a bubble, despite the long history of giant bubbles in real estate markets, including a disastrous one in Japan just a few years earlier. More to the point, Greenspan argued in 1999 that government has no place monitoring markets for bubbles, since that "requires a judgment that hundreds of thousands of informed investors have it all wrong."[7] This was typical of what economist Robert Brenner called Greenspan's "touching faith in the optimistic predictions of equity analysts," referring to Greenspan's outlook during the *1990s* stock bubble, the 2000 crashing of which did nothing to temper hopes for the housing bubble the next decade.[8] The London *Financial Times* tellingly remarked, "Any central banker who could not see the Japanese stock market and property bubbles of the late 1980s, the UK housing bubble of same period and the high-tech bubble of the late 1990s was in the wrong job," adding that many business media, including their own editorial board, had been calling them for years.[9]

Greenspan, of course, is now notorious for overseeing the expansion of the housing bubble in the US in the early part of this century, so it's relevant to look back at his views on government policing of companies' structural inability to consider externalities, such as system stability. A fan of Ayn Rand's blame-it-on-the-government style of analysis, Greenspan often stated his pessimism that government could prevent crises.[10] Amazing, considering that in the several decades after the sweeping financial reforms of the Great Depression, no financial crises occurred. Only when market deregulation was demanded by capital and defended by economists did the fearful visage of financial crisis appear again.

Greenspan's, and many economists', claim that bubbles such as the real estate mania are impossible to detect is also hard to justify, given the fact that so many less-ideological economists saw it years in advance. Consider Stephen Roach, chief economist at Morgan Stanley and an exceptional analyst, and his view of the developing housing bubble:

> Nearly five years after the bursting of the equity bubble, America has done it again. This time, it is the housing bubble ... income-short US consumers are playing this latest bubble for all it is worth—enjoying the psychological benefits of the so-called wealth effect and utilizing refinancing and second mortgages to extract purchasing power from over-valued property and ultimately depleting income-based saving rates ... [the Federal Reserve] has long suffered from bubble-denial syndrome, unwilling or unable to address speculative excess in asset markets until it is too late ... While it is only a few years since the bursting of the equity bubble, memories of that speculative excess have already dimmed ... The debate over a US housing bubble is now over.[11]

To Roach's chagrin, the "debate" would go on until the reality was undeniable, as the bubble popped in 2007–08. But despite Greenspan's insistence that investors are rational and that neither government nor others could identify a bubble significantly in advance, we might note that Roach's comments were written in 2004, three years before the climax.

Greenspan's "denial" might have been due in part to another classic assumption of economic modeling, "rational expectations," which insists that investors' expectations of future conditions are not wrong in any nonrandom way. In other words, investors do not irrationally assume that prices are more likely to go up or down in the future. This hypothesis is, of course, rather summarily contradicted by the long, long historical record of financial bubbles and subsequent panics and crashes.

Indeed, Charles Kindleberger, the author of a standard book on the subject, *Manias, Panics, and Crashes*, finds that the assumption of investor rationality is fairly well refuted by the record:

> The "rational expectations" assumption used in economic models is that investors react to changes in economic variables as if they are always fully aware of the long-term implications of these changes, either because they are clairvoyant or because they have Superman-like kryptonic vision. Thus the cliché that "all the information is in the price" reflects the view that prices in each market react immediately and fully to every bit of news so that no "money is left on the table" ... Rationality is thus an a priori assumption about the way the world should work rather than a description of the way the world has actually worked.[12]

The closest parallel to this destabilizing aspect of externalities among the environmental ones discussed in Part I involves the example most focused on risk, the Deepwater Horizon disaster (see Chapter 4). There, BP continually cut costs by omitting technical elements and practices that provided additional safety against blowouts and other potentially catastrophic accidents. While saving money, BP was considering only the risks to itself of an accident, not the monumental risks to the Gulf of Mexico, including significant damage probably lasting for decades, and to an ecosystem that was already rather battered. Likewise, an investment bank or hedge fund will clearly conduct any transaction likely to reward the firm, even if it will very likely have significantly destructive effect on the broader marketplace. In both cases, major disasters are made rather likely, due to the institutional structure of firms, influenced by their close ownership by families in the top few percent of America.

Kindleberger's book ends with a moving Appendix, presenting what the author calls a "partial but suggestive" list of financial crises around the world, over the last four hundred years. The entries include the scale of the bubble's expansion, the assets speculated upon, and so on. The list is not short, and the crises are seldom separated by great stretches of time, except by strong regulatory regimes like that after the Great Depression. The list is a sobering reminder of the reality of the abstract external costs written off under efficient market theory, and a reminder not to trust sober-seeming authority. Or economists.

15
Not Too Big Enough:
How America's Banks Got Too Big to Fail

The government bailout of America's biggest banks set off a tornado of public anger and confusion. When the House of Representatives initially rejected the bailout bill, the *Wall Street Journal* attributed it to "populist fury," and since then the public has remained stubbornly resentful over the bailout of those banks considered "too big to fail."[1] Now, the heads of economic policy are trying to gracefully distance themselves from bailouts, claiming that future large-scale bank failures will be avoided by new regulation and higher insurance premiums.[2]

Dealing with the collapse of these "systemically important banks" is a difficult policy issue, but the less-discussed issue is how the banking industry came to this point. If the collapse of just one of our $600 billion "systemically important" financial institutions, Lehman Brothers, was enough to touch off a crisis-level contraction in the supply of essential credit, we must know how it and a number of other banks became "too big to fail" in the first place. The answer lies in certain incentives for bank growth, which after the loosening of crucial industry regulations drove the enormous waves of bank mergers in the last 30 years.

ALL BANKS, GREAT AND GREAT

Prior to the 1980s, American commercial banking was a small-scale affair. State-chartered banks were prohibited by state laws from running branches outside their home state, or sometimes even outside their home county. Nationally chartered banks were likewise limited, and federal law allowed interstate acquisitions only if a state legislature specifically decided to permit out-of-state banks to purchase local branches. No states allowed such acquisition until 1975, when Maine and other states began passing legislation allowing at least some interstate banking. The trend was capped in 1994 by the Riegle-Neal Act, which removed the remaining restrictions on interstate branching and allowed direct cross-state banking mergers and acquisitions.

This geographic deregulation allowed commercial banks to make extensive acquisitions, in-state and out. When Wells Fargo acquired another large California bank, Crocker National, in 1986, it was the largest bank merger in US history.[3] Since "the regulatory light was green," a single banking company could now operate across the uniquely large US market, opening up enormous new opportunities for economies of scale in the banking industry.

Economies of scale are savings that companies enjoy when they grow larger and produce more output. The situation is similar to a cook preparing a batch of cookies for a Christmas party, and then preparing a batch for New Year's while all the ingredients and materials are already out. Producing more output (cookies) in one afternoon is more efficient than taking everything out again later to make the New Year's batch separately. In enterprise, this corresponds to spreading the large costs of start-up investment over more and more output, and is often thought of as lower per-unit costs as the level of production increases. In other words, there's less effort per cookie if you make them all at once. Economies of scale, when present in an industry, create a strong incentive for firms to grow larger, since profitability will improve. But they also give larger, established firms a valuable cost advantage over new competitors, which can put the brakes on competition.

Once unleashed by the policy changes, these economies of scale played a major role in the industry's seemingly endless merger activity. "In order to compete, you need scale," said a VP for Chemical Bank when buying a smaller bank in 1994. Indeed, in 1996 Chemical would itself merge with Chase Manhattan Bank.[4]

Economies of scale are common in manufacturing, and in the wake of deregulation the banking industry was also able to exploit a number of them. Spreading big up-front investment costs over more output is the main source of generic economies of scale, and in banking, the large initial investments are in sophisticated computer systems. With the growth in importance of large-scale computing power and sophisticated systems management, the cost of investing in new computer hardware and development is now recognized as a major investment obstacle for new banks. However, once installed by banks large enough to afford them, the great cost of that initial investment can be "spread out" over more product, so that the cost per unit decreases as more output is produced, making them highly profitable.[5] The *Financial Times* describes how "the development of bulk computer processing and of electronic data transmission ... has allowed banks to move their back office operations away from individual branches to large remote centers. This had helped to bring real economies of scale to banking, an industry which traditionally has seen diseconomies set in at a very modest scale."[6]

Consolidation of functions is another general source of scale economies. The modern workforce is no stranger to the massacres of "redundant" staff after mergers and acquisitions. If one firm's payroll staff and computer systems can handle twice the employees with little additional expense, an acquired bank may see its payroll department harvest pink slips while the firm's profitability improves. When Citicorp merged with the insurance giant Travelers Group in 1998, the resulting corporation laid off over 10,000 workers—representing 6 percent of the combined company's total workforce and over $500 million in reduced costs for Citigroup.[7] This practice can be especially lucrative in a country like the United States, with a fairly unregulated labor market where firms are quite free to fire. Despite the economic peril inflicted on workers and their families, this consolidation is key to increasing company efficiency post-merger. Beyond back-office functions, core profit operations may also benefit from consolidation. When Bank of America combined its managed mutual funds into a single fund, it experienced lower total costs, thanks to trimming overhead from audit and prospectus mailing expenses.[8] Consolidating office departments in this fashion can yield savings of 40 percent of the cost base of the acquired bank.[9]

Another important source of returns to scale in the financial sector is the "funding mix." The funding mix used by banks refers to where banks get the capital they then package into loans. Smaller institutions, having only limited deposits from savers, must "purchase funds" by borrowing from other institutions. This increases the funding cost of loans for banks, but larger banks will naturally have access to larger pools of deposits from which to arrange loans.[10] This funding cost advantage for larger banks relative to smaller ones represents another economy of scale.

Finally, in any market, advertising is an important source of scale economies, because the nature of advertising requires a certain scale of operation to be viable. Advertising can reach large numbers of potential customers, but if a firm is small or local many of those customers will be too far afield to act on the marketing. Large firm size, and especially geographic reach, can make the returns on ad time worth the investment. All these economies of scale give existing giants in an industry an advantage over new competitors, who are discouraged from trying to break into the market by the massive up-front costs and unlevel playing field.

Business Week's conclusion is that the banking industry "has produced large competitors that can take advantage of economies of scale ... as regulatory barriers to interstate banking fell," although not until the banks could "digest their purchases."[11] The 1990s saw hundreds of bank mergers and acquisitions annually, and hundreds of billions in acquired assets as old regulatory barriers fell. Economies of scale have limits, of course: as institutions grow, they tend to develop additional intervening layers of management and bureaucracy. But as we will see, by this time the large institution may have sufficient money and power to get away with it.

ACE OF ALL TRADES IN A STACKED DECK

But an additional step toward too-big-to-fail came with the deregulatory Gramm-Leach-Bliley Act of 1999, which further loosened restrictions on bank growth, this time not geographically but industry-to-industry. After earlier moves in this direction by the Federal Reserve, GLB reversed 60-year-old bans on mergers between commercial banks, insurance firms, and the riskier field of investment banking.[12] These had been separated by law for decades, on the grounds that the availability of commercial credit was too important to the overall economy to be tied to the volatile world of investment banking.

GLB allowed firms to grow further, through banks merging with insurers or investment banks. The world of commercial credit was widened, and financial mergers this time exploited economies of scope—where production of multiple products jointly is cheaper than producing them individually. As commercial banks, investment banks, and insurers have expanded into each others' fields in the wake of GLB, their different lines of business can benefit from single expenses—for example, banks perform research on loan recipients that can also be used to underwrite bond issues. Scope economies such as these allow the larger banks to both run a greater profit on a per-service basis and attract more business. Thanks to the convenience of "one stop shopping," Citigroup now does more business with big corporations, like IT giant Unisys, than its component firms did pre-merger.[13]

Exploiting economies of scope to diversify product lines in this fashion can also help a firm by reducing its dependence on any one line of business. Bank of America weathered the stock market downturn of 2001 in part because its corporate debt underwriting business was booming. Smaller, more specialized banks can become "one-trick ponies" as the *Wall Street Journal* put it—outdone by larger competitors with low-cost diversification thanks to scope economies.[14]

These economies of scope are parallel to the scale economies, since both required deregulatory policy changes to be unleashed. Traditionally, banking wasn't seen as an industry with the strong economies of scale seen in, say, manufacturing. But the deregulation and computerization of the industry have allowed these firms to realize returns to greater scale and wider scope, and this has been a main driver of the endless acquisitions in the industry in recent decades.

FREE MARKET MUSCLE-FLEXING

The enormous proportions that the banking institutions have taken on following deregulation have meant serious consequences for market performance. A number of banks have reached sufficient size to exercise market power—the ability of firms to influence prices and to engage in anticompetitive behavior. The market power of our enormous banks allows them to take positions as price leaders in local markets, where large firms use their dominance to elevate prices (that is, increase fees and rates on loans, and decrease interest rates on deposits). Large firms can do this because smaller firms may perceive that lowering their prices to take market share could be met by very drastic reductions in prices from the larger firm in retaliation. Larger banks, having deeper pockets, may be able to withstand longer periods of operating at a loss than the smaller firms.

Small banks are likely to perceive that the colossal size and resources of the megabanks make them unprofitable to cross—better to follow along and charge roughly what the dominant, price-leading firm does. Empirical research by Federal Reserve Board senior economist Steven Pilloff supported this analysis, finding that the arrival of very large banks in local markets tended to increase bank profitability for reasons of price leadership, due to the larger banks' economies of scale and scope, financial muscle, and diversification.[15]

Examples of the use of market power in the finance industry are easy to find. A recent Congressional bill dealt with the fees that retail businesses pay to the banks and the credit card companies. When consumers make purchases with credit cards, two cents of each dollar go not to the retailer but to the credit card companies that run the payment network and the banks which supply the credit for cards branded Visa and Mastercard. These "interchange fees" bring in over $35 billion in profit in the United States alone, and they reflect the strong market power of the banks and credit card companies over the various big and small retailers.[16] The 2 percent charge comes to about $31,000 for a typical convenience store, just below the average per-store yearly profit of $36,000, and this has driven a coalition of retailers to press for congressional action.

Visa has about 50 percent of the debit-credit card market, and Mastercard has 25 percent, which grants them profound market power and strong bargaining positions. Federal Reserve Bank of Kansas City economists found the United States "maintains the highest interchange fees in the world, yet its costs should be among the lowest, given economies of scale and declining cost trends."[17] The *Wall Street Journal*'s description was that "these fees ... have also been paradoxically tending upward in recent years when the industry's costs due to technology and economies of scale have been falling."[18] Of course, there's only a paradox if market power is omitted from the picture. The dominant size and scale economies of the banks and the credit card oligopoly allow for high prices to be sustained—bank muscle in action against a less powerful sector of the economy. The political action favored by the retailers includes proposals for committees to enact price ceilings, or collective bargaining by the retailers, again reflecting the understanding that organization is key to power and political success.[19] As is often the case, the political process is the reflection of the different levels and positions of power of various powerful institutions, and the maneuvering of their organizations.

Market power brings with it a number of other advantages. A powerful company is likely to have a widespread presence, make frequent use of advertising, and be able to raise its profile by contributing to community organizations like sports leagues. This allows the larger banks to benefit from stronger brand identity—their scale and resources make customers more likely to trust their services. This grants a further advantage in the form of customer tolerance of higher prices due to brand loyalty.

Large firms additionally enjoy more clout with other firms they deal with. In the deteriorating economic circumstances of the 2007–09 recession, the *Journal* reported that "Large corporations are tightening the screws on their smaller counterparts as the credit crunch intensifies companies' efforts to hold on to their cash. In an example of corporate Darwinism at work ... companies with annual revenue of more than $5 billion sped up their collection of cash from customers while slowing their own payments to suppliers."[20] A former Wells Fargo economist concludes, "Big firms can force their terms on suppliers and customers. And if you're a small business or a small store in a mall, you have no bargaining power and have to take what's given, which is not much today."[21]

And crucially, large firms with market power are free to participate meaningfully in politics—using their deep pockets to invest in electoral campaigns and congressional lobbying. The financial sector is among the highest-contributing industries in the United States, with total 2008 campaign contributions approaching half a billion dollars, according to the Center For Public Integrity.[22] So it's unsurprising that they receive so many favors from the state, since they fund the careers of the decision-making state personnel. This underlying reality is why influential Senator Dick Durbin said of Congress, "The banks own the place."[23]

Finally, banks may grow so large by exploiting scale economies and market power that they become "systemically important" to the nation's financial system. In other words, the scale and inter-connectedness of the largest banks is considered to have reached a point where an abrupt failure of one or more of them may have "systemic" effects—meaning the broader economic system will be seriously impaired. These are the banks called "too big to fail," and which were bailed out by an act of Congress in fall 2008. Once a firm becomes so enormous that the state must prevent its collapse for the good of the economy, it has the ultimate advantage of being free to take far greater risks. Riskier investments come with higher returns and profits, but the greater risk of collapse that accompanies them will be less intimidating to huge banks that have an implied government insurance policy.

BUYING INTO BAILOUTS

Some analysts have expressed doubt that such firms truly are too large to let fail, and that the banks have pulled a fast one. It might be pointed out in this connection that in the past the banks themselves have put their money where their mouths are—they have paid out of pocket to rescue financial institutions they saw as too large and connected to fail. An especially impressive episode took place in 1998, when several of Wall Street's biggest banks and financiers agreed to supply billions in emergency loans to rescue Long Term Capital Management. LTCM was a high-profile hedge fund that borrowed enormous sums of capital to make billion-dollar gambles on financial markets.

America's biggest banks aren't in the habit of forking over $3.5 billion of good earnings, but they had loaned heavily to LTCM and feared losing their money if the fund went under. The Federal Reserve brought the bankers together, and in the end, they paid up to bail out their colleagues; the *Wall Street Journal* reported that it was the Fed's "clout, together with the self-interest of several big firms that already had lent billions of dollars to Long-Term Capital, that helped fashion the rescue."[24] Interestingly, the banks insisted on real equity in the firm they were pulling out of the fire, and they gained a 90 percent stake in the hedge fund. Comparing this to the less-valuable "preferred stock" the government settled for in its 2008 bailout package of the large banks is instructive. The banks also got a share of control in the firm they rescued, again in stark contrast to the public bailout of some of the same banks.

In fact, the financial crisis and bailout led only to further concentration of the industry. The crisis gave stronger firms an opportunity to pick up sicker ones in another "wave of consolidation," as *BusinessWeek* put it. And a large part of the government intervention itself involved arranging hasty purchases of failing giants by other giants, orchestrated by the Federal Reserve.[25] For example, the Fed helped organize the purchase of Bear Stearns by Chase in March 2008 and the purchase of Wachovia by Wells Fargo in December 2008. Even the bailout's "capital infusions" were used for further mergers and acquisitions by several recipients. The Treasury Department was "using the bailout bill to turn the banking system into the oligopoly of giant national institutions," as the *New York Times* reported.[26]

The monumental growth of the largest banks owes a lot to the industry's economies of scale and scope, once regulations were relaxed so firms could exploit them. While certainly not unique to finance, these dynamics have brought the banks to such enormous size that their bad bets can put the entire economy in peril. Banking therefore offers an especially powerful case for the importance of these economies and the role of market power, since it's left the megabanks holding all the cards.

In fact, many arguments between defenders of the market economy and its critics center on the issue of competition vs. power—market boosters reliably insist that markets mean efficient competition, where giants have no inherent advantage over small, scrappy firms. However, the record in banking clearly shows that banks have enjoyed a variety of real benefits from growth. The existence of companies of great size and power is a quite natural development in many industries, due to the appeal of returns to scale and power. This is why firms end up with enough power to influence state policy, or such absurd size that they can blackmail us for life support.

And leave us crying all the way to the bank.

*   *   *

An article containing the above argument was first published in August 2010. While it waited for publication, an interesting article appeared in the very pro-large bank *Wall Street Journal*, "A City Feels the Squeeze In the Age of Mega-Banks."[27] Taking Orlando, Florida as an example, the reporting pretty closely tracked the above conclusions, finding that local banks were closing down, not because of the general economic downturn, but because they are "surrounded by giant banks that keep getting bigger and bigger ... Market power is concentrating in the hands of the nation's biggest banks." The article expects that the new "Dodd-Frank" finance reform bill (discussed in the next chapter) will reduce earnings for the megabanks somewhat, but "their growing supremacy will help them absorb the blow."

"Bank of America, J.P. Morgan and Wells Fargo now have 33% of all U.S. deposits ... Measured in loans and other assets,

Citigroup Inc. and the three other giants had $7.7 trillion as of March 31 [2010] ... Their combined assets are nearly twice as big as the assets of the next 46 biggest banks." Large banks justify their dominance with their ability to offer more ATMs, but, to quote a former FDIC chairman: "To keep their costs down, however, the big banks generally pay lower rates on certificates of deposit and other types of savings products," getting away with it because of their dominant position and remaining highly profitable thanks to "their low costs and volumes of scale ... Possibly even worse, the consolidation puts more risk 'in fewer and fewer hands, so when mistakes are made, they are doozies.'"

While the *WSJ*'s editorial page may defend any venal action of the finance majors, their real-world reporting pulls no punches: "Right after J.P. Morgan barreled into town, the bank hired a top commercial banker" from a regional bank, "to woo corporate customers. Billboards, print and television ads and junk mail have surged." A local bank, unable to compete with Chase's billboards and mailings with its newspaper ads, "was about to snatch several corporate customers away from the big banks when the borrowers suddenly were told to keep their accounts right where they were, or else the companies shouldn't bother trying to get credit from the big banks."

The picture backs up this chapter's analysis: "The giant banks are gambling that their vast array of products and convenient locations are enough to keep a grip on most customers no matter how low deposit rates sink. Frustrated depositors often can't find better rates elsewhere, though, because smaller financial institutions tend to quickly follow the lead of bigger banks when they come to town ... On loans, lower funding costs allow the big banks to be more aggressive, freeing them to undercut rivals," with bank funding rates a half-percent lower than for smaller firms.

When you do billions in business annually, those half-percents add up to a king's ransom.

16
Bonanzas as Usual: How Sky-high Bank Profits Persist Despite Bad Loans

After the catastrophic bank collapses of 2008 and the government rescue of the finance industry, Wall Street staged an impressive comeback. Post-bailout, profits were up, capital reserves were up, stock prices were up, government direct aid was repaid, and executive compensation exploded. But bank stability is just skin-deep, and dense accounting rules hide a powderkeg of bad debt and mounting funding issues. While the recent paper-thin re-regulation of finance has been a major political victory for the banks, their core business is headed downhill and even worse trouble seems to lie ahead.

All of the Big Four American megabanks—Bank of America, Citigroup, Chase, and Wells Fargo—reported decreases in their enormous profitability in early 2010. But the drop would have been even more disappointing without a pair of accounting maneuvers.[1] One was a bookkeeping measure allowing banks to book projected profit from buying back their debt when their bonds become cheaper. But the banks rarely buy back their debt, so this is essentially a paper gain. The other penstroke boosting profit was consumption of money set aside to protect against losses on loans—as banks grew more outwardly confident about the economic recovery, they lowered their stated expectations of bad loans and designated some of their capital cushions as profit. This same number-shuffling helped elevate reported bank income through 2011, although only some of the megabanks relied upon it.[2]

These shallow techniques for elevating profit weren't enough, however, to compensate for the decline in banks' core business, which is interest income, that is, the money collected from loans minus that paid out to depositors. That income diminished significantly over 2008–12, by as much as 6.2 percent for Bank of America, mainly due to falling loan volume. Banks were making fewer loans to consumers and businesses, citing a "lack of demand," which obscured the quite favorable credit rating they now required for extending credit.[3] During the real estate bubble, anyone ducking into a bank to escape the cold could get a loan, whereas now only sparkling credit ratings need apply. The lower supply of these applicants as job losses persist, combined with locking out applicants with spottier credit history and a general consumer preference to reduce total debt, were responsible for bank loan books continuing their shrinkage in the feeble recovery.

The market did not much reward the banks for the elaborate camouflage of this weakness in their core income source, and as a result their stocks barely traded above book. Executive compensation was another story, of course, with traders' pay rebounding into the $200,000–500,000 range. Meanwhile Obama's much-hailed "pay czar" in charge of monitoring finance executive compensation, Kenneth Feinberg, issued a moderately damning report or two, finding that within three months of receiving their bailouts, the megabanks had paid out $1.6 billion in bonuses—up to a quarter of their TARP rescue totals.[4] However, the "czar" has no formal power to rescind exorbitant pay now that the majors had repaid their government capital infusions, and compensation will now be monitored by a rather unintimidating consortium of regulators, including the FDIC, the Federal Reserve, and the Comptroller of the Currency. No upward limit is in sight for financier compensation, although the banking institutions themselves may have some bumpy days ahead.

EXTEND AND PRETEND AND DESCEND

While the banking majors were relieved of much of their bad mortgage-based investments by Federal Reserve purchases in the course of the financial crisis and aftermath, large loans related to commercial real estate remained on banks' books. Many of these loans were to growing businesses and over-optimistic developers, and have frequently failed to perform, as the recession rendered projects unprofitable, reducing borrowers' ability to repay.

But the loans are often for sobering amounts, upwards of tens of millions of dollars, and rather than foreclose on such large credit lines (as opposed to a typical home loan), banks large and small engage in what has come to be called "extend and pretend." The practice involves not taking legal measures on underperforming commercial real estate loans, but rather "restructuring" loans with new, more favorable terms for the borrowers, such as extended timelines for repayment or below-market interest rates. The goal of the practice is to prevent foreclosure on large loans, with the hope that extending maturities will give borrowers enough time to recover their business and repay.[5]

There are several problems with this practice—first, it conceals the real condition of the commercial real-estate market.[6] Secondly, the restructured loans are usually still foreclosed upon in the end—in the first quarter of fiscal 2010, 44 percent of loan restructurings were still a month or more delinquent, a fact related to the startling two-thirds of commercial real-estate loans maturing by 2014 that were underwater—meaning that the property is worth less than the bank loan itself.[7] Finally, the bad loans take up space on bank balance sheets that could go to real lending. This suggests that many banks may come to resemble a miniature version of 1990s Japan, where refusal to accept real-estate loan losses led to a decade of slow growth, in part due to banks' inability to make fresh loans.

However, the "extend and pretend" policy presents one major benefit to the big banks: restructuring these loans allows banks to count them as "performing" rather than delinquent or worse, which means banks may reduce their capital reserves against losses. This enables banks to claim their capital cushions as profit, so firms can remain in denial about their bad loans, and this itself allows profit increases today. And when banks are one day obliged to confront these serious losses, they may find they no longer have the capital cushion to absorb the damage.

This ominous hidden liability is on top of the banks' better-publicized underperforming residential mortgage holdings.

Within two years of the 2008 crisis, the mortgage delinquency rate hovered around 10 percent nationwide, and, when including those behind on payments and those on the verge of eviction, fully one American mortgage in seven was in some kind of trouble. Importantly, the bad mortgage debt on banks' books ceased to be a primarily "subprime" phenomenon of low-income loan recipients; over a third of new foreclosures in early 2011 were prime fixed-rate loans, as the layoff-intensive recovery pulled the rug out from under mortgage recipients.

Notably, the home mortgages still held by the banks were listed on bank balance sheets at inflated values, since they were bought at the housing bubble's peak, and the government did not force the banks to account for them at any reasonable value. And beside this additional hidden weakness and the space taken up on bank balance sheets by this bad mortgage debt, the banking majors were vulnerable by moves by insurers and other purchasers to force the banks to repurchase securitized home loans sold to them at wildly inflated values. So far, losses on effected and expected repurchases have cost the biggest four US banks nearly $10 billion, with additional losses anticipated, weakening megabank positions.[8]

Meanwhile, the banks have allowed extremely few mortgage borrowers to modify their mortgages or reduce their principal—the National Bureau of Economic Research found that just 8 percent of delinquent borrowers received any modification, while a pitiful 3 percent received reductions in their total owed principal.[9] On the other hand, about half of all seriously delinquent borrowers had foreclosure proceedings brought by their bank. Of course, banks ultimately benefit more from a renegotiated loan that is paid off than from a foreclosure, but the long timeline required in the foreclosure process allows the banks to once again push back acknowledgement of the loss.

Banks face other market difficulties in the near future. One involves the increased reliance of the large banks on short-term borrowing to fund their loan portfolios. While banks have issued bonds to raise loan capital for years, lately they have grown increasingly dependent on short-term borrowing—the average maturity of recent bank bond issues is under five years, the shortest average in decades. Banks have grown more inclined to near-term borrowing as the financial services world has grown more volatile, and this is one reason why the seizing-up of the credit markets in 2008 was such a big deal—banks were in immediate trouble if they couldn't borrow. Of course, the government bailout included guarantees for short-term bonds, leading the banks to become even more reliant upon them.

This means banks must "turn over" their debt more frequently—they must issue fresh bonds to raise capital to pay off the maturing older bonds—and US banks needed to refinance over a trillion dollars through 2012. The problem is that the banks will be competing with huge bond rollovers from governments, which are heavily indebted from upper-class tax cuts, expensive wars, and recent rounds of stimulus. Even the powerful megabanks may struggle in this environment—as the *New York Times* put it, "The cost of borrowing is likely to rise faster than banks can pass it on to customers."[10] The total demand for institutional credit may significantly spike in coming years, meaning perhaps higher interest rates as states and finance houses compete for the bond market's favor, or a further decline in lending by banks due to prohibitive funding costs.

And in a related development, the US banks face a significant threat of exposure to the European finance crisis. Brought on by the chronic weak budget positions of countries like Greece and Spain (see Chapter 8), the fear is that defaults by these countries (announcing a failure to pay debts) or a restructuring (a reduced payment of debts) would mean losses for the major banks that have lent to Greece, especially France and Germany, the heart of the Eurozone. Many US financial institutions have held significant amounts of public debt issued by these nations, and especially the debt of private French and German banks. So if the working majorities in these weak, "peripheral" European nations succeed in preventing their governments and mobile capital from imposing austerity, a default may follow, meaning losses for those countries' creditors. This has indeed happened with Greece's partial default in 2012, in which it was able to force creditors to accept losses, leaving it however with sterner lenders in the form of European governments and the IMF. In

2012, US financials reduced their exposure to European debt, although the Congressional Research Service estimated US bank exposure as about $640 billion, not counting non-bank financial firms.[11]

Meanwhile, smaller banks experienced a different post-crisis environment. Despite some TARP bailout crumbs, they went under in record numbers—140 failed in 2009, and 157 in 2010. Most of these smaller fry succumbed to losses or suffocated under bad loans following the real estate bubble of the last decade. This sector of the industry was ironically on track to cause more taxpayer losses from non-repayment of bailout funds than the majors.[12] The Congressional Oversight Committee, charged with monitoring the banks' repayment of TARP money, reported in July 2010 that smaller banks are having a more difficult time than the majors paying their bailout funds back, and "because many of the smaller banks are lightly traded or private [the Treasury's options for selling their bank shares] are more limited ... thereby making the federal government a player in the small bank market for the indefinite future."[13]

Compounding these stabilized but still shaky banking positions, the industry was now subjected to a significantly reshaped regulatory environment. In addition to the major finance reform bill enacted in July 2010, banks faced new international capital standards in the Basel Rules and new regulatory scope for the Federal Reserve as well. But all these reforms have been limited by massive lobbying spending by Wall Street, including $476 million spent by the financial sector in 2010, according to the Center For Responsive Politics.[14]

ONE HAND REGULATES THE OTHER

July 2010's Wall Street Reform and Consumer Protection Act, or "Dodd-Frank" for its Congressional sponsors, was expected to be a return to at least moderately punishing finance industry regulation, even if a far cry from the more sweeping controls that followed the Great Depression. But the slap-on-the-wrist nature of the bill was clear when stock prices of the megabanks *rose* 3 percent on its passage.[15] The bill was in many places rather vague and delegates dozens of decisions to the regulatory agencies themselves, from what constitutes a systemically important bank to credit rating disclosure. Crucially, bank regulators were expecting what the press calls a "lobbying blitz," as former employees of the regulators were bankrolled by Wall Street to lobby for industry discretion and relaxed standards on every rule.[16]

This industry's effort to neuter any reform has been led by the Financial Services Roundtable, the organization through which Wall Street primarily organizes itself (see Chapter 8). Its head is Steve Bartlett, who is described in a business organ of the *New York Times*:

> An unexpected voice dominated a closed-door meeting a few months ago on Capitol Hill, where senior Senate aides were discussing the financial regulatory overhaul adopted last summer. It was not a lawmaker, or even a Congressional staff member. It was a Wall Street lobbyist ... Mr. Bartlett, wearing ostrich leather cowboy boots, barked orders to surprised Congressional staff members ...

and indeed "acted like someone running the meeting."[17]

The Roundtable has overseen the "fierce and frenetic behind-the-scenes effort that has successfully delayed or watered down many of the major regulatory changes passed by Congress in the wake of the financial meltdown. Wall Street has spared little expense, spending nearly $52 million to woo Washington in the first three months of the year." Bartlett concedes that "We are trying to reform the reform," and this is considered legitimate despite the fact that the Roundtable's members bear primary responsibility for the crisis in the first place. The Roundtable head himself makes $2 million a year and was first hired to "secure passage" of the Gramm-Leach-Bliley Act (see Chapter 15), as he is a former Congressman. The "reform" legislation that emerged from this process is as weak-sauce as you'd expect:

- While now stuck with mild limits on overdraft fees and the "interchange fees" charged to merchants for debit card processing, banks have attempted to phase out free checking accounts, and been surprised at the outraged reactions from customers. This is because many depositors are unable to afford checking account fees, of course, but the *New York Times* journalists still expect the banks to "jettison unprofitable customers."

- The Volcker Rule would limit banks' "proprietary trading," investments made with a bank's own money rather than clients' funds. The practice was damaging during the finance crisis, but banks have already found a work-around for the new rule. Banks are moving star proprietary traders to client desks, where they will primarily conduct derivatives trades for corporate clients, but will also be able to engage in the barred practice on the side, further blurring the client/proprietary distinction.[18]

- The bill moved derivatives into the realm of "regulated" finance. Previously traded ad-hoc by individual banks, derivatives will now be listed on established indexes and will require collateral as a cushion against losses. This removes significant risk from the banks themselves, but reduces them to competing on service rather than deriving assets from existing debt for large fees. Importantly, businesses that use derivatives for legitimate purposes, such as farmers buying futures contracts to secure favorable grain prices, are exempted from the bill's indexing and collateralizing requirements (see Chapter 18).[19]

- The bill includes a resolution authority that gives regulators a procedure to "unwind" a bank—to oversee its bankruptcy in an orderly fashion and at its creditors' expense. Additionally, the Kanjorski amendment to the bill gives regulators the authority to break up any financial institution considered to be a systemic threat to the financial system. But the specifics are subject to heavy industry lobbying, and it seems unlikely that regulators, typically close to the firms they regulate, would let a titan go down regardless of their resolution authority.[20]

- The new Consumer Financial Protection Bureau requires more information transparency from banks in their communications with customers. However, despite apocalyptic predictions from bank spokespeople, it is notable that banks with under $10 billion in assets are exempt from its rules. This excludes the small and medium-sized lenders that make up 98 percent of US banks, but does include the large proportion of the industry run by the majors.

BASEL FAULTY

The Basel bank guidelines are meant to be the G-20's coordinated, worldwide response to the crisis of 2008, establishing consistent guidelines limiting banking risk and other practices. Much of the American reform bill's vagueness was justified on the grounds that Congress was awaiting the final version of the global Basel standards. But like the American bill, the lightweight standards have been greeted by stock jumps for the bank majors, since the process was heavily influenced by massive financial industry lobbying and other, nationalist factors.

The negotiations were run by regulators from across the G-20 group, and as the negotiations proceeded, the prevailing attitude was "if in doubt, take it out."[21] This is due to the national negotiators' diverging interests as well as the finance industry's insistence that stiffer limits on risk-taking will deprive the world economy of needed capital. (However, since the banks are facing a mostly demand-side problem with their lending, this argument doesn't hold much water.)

Perhaps most notably, the biggest banks' minimum leverage ratio—how much capital banks must hold to cushion against sudden losses—has been set at a modest 7 percent of assets, with the possibility of increasing that level for large, more systemically important banks.[22] However, banks need not meet this requirement until 2019, with only a 2.5 percent requirement by 2015. Further, the Basel Committee caved to industry demands to count assets like deferred-tax funds, mortgage-service rights, and investments in other firms as capital. These are now being limited to 15 percent of a bank's capital cushion, rather than not being counted due to their illiquidity. These assets are "risk-weighted," meaning the holdings are given different values based on how risky they're thought to be. Unfortunately, the 2008 crisis demonstrated the banks are poor at gauging just how risky their assets are, and again they have significant influence over the regulators' decision.[23]

A related issue is how much long-term funding (vs. short-term bonds) the banks issue, making them less vulnerable to sudden credit market lockups, as in 2008. The Committee failed to reach agreement on this issue, and the rule was postponed until 2015, along with many others, including "calibration," that is, the specific required reserve level banks must maintain based on their importance to the overall finance system.

One obstacle to progress is the distinctly nationalist approach taken by the regulators, who aim to minimize the weight of regulations that will affect the banks based in their home countries.[24] The United States has pushed aggressively for broader definitions of capital, since US banks still hold large volumes of mortgage securitization rights. Germany wants "flexible" enforcement of the reserve requirements for its undercapitalized banks; France wants allowances for its banks to continue to own insurers, and so on.[25] The result is banking regulators fighting tooth and nail against regulating their own banks.

In this way, the standards meant to prevent banks from reverting to their old systemically risky ways have been heavily diluted, diminishing Basel to a fig leaf. As the *Wall Street Journal* put it, "significant moves by the Basel Committee to back away from its initial proposals … [are] likely to provoke criticism that regulators are caving to industry pressure and missing a chance to impose restraints that could reduce the risk of future costly crises."[26]

In the end, moderately higher capital requirements and the public listing and indexing of derivatives may take the financial system a step back to short-term stability, but banks remain stuck with significant bad loans limiting core interest income, and continue to rely on market bubbles and their outsized political power. They also face a difficult short-term bond market in the near future, and besides being weighed down with the bad commercial real-estate debt and some higher regulatory costs, their core business is further limited by weak credit demand in the low-expectations recovery. Ominously, they have also seen their insurance premiums go up: in November 2011, it cost around $475,000 to insure $10 million worth of Bank of America's debt; in January the same year, it was $150,000. This increase suggested that, as the *Journal* puts it, "the bond vigilantes are on the prowl," meaning they are looking skeptically at the banks and driving up their borrowing costs. But unsurprisingly, compensation has not fallen in the face of these circumstances.

So far, despite Occupy Wall Street, the megabanks have had their traders instead of Hell to pay.

17
Fed Up:
The Desperation of Quantitative Easing

After suffering for years from a dizzyingly high unemployment rate, Americans are eager for meaningful increases in hiring. In the past, the government jump-started economic growth with fiscal policy—increasing spending in order to create new demand for goods and services, which companies could fulfill only by hiring. After the nation languished through a decade of depression in the 1930s, the monumental fiscal outlays for World War II created an enormous "stimulus" to total demand and hiring. The massive spending for the war effort, financed in large part by aggressive 80+ percent tax rates on the richest households, created demand that gave employers reason to create millions of jobs.

Most people regard social spending, such as on education or public health, as a more acceptable form of stimulus than military spending. But apart from government programs started in the 1960s due to popular demand, stimulus has proven "politically difficult" unless it takes the form of military adventure or tax cuts that are typically skewed toward the richest households. Unfortunately, tax cuts for the wealthy are the weakest form of stimulus and have relatively little job-creating impact; and non-military stimulus plans, including the inadequate 2009 stimulus bill, have been blocked by deficit hawks.[1]

Yet in this climate of public-spending cutbacks, policy makers recognize that some new government response to the desperate job-market situation is clearly needed. The traditional alternative to fiscal policy is monetary policy—encouraging economic growth by lowering short-term interest rates through the Federal Reserve Bank's interventions. But traditional monetary policy has failed—short-term rates remain near zero while the economy continues to show little response. So attention has turned to the Fed's new alternative, "quantitative easing," an enormous program of purchases of financial assets. Fed policymakers hope to make long-term borrowing cheaper and therefore spur hiring, but the result so far has been to load up the Fed's balance sheet while enriching bond investors and rescuing more banks, with little effect on job creation.

BALANCING ACT

All companies have balance sheets, listing a company's "Liabilities"—what the company owes—and "Assets"—what the company owns. Assets and liabilities always balance, due to how they are counted. For example, on the balance sheet of a typical commercial bank, the main assets are bank loans extended to consumers and businesses, because they provide the bank with an interest income. The main liabilities are the depositors' account balances, which the bank is obliged to produce at any time. The Federal Reserve is different, however, because it can essentially print money by electronically increasing the account balances it owes other banks. With the government's current refusal to run sensible fiscal deficits targeted at creating jobs, the Fed's ability to massively expand its balance sheet (and to even run a profit doing so) has attracted new attention.

Historically, the Fed's main role has been to influence interest rates, in order to moderate the business cycle of growth and recessions. Interest rates affect economic growth and hiring because these usually involve at least some borrowed money, and since interest rates are the cost of borrowing, decreasing interest rates encourages growth and jobs. Likewise, cranking interest rates up makes credit more expensive and tends to put the brakes on a fast-growing economy. The Fed most commonly pushes interest rates up or down by contracting with the largest US banks to buy or sell large amounts of US Treasury bonds, which are pieces of government debt. This moves money in and out of the banking system, which pushes interest rates up and down across the economy. So the Fed's main asset has been

US Treasury bonds, meaning that the Fed generally has large volumes of these interest-bearing government bonds among its assets.

The Fed has historically held a number of liabilities, including the reserve accounts of the many private banks in the Federal Reserve system, held as cushions against losses. The US Treasury Department's own "general account," used for government payments, also falls on this side of the balance sheet. But Fed liabilities also include the US paper currency used across the economy, hence the "Federal Reserve Note" on dollar bills. So the Fed is "liable" for the balances of the rest of the government, the private banks' reserve accounts it maintains, and for US cash, which can be exchanged for other assets.

THROWING MONEY AT THE PROBLEM

Over the course of the 2008 financial crisis, the Fed quickly shot most of its conventional ammo—the interest rates it has influence over were cut down to almost zero. But since banks drastically cut back their lending regardless of rates (see Chapter 14), essentially cutting off the supply of important credit to the broader economy, the Fed's balance sheet has taken on a very different look. It has swollen with different types of asset purchases: first, the Fed bought devalued "toxic assets" from the banks as part of the 2008 bank bailout, and then subsequently in large "quantitative easing" programs of buying various financial assets in order to inject more cash into the economy. The Fed's large-scale buying tends to push bond prices up, which lowers long-term interest rates. The Fed bought great volumes of these financial assets, with its balance sheet rocketing from $800 billion in 2007 to over $2 trillion in February by year's end 2011.

The mountain of new Fed assets is composed of three broad asset categories. The first is the extension of short-term credit to financial firms—lending on favorable terms to banks that are in dire need of immediate cash. This is an extension of the Fed's original role of "banker of last resort," lending cheaply to banks in need of money overnight or even facing a "run" of panicking depositors. This included lending through both the Fed's normal "discount window" and the "Term Auction Facility," which was set up to allow staggering banks to borrow with more anonymity. "Currency swaps" to foreign central banks, in which the Fed bought foreign currency from banks needing US dollars, were also part of the program. This category of Fed assets reached its high point during and immediately after the 2008 financial crisis, when the short-run lending markets dried up amid fears of borrower insolvency, leaving many enormous banks, insurers, and other financial companies on the edge of failure. As the financial industry has recovered its footing, this category declined as a share of the Fed's balance sheet.

The second category of the Fed's new asset pile is loans to borrowers in the broader economy, primarily short-term corporate bonds, or "commercial paper," from many US corporations. Companies often rely on short-term borrowing to cover regular operating costs, like payroll or supplier bills, while waiting for receivables to come in. During the 2008 crisis, struggling investment groups like money market funds faced huge withdrawals, leaving them without the cash to continue investing in these short-term bonds. Therefore the commercial paper market "locked up:" rates spiked and borrowing became almost impossible. The Fed stepped in to supply the market with emergency short-term credit, and its program earned headlines for the "bedrock" corporations revealed to have relied heavily on the program—including Caterpillar, GE, McDonald's, Toyota, and Verizon.[2] This category of assets also includes the TALF program (the Term Asset-Backed Securities Loan Facility), which sought to restart "securitization"—the packaging of loans into tradeable assets that may be bought and sold. Car loans, credit card debt, and student loans are among the forms of packaged debt the Fed invested in. As these short-term markets returned to somewhat normal functioning, this component also diminished as a proportion of the Fed's total assets.

TALF and its related programs became particularly notorious for being "gamed" by financial firms and what the *New York Times* called "a cross-section of America's wealthy." The super-low interest rates provided by the Fed for desperate and important corporations were also used by canny investors to make enormous sums off the public aid. One investor, having seen impressive returns of up to 10 percent, referred to getting "a gift from the Fed."[3] In this connection, it is notable that at every stage the Fed's policy has been to pursue options that preferentially benefit the rich. Bond ownership is skewed toward upper-income households, so supporting bond market conditions is of disproportionate benefit to them. Likewise, the Fed's actions during and after the 2008 financial crisis meant few losses for the well-off creditors of banks and insurers, with their institutions rescued at taxpayer expense. The Fed richly deserves its reputation as a "captured" regulator, being predominantly run by former Wall Street bankers who often return to the finance industry after leaving the Fed.

The third main category of the Fed's asset purchases is what the Fed calls "high-quality" securities, meaning debt instruments with relatively low risk. This is the component that has taken on enormous proportions as part of the Fed's QE program. This program of asset purchases, which played the biggest role in raising the Fed's balance sheet to over $2 trillion, made massive acquisitions of US Treasury bonds, "agency debt" issued by the government mortgage agencies Freddie Mac and Fannie Mae, and mortgage-backed securities. In late 2011, the Fed announced it was continuing this strategy with its "Operation Twist," trying to muscle down longer-term interest rates by rolling $400 billion earned from the Fed's bond investments into assets with longer maturities, hoping to drive investors into private bond markets.[4]

After these moves from the Fed, some rates were lowered for different amounts of time, but the bond market has mostly seen rate increases instead, defying Fed policy. Bond investors evidently expect borrowers to have difficulty repaying loans in today's weak recovery and are demanding higher rates as compensation, and may also be "spooked" at the huge supply of public and private bonds for purchase today.[5] Higher interest rates, of course, act as a drag on the economic recovery, such as it is. This "overruling" of the Fed by the bond market has been surprising, but runs parallel to other recent reductions in the Fed's power, such as the creation of more unregulated "shadow" finance institutions which have partially taken the place of the commercial banks the Fed regulates. This has reduced the Fed's ability to influence the economy through interest rate changes for the banks in its system.

Notably, the QE program has had a secondary effect as a semi-bailout for America's mid-size banks, which are still failing at a rate on course to swamp the FDIC, which insures their deposits. Since these second-tier banks received relatively little bailout money, the Fed propped up many by buying their bad mortgage debt. QE is presumably also executed with the expectation that it will contribute to driving down the value of the US dollar relative to other world currencies, as the Fed's buying spree effectively dumps the currency into world markets. This may have a positive effect in encouraging US exports, which are cheaper for foreign buyers when the dollar loses value, but it also risks setting off a global currency war as other nations strive to weaken their own currencies in order to boost exports. Competition among trading blocks to deflate currencies was a prominent feature of the Great Depression and not an encouraging model for world economic recovery.

The currency swaps discussed above were also making a return as the Fed strove to help its central bank colleagues at the European Central Bank deal with the fallout of the Greek/Euro finance crisis (see Chapter 10). Many central banks in the EU had made loans in dollars, usually borrowing those dollars on the market, but when lending dried up the Fed intervened to prevent these banks from experiencing a dollar crunch to add to their existing problems, for example, keeping their own private banks afloat after losing money on the housing crash and now sovereign debt (such as Greek bonds).[6]

In the shadow of this still-growing mountain of Federal Reserve asset purchases, the Fed's liabilities have grown in parallel, but with less public attention. This is because most of the Fed's new assets were purchased from banks in the Federal Reserve regulatory system, which maintain their own reserve accounts with the Fed.[7] So when the Fed buys some of a private bank's assets, like US Treasury bills or mortgage-backed debt, rather than mail a check it simply increases the banks' deposit account balance. The Fed may be called on to give the bank the money in its Fed account, so these payments are a liability for the Fed, and have grown as a mirror image of the assets bought in the QE purchase program.

QUANTITATIVE UNEASE

The QE gambit—and its effects on the Fed's balance sheet—are by no means unanimously popular at the Fed. It is widely reported that QE is a contentious move among the Federal Reserve Open Market Committee (FOMC), which decides monetary policy. Prominent Fed members, including the presidents of the Dallas, Philadelphia, and Minneapolis Federal Reserve Banks, have stated discomfort with QE.[8] Dissenters also include Kansas City Federal Reserve Bank President Thomas Hoenig, who has described QE as "risky," and prefers breaking up the "too-big-to-fail" banks. And in language somewhat unusual for a Fed Bank president, he has openly discussed the "Wall Street-Washington axis of influence" and decries the "enormous power" of the "oligarchy" of powerful banks.[9]

But most of QE's critics are inflation "hawks"—investors and FOMC members who advocate an aggressively anti-inflationary posture. They oppose QE for two reasons. The first is a fear of runaway inflation caused by injecting so much money into the economy. However, this concern seems remote in an economy which, in 2010, had a double-digit real unemployment rate and usage of manufacturing capacity at an embarrassing 72 percent.[10] Also, the inflation rate itself by that time had not reached 3 percent since the finance crisis, although significant inflation could originate in imported products should the dollar fall quickly. The hawks' second concern about QE is that the Fed will become unwilling to raise interest rates in the future. Increasing interest rates would reduce the value of the Fed's own large bond investments, when investors would sell them for higher-yielding assets.[11] Furthermore, higher rates would mean the Fed would have to pay more in interest to banks with deposits at the Fed. For these twin reasons the hawks fear a loss of the Fed's willingness to raise rates later, thus damaging its inflation-fighting "credibility."

Conservative critics also fear that QE jeopardizes the large payments the Fed makes to the government. By law, any profit the Federal Reserve Bank makes on its now-large investments must be paid to the US Treasury, after covering the Fed's own expenses. In 2009 the Fed made $47.4 billion from its huge investments, politically valuable income in a time of widening budget deficits.[12] A Fed rate increase could eliminate that payment, and indeed the Fed could ultimately lose money on its investment—as the bond market has declined, the Fed's portfolio was down a few percent in late 2010.[13]

Whatever the long-term impact on the Fed of its asset purchasing campaign, it is difficult to see significant positive effects on the broader economy. Even if the Fed ultimately succeeds in pushing down long-term interest rates, cheap borrowing won't boost the economy the way a targeted spending program would. Companies may appreciate cheap borrowing, but why create jobs without sufficient demand for goods, so that the new workers' output will be bought? Likewise, while cash-strapped and indebted consumers will benefit from low interest rates, they're unlikely to increase spending again without the feeling of security that comes from a steady job. Aggressive fiscal outlays in energy and infrastructure would create far more jobs than quantitative easing is likely to do, and indeed, by April 2011, the results of trillions in QE investment had been disappointing, with Fed figures and many economists concluding its experiment had failed to meaningfully lower interest rates, let alone create jobs.[14] No wonder popular discontent with the Fed has reached the point that it's one of the institutions most blamed for the crisis by the rising American movements.

PUPPET MASTER OR SOCK PUPPET?

The Federal Reserve retains a strong reputation in mainstream economic circles. Its Chairs, for instance, Paul Volcker or Ben Bernanke, are treated reverently as high priests, even if their images are later tarnished by their disastrous policy decisions, as with Alan Greenspan (see Chapter 14).

However, among the American public the Fed's reputation is in flux. Many street-level activists see the Fed as a key to the current economic depression, since it prevented the megabanks from going bankrupt, the idea being that the failure of firms is an important part of recessions. Many waver in this view when reminded that given the monumental scale of the megabanks (see Chapter 15), the bankruptcy of even one of which would have meant major disruption of the credit system, the loss of hundreds of billions of dollars in savings and assets, and a near-certain depression. The more modest firm Lehman Brothers' bankruptcy brought disruption enough. But the Fed is also blamed for reducing market efficiency through its regulation of finance, and its failure to stop the growth of the housing bubble, despite the clear association of financial deregulation and bubbles over the last 30 years. Finally, the advent of QE1 and 2 have driven the right to decry the "hyperinflation" it will bring about, somehow overcoming the strong deflationary pressures of our slack job market. The "End the Fed" campaign associated with Republican presidential candidate Ron Paul is an incarnation of this tendency, often seen during Tea Party protests.

On the other hand, given its consistently expressed view that government is run by big business, the Occupy Wall Street position might begin with the recognition that the Fed's policy-making bodies are visibly controlled by Wall Street. From regular staffers all the way to senior policy makers, there is a standard practice of Fed staff working for large commercial or investment banks before joining the Fed, and an understanding that often they will return to the financial industry later in their careers. Further indicators that the Fed is to a large extent a pawn of the financial industry include its surrender of a significant part of its influence, as government deregulation has allowed the huge growth of "shadow banking" institutions outside the Fed system, seriously weakening the Fed's monetary policy effectiveness. Despite some complaints from Fed leaders, the central bank generally accepted these changes since they were demanded by Wall Street, the center of economic power and, again, where many Fed figures expected to return. It's hard to picture a more powerful institution taking orders from less powerful ones, unless indeed the phenomenal volume of money and power of the modern finance industry is a real power center.

So the left picture is of a "captured regulator," a government body run by the industries it's supposed to regulate. From this point of view, moves to reform the Fed would include more democratic influence over policy moves, rather than banking industry influence, along with an increased emphasis on creating jobs instead of treating inflation as the main threat to the economy. After years of disbursing literally trillions in aid to the rich and their institutions, with a pitiful trickle going to the majority, the public is fed up with the Federal Reserve.

18
Starved for Attention:
Financial Speculation and
Rising Food Prices

Financial markets have extended their scope widely over the last few decades of neoliberalism. As finance has shed one regulatory burden after another, it has become more volatile (see Chapter 14) and more powerful (Chapter 16). One marketplace that has recently become regarded by finance as fair game for speculation is commodities—including oil, important industrial minerals, and food.

Speculation, of course, is the practice of buying an asset with the plan of selling it later for a higher price. Some speculation is helpful in markets, as it helps them arrive at a regular price level. But as discussed in Chapter 14, speculation can cause severe market turbulence, and even form destructive bubbles. Speculation in oil has become a major contributor to driving up prices at the pump, which has bitten into household budgets at a time when they're already stretched past their limits. But speculation on food has a far darker effect, especially for households in the developing world, where a far larger share of incomes go to food, and where millions of people are already facing malnutrition and hunger.

THE FOOD PYRAMID SCHEME

Over 2007 and 2008, the world experienced a very sharp spike in prices for basic foods, including rice, wheat, and corn. In this short period, prices for these commodities doubled and even tripled; however, they reached a sharp peak in autumn 2008, just as the financial crisis was breaking. Then prices plummeted, and by January 2009 their prices were at or returning to their January 2007 levels. But while they were sky-high, the food prices did some enduring damage: tens of millions of additional people experienced malnutrition, including children whose growth will be permanently stunted.

The extremely sharp, and short-lived, character of the price jump is rather anomalous, and many researchers have concluded that such a fast and intense jump and then abrupt reversal can't possibly be accounted for simply by changes in supply and demand. As one group of economists put it, "While demand-supply imbalances have been touted as reasons, this is largely unjustified given that there has been hardly any change in the world demand for food in the past three years," noting that levels of demand for food grains in even fast-growing India and China

> ...have actually fallen in both countries. Supply factors have been—and are likely to continue to be—more significant. These include the short-run effects of diversion of both acreage and food crop output for bio-fuel production, as well as more medium-term factors such as rising costs of inputs, falling productivity because of soil depletion, inadequate public investment in agricultural research and extension, and the impact of climate changes that have affected harvests in different ways.[1]

So if supply and demand for food didn't cause the price spike, what did? The timing and pattern of the spike are suggestive—sudden price swings are common in markets that are characterized by speculation (see Chapter 14). The timing considers the fact that the huge price run-up ended just as financial institutions needed to withdraw from investments in order to pile up desperately needed cash at home. Several research groups have attempted to ascertain the degree of connection here, and leading the pack are agencies associated with the United Nations.

The Food and Agriculture Organization is a UN-affiliated body that provides research and support programs for world agriculture. In June 2010, they caused something of a stir when they published a brief suggesting that financial speculators drove the bubbles in the food market, or more specifically, food commodity futures markets. Futures are financial contracts where two parties agree to exchange a specified commodity at a future date. They're often used by farmers to hedge against future changes in the prices of their crops (see Chapter 16). However, because these contracts can be traded prior to their maturities, investors can buy and sell them without ever necessarily holding any of the actual commodity involved.

The FAO found that since

> ... only 2 percent of futures contacts end in the delivery of the physical commodity ... futures contracts also attract investors who are not interested in the commodity as such, but in making a speculative gain. In fact, commodity futures have become increasingly appealing to non-commercial investors as their returns seem to be negatively correlated with returns to equities and bonds.[2]

In other words, once the housing bubble began to plateau in 2007, hedge funds, investment banks, and other well-capitalized financial institutions began to view assets representing food as a great place to make quick returns.

While noting that conventional efficient-market theory (see the Introduction) holds that speculation should reduce volatility, the FAO suggests that

> Such theory, however, may not hold in the presence of trend-following investors or those with market power. For example, in the short term an investor might be attracted by the opportunities offered by the upward trend of a commodity price although this development may not be based on any fundamental data. These speculative investments could strengthen the trend and push the futures price further from its true equilibrium, if many investors jump the bandwagon ("herd behavior") or those who invest have sufficient funds to influence the market. Index funds are an example of such powerful investors. They have become key players in the market, holding about 25-35 percent of all agricultural futures contracts.[3]

These "index investors" are usually run by the larger financial institutions like Goldman Sachs and AIG, which received one of the biggest government bailouts in 2008.

Another UN body's research on this subject shed more light. UNCTAD, the UN Conference On Trade and Development, published a report on the global economic crisis and the commodities spike. UNCTAD's conclusion is stronger than the FAO's, pointing to one strong indicator of the role of speculation in the price hike—that since not only food but other commodities like oil and metals also experienced the dizzying rise and simultaneous crash, "This parallel development of commodity prices and financial investment on commodity futures markets is a first indicator for the role of large-scale speculative activity in driving commodity prices first up and then down."[4]

The UNCTAD report addresses the mainstream economic theory that speculators should decrease market volatility and that efficient markets have freely adjusting prices that immediately adapt to incoming information. Noting that the supply of physical commodities like oil and food are "inelastic," or slow to adjust to price changes:

> Prices can be driven up by the mere fact that everybody expects higher prices, which in itself may be driven by rising futures prices following rising demand for futures by financial speculators ... Hence, large orders may ... cause significant price shifts. This implies the possibility of a 'weight-of-money' effect: position changes that are large relative to the size of the total market have a temporary, or even a persistent, price effect.[5]

In other words, a big enough financial institution can invest enough money in a market to drive up prices, which may be thought to continue if investors are the least bit not perfectly rational, creating the expectation of rising prices and the potential for a bubble.

Swimming as it is against the tides of economic orthodoxy regarding rational investor behavior, the report sites as evidence the "strong correlation between the unwinding of speculation in different markets that should be uncorrelated." Reviewing the data on crashing asset prices across the board in 2008/09, "there are phases of speculative activity where currencies, even those of small countries like Iceland, and commodity prices are clearly driven by factors beyond fundamentals because the fundamentals underlying the different prices cannot go in the same direction."

The "weight-of-money" effect alludes to the "market power" brought up in the FAO report, meaning that a market of certain size can be steered upward by large enough infusions of money, which is possible if financial firms are large relative to the market. Here the suspects would be the "index investors," the funds and investment vehicles managed by the great banks and money managers like Goldman and AIG:

> The weight-of-money effect relates primarily to index-based investment, which allocates positions across many commodities in proportions that depend on the weighting formula of the particular index. As a result, index-based investment generates price pressure in the same direction across a broad range of commodities. Moreover, index-based investment positions can be large relative to the size of the entire market.[6]

Once again, it's clear that the size of the companies in a market, including financial markets, has serious consequences for market performance. Analyzing data from the main commodities trade regulator (more on which below), the agency finds that

> While the number of index traders is relatively small, their average long position is very large ... sometimes more than ten times the size of an average long position held by either commercial or non-commercial traders. [Long positions indicate an expectation, or a bet, that the price of a commodity will increase.] Positions of this order are likely to have sufficiently high financial power to drive prices ... As a result, speculative bubbles may form and price changes can no longer be interpreted as reflecting fundamental supply and demand signals.[7]

Put more simply, the data implies that the large financial institutions are making money by betting that food prices will increase, and their raw size allows them to make that a self-fulfilling prophecy, by pouring huge amounts of liquidity into the futures markets. Indeed the Commodity Futures Trading Commission (CFTC) data suggests that Index positions are four to ten times the size of other market participants, and hugely weighted toward long positions prior to December 2008.

These conclusions are rather strong, but received added strength when the *Guardian* and *Bloomberg Businessweek* reported some advice from major commodity future index trader Goldman Sachs, for its wealthy clients, specifically on petroleum commodity investments: "The record levels of speculative trading in crude have pushed their prices up so much in recent months that in the near term, risk reward no longer favors holding those commodities."[8] This speculation is not limited to the finance majors, but is also a growing focus for the giant agricultural companies like Cargill, a "food company" where the president of the Financial Markets Division remarked that "This business is built on the recognition that money is the ultimate commodity … Financial assets are repackaged and redistributed to add value to the products."[9]

IMPACTS OFF THE MENU

In addition, we might take note of some other serious developments in world agriculture. In 2010, *Science* published a special issue covering the desperate need to increase food production to feed the additional 2 billion people (bringing the world's population to 9 billion), expected by the middle of this century. Notably, almost every article in the collection at some point discusses the increased stress that rising temperatures and shifting climate patterns will bring to already-stressed food production. The flagship article is a very broad analysis of the difficulty of increasing production in the face of the enormous costs modern agriculture has on the environment, noting early on that "[t]he long-term nature of returns on investment for many aspects of food production and the importance of policies that promote sustainability and equity also argue against purely relying on market solutions." The basic picture is that

Food production has important negative "externalities," namely effects on the environment or economy that are not reflected in the cost of food. These include the release of greenhouse gases, environmental pollution due to nutrient run-off, water shortages due to overextraction, soil degradation and the loss of biodiversity through land conversion or inappropriate management, and ecosystem disruption due to the intensive harvesting of fish and other aquatic foods.[10]

These issues are complex in their interrelations and are impossible to value through simple market prices. Additionally, the article maintains that while globalization helps some farmers through increased market access, it comes with not only higher "external" costs from transporting goods further, but also

An unfettered market can also penalize particular communities and sectors, especially the poorest who have the least influence on how global markets are structured and regulated. Expanded trade can provide insurance against regional shocks on production such as conflict, epidemics, droughts, or floods—shocks that are likely to increase in frequency as climate change occurs. Conversely, a highly connected food system may lead to the more widespread propagation of economic perturbations, as in the recent banking crisis, thus affecting more people. There is an urgent need for a better understanding of the effects of globalization on the full food system and its externalities.[11]

The piece ends with the conclusion that "The goal is no longer simply to maximize productivity, but to optimize across a far more complex landscape of production, environmental, and social justice outcomes."

HUNGRY FOR RE-REGULATION

When the Dodd-Frank financial reform bill was passed (see Chapter 16), one of its provisions obliged the main regulator of futures trading, the Commodity Futures Trading Commission, to reimpose position limits. Position limits are restraints on how large of a share of a market a single firm can hold at one time, and were in force for the many crisis-free decades that followed the tight regulation of finance after the Depression. After a year-long delay, the CFTC voted to reimpose some position limits on futures trading. The limits restrict the number of futures contracts that can be held by a single firm to 25 percent of deliverable supply, down from the 30 or even 40 percent that has become common today. This "position limit" rule obviously still allows big investors to hold a very large proportion of the market.[12]

But not large enough for Wall Street, which is suing the CFTC over the rule. The *New York Times*' business blog *DealBook* put it best: "Wall Street sought to deliver another blow to the financial regulatory overhaul on Friday, as two industry trade groups sued a federal regulator over a new rule restricting speculative trading," arguing that the regulator

> … failed to evaluate the rule's economic impact on Wall Street … The lawsuit is the latest indication that Wall Street is shifting fronts in the battle over Dodd-Frank, moving from backroom lobbying to the courtroom [see Chapter 12]. A federal appeals court in July struck down the Securities and Exchange Commission's so-called proxy access rule, a Dodd-Frank policy that would have made it easier for shareholders to nominate company directors. The court ruled that the S.E.C.'s cost-benefit analysis [see Chapter 5] on the rule was inadequate.[13]

Since Dodd-Frank left so many of its details up to the decisions of individual regulatory agencies, the finance industry organized a "lobbying blitz" to weaken new regulations as much as possible, despite the fact that the US experienced no financial crises in the years of regulated finance. In the case of these limits on commodity futures positions, "The groups pushed regulators to interpret the fine print to mean that in essence, no limits were appropriate." Despite this "blitz" of lobbying, the industry groups also accuse the CFTC of "not allowing the industry to adequately comment on the rule proposal."

Depending on how this money-driven process turns out, we'll see whether millions of poor people, and even middle-class developed-world consumers, will have to carry the burden of speculative megabanks in the form of higher food prices. But as discussed before, the amount of public activism influences judicial decisions, and will play a major role in deciding if we will be able to keep food on the table and out of portfolios.

Conclusion
Invisible Sleight-of-hand:
Economics as a Failed Science

The failure of the dominant "neoclassical" schools of economic theory is now pretty clear. Mainstream theory fails to capture critical aspects of the market economy, including "external" social and natural costs, economic power and its use in bargaining over prices and wages, and financial instability through disregard of systemic risk and the tendency of people's excited expectations to form speculative bubbles.

The failure of the giant majority of the profession to anticipate the catastrophic collapse of the housing bubble in the US is itself a powerful indictment of the profession, which had insisted that each step over the last 40 years toward deregulating finance, cutting high-income taxes, and weakening unions, would all encourage prosperity and job growth. The reality has turned out to be rather different, and even conservative *Bloomberg Businessweek* ran a full cover story titled "Hey, Economics Geniuses! What Happened?": since "[e]conomists mostly failed to predict the worst economic crisis since the 1930s ... People are starting to wonder: What good are economists anyway? ... The rap on economists, only somewhat exaggerated, is that they are overconfident, unrealistic, and political ... Those few who defy the conventional wisdom are ignored."[1]

Indeed, in the hard sciences, if a scientific recommendation produced major disasters that were the exact opposite of what was claimed would happen, the science would be expected to change significantly, and scientists would have to seriously change their positions in order to get closer to the truth. The fact is that the last three decades have been ones of deregulation and tax cuts. The data show significant deterioration in most economic indicators, including the traditional ones, that is, GDP and productivity growth. This would be considered data in a real science. Most economists will now admit that systemic risk is perhaps undervalued by market forces, but that is usually as much contrition as you'll get.

THE DISMAL "SCIENCE"

The task of reforming economics is a very broad one, beyond the scope of this concluding chapter. However, after all the contrasting of theory and reality in this book, one direction for research suggests itself: taking a step toward respecting the scientific method, by prioritizing empirical analysis in economics. Empirical research simply refers to collecting real data on the economy, rather than relying on theoretical modeling on paper or software programs. In each year's flood of economic papers, the component engaged in this research is a trickle. But these drops of real data analysis are a precious suggestion of what real economics could look like.

Before considering some empirical studies in economics, a caveat is necessary: the social sciences are inherently different from the natural sciences. When studying people and their societies, there are far more different variables than when studying a chemical reaction in a lab environment. In the hard sciences, holding all the variables in an experiment fixed allows us to prove objective conclusions. For example, when studying cancer in lab rats, variables like group size, diet, and exercise can be held constant by the experimenter to isolate the variable of interest. This allows scientists to prove in a lab environment that in the presence of some element, rats will develop cancer, and in its absence, they will probably not. Since the lab setting allows control over all the factors relevant to an experiment, conclusions are very strong, and form the basis of the modern science-driven world, from disease eradication to computers to flight.

But in the social sciences, the level of confidence that comes from controlled experimentation is not available, simply because social variables are uncontrollable. In human societies, few variables can be held constant even in principle, and the reality is that large numbers of social variables are always changing simultaneously—prices of different products, preferences of different consumers, corporate expenses, government policies, and natural changes like weather and crop yields. This means that in the social sciences, firm conclusions are harder to draw, and even with a good deal of evidence in their favor can't be called certain.

The perhaps more obvious second problem is that economics doesn't study chemicals and rats, about which no powerful institution has an opinion; it studies the economic system, where huge amounts of money and power are at stake. Much as money works to influence politics, it works to influence the disciplines that pronounce conclusions about it, making economics a "politicized 'science,'" as business economist Edward Herman put it.[2] Most economic arguments involve money, powerful institutions, and policy arguments, and we've seen how the dominant conclusions in the discipline tend to rationalize money and power.

That said, many trends in social science data can be seen clearly, and careful study brings them out. But the key is to actually look at the data and consider it of crucial importance in any enterprise that claims the name of science. Most of this book has been an effort to hold up the predictions of economic theory against actual events. But on a more formal basis, let's consider some examples of research in hard data.

IN THEIR OWN WORDS

One especially useful empirical study was conducted by Alan Blinder at Princeton, who in the late 1990s used a foundation grant to conduct a very broad and thorough survey of businesses, especially larger ones, in face-to-face interviews with CEOs, presidents, vice-presidents, managers and accountants. Blinder's test sample reflected the composition of the US economy, excluding farms and small firms. Two hundred companies replied to the survey, with average company annual sales of an impressive $3.2 billion, and themselves representing a full 7.6 percent of the total US economy.[3]

Blinder's survey was wide-ranging, requesting executives' views on several subjects. We'll just look at one or two examples. One relevant subject to bring up was addressed in Chapter 15, the question of economies of scale and why firms grow large. As that chapter shows, companies often report scale economies, where per-unit costs fall as production grows, making production more profitable the more you produce. However, economic theory is based on a very different circumstance called "diminishing returns."

Simply put, diminishing returns means that firms have rising costs the more output they produce, so as they produce more and more output, their marginal costs—the expense of producing another unit of output—get higher and higher. This comes from the idea that companies make their output decision, about how many products to produce, in the short run, a period of time too short to change their production setting, such as a factory. This means that to produce more output, more workers must be packed into a factory of a given size, making workers less productive, meaning that to produce more output, more workers must be used, driving up costs. This means companies get "diminishing returns" on their hiring and production hikes—they get less and less profit growth for each increase in production. Diminishing returns are thought to limit production and keep firms small relative to the market, being essentially the opposite of economies of scale (see Chapter 15) and restricting the output levels at which a firm will be profitable. This would limit the size of companies relative to the marketplace, and thus keep close to the competitive market structure where numerous companies compete, which is required for models of efficient market performance.

Well, what did the actual executives report? They contradicted the expectations of theory on a pretty impressive scale: instead of rising costs, 48 percent of the companies surveyed in Blinder's project reported constant marginal costs. Another 41 percent reported falling marginal costs, consistent with the reports of economies of scale in many industries. Only *11 percent* reported the rising costs that are the cornerstone of the modern theory of the firm.[4] Not exactly robust support.

These results were a strong confirmation of studies done along similar lines by little-known economists Wilford Eiteman and Glenn Guthrie, who conducted their own research survey with manufacturing firms, asking for them to describe which of a series of per-unit cost curves most looked like their own figures.[5] The curves are reproduced in Figure C.1. Curves no. 3, 4, and 5 come closest to the diminishing returns predicted by theory—notice the rising costs as production increases. On the other hand, curves 6 and 7 more closely correspond to economies of scale—notice the falling per-unit costs as output increases. Eiteman and Guthrie's survey had a total of 366 firms respond, and of those, only *18* chose curves nos. 3–5, while a whopping 113 chose curve 6, and 203 chose curve 7, the one most clearly illustrative of consistent returns to scale.

What this means is that, for manufacturing especially, economies of scale are very real, and they give firms strong incentives to grow and become profitable, and powerful. Again, the diminishing returns anticipated by the dominant schools of economic theory today are not to be seen for the large majority of real-world respondents—in fact, less than 5 percent of manufacturing firms in the survey reported them. And indeed, economies of scale are considered to be most pervasive in industries with large up-front costs, because producing more output "spreads" that start-up expense over more units. Manufacturing involves very large start-up costs, involving the construction of new factory capacity, equipping it with modern machinery, arranging for basic staff, getting utilities hooked up, and so on. As we saw in Chapter 15, as high-tech computing has come to new industries, like finance, economies of scale have come to exist in those industries as well. But without empirical research like Blinder's and Eiteman-Guthrie's, we wouldn't have direct confirmation of these trends.

This research helps to explain why markets somehow end up with small numbers of large firms dominating many industries. The data on this are rather clear—the Economic Census, part of the regular US Census surveys, finds that high levels of concentration are the norm in many industries. For example, in 2007 the four largest cigarette manufacturers produced 97.8 percent of America's cigarettes, the four biggest beer brewers produced 89.5 percent of its beer, the four largest petroleum refining firms produced 47.5 percent of its gas and diesel, and the four biggest soybean processors produced 81.5 percent of all soy products.[6] These numbers are not uncommon, and indicate market structures that are a pretty far cry from the theoretical expectation of competitive markets made up of tiny firms. The competitive marketplace remains a cornerstone of most economic theory, and is required for the model of supply and demand as well as claims of corporate efficiency. But the data tell another story, and we can understand where the surprising numbers come from using empirical analyses like Blinder's and Eiteman-Guthrie's.

But an additional highlight in empirical economics is the part of Eiteman and Guthrie's corporate survey that allowed for executive commentary. After being informed of economists' expectations regarding what their costs looked like, they were given a chance to respond. Regrettably, only two are included in the original 1952 paper, but they are very interesting: "The amazing thing is that any sane economist could consider No. 3, No. 4 and No. 5 curves as representing business thinking. It looks as if some economists, assuming as a premise that business is not progressive, are trying to prove the premise by suggesting curves like Nos. 3, 4, and 5." A manufacturer of road building equipment wrote, "Even with the low efficiency and premium pay of overtime work, our unit costs would still decline with increased production since the absorption of fixed expenses would more than offset the added direct expenses incurred."

These comments from businessmen and women suggest a major problem we've seen in this book: economists have shaped data to their theory, rather than vice versa. This is possible in the social sciences rather than the natural sciences, again due to the high number of variables that can't be controlled, allowing economists to insist their pet theory hasn't been disproven by pointing to other uncontrollable factors.

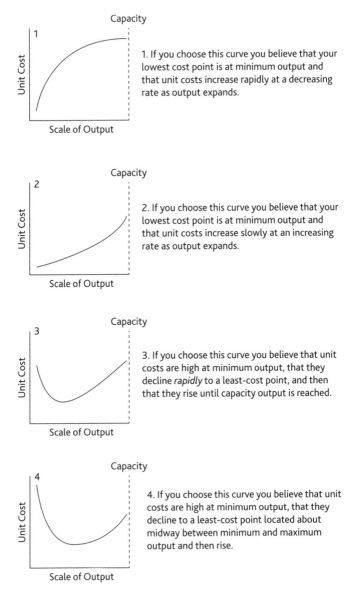

1. If you choose this curve you believe that your lowest cost point is at minimum output and that unit costs increase rapidly at a decreasing rate as output expands.

2. If you choose this curve you believe that your lowest cost point is at minimum output and that unit costs increase slowly at an increasing rate as output expands.

3. If you choose this curve you believe that unit costs are high at minimum output, that they decline *rapidly* to a least-cost point, and then that they rise until capacity output is reached.

4. If you choose this curve you believe that unit costs are high at minimum output, that they decline to a least-cost point located about midway between minimum and maximum output and then rise.

Figure C.1

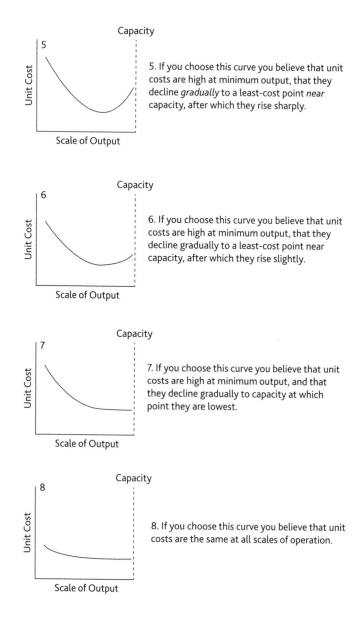

5. If you choose this curve you believe that unit costs are high at minimum output, that they decline *gradually* to a least-cost point *near* capacity, after which they rise sharply.

6. If you choose this curve you believe that unit costs are high at minimum output, that they decline gradually to a least-cost point near capacity, after which they rise slightly.

7. If you choose this curve you believe that unit costs are high at minimum output, and that they decline gradually to capacity at which point they are lowest.

8. If you choose this curve you believe that unit costs are the same at all scales of operation.

THE BIG IDEA

Having put the theory aside, looking back over this book it becomes clear that our economic system is struggling. In its current deregulated form, at least, it is incapable of providing a job to enormous numbers of people, and it's run by the financial power centers that dominate the republics in which it operates. Not exactly a glowing report card.

Just to crystallize the point, consider driving through the downtown of almost any American city. Do you see people who need work? With our astronomical unemployment rate, you can't avoid it. Do you see work to be done? America is in a state of some decay. Bridges collapse at rush hour, the roads are often pockmarked with potholes, and the American Society of Civil Engineers gave the country's infrastructure an overall D grade.[7] Finally, is there money to pay people to do the work? Well, today's income and wealth inequality, as we've seen, is bigger than ever, and corporate America itself is sitting on retained cash to the tune of $2 trillion—"hoarding cash," as the *Wall Street Journal* calls it.[8] So our society has a lot of work to do, lots of people who want to do it, and lots of money to pay them to do it. If our economic system can't bring those things together, it may be time to put aside the current system and create a new one.

In order to deal with this economic system failure, I would suggest that making the economy more democratic would be a productive way to go, since it would go a long way to addressing most of the problems discussed in this book. The US is a heavily polled country—having a large marketing and PR sector, money is invested in shaping and keeping track of public opinion. Well, if Americans were to actually get what they want from their government and economy, we'd have a return to progressive taxation of the wealthy, reimposed regulations on banks and finance, far wider labor union membership, more limited environmental destruction and significant moves toward a new energy system, with all the jobs that would accompany that.[9]

But beyond what people want from the current system, the goal of economic democracy is hard to fulfill in a capitalist economy—a system run by small slices of society, through their concentrated ownership of money and productive resources. Even when Americans and other peoples have organized themselves, and laboriously fought for and won many of the above reforms, the concentration of wealth and resources leaves enormous power in the hands of the economic elite and the corporate institutions they own. During the postwar era, for example, when the economy was more regulated, unions were stronger, and the system worked better, business was always pushing for lower taxes, using political muscle for subsidies and government business, and hiring PR firms to polish their image and shape people's perceptions. Starting in the 1970s, these demands were dialed up in the push for neoliberalism, and the rich have been winning a bigger share ever since.

This lack of democratic control over the economy can be seen especially clearly when looking at international outsourcing. As we saw in Chapter 13, today's job market is disastrous, with huge numbers unemployed, and those with jobs failing to make ends meet. A significant part of this disaster is the loss of the manufacturing sector, previously the heart of the economy with its decent-paying jobs, to international outsourcing. This process has significantly reshaped American society. Well, when did we all vote on that? Of course, no referendum was ever put to actual American citizens; outsourcing was an investment decision for multinational corporations to make. Well, if we don't have the power to even somewhat influence the course of the economy, and the investment decisions that drive it, what control over our own lives do we have?

So at least some economic democracy would be a good idea, to turn our economy in directions the American people want but can't get through the current social system. The more democratic power we have, the less power will remain in the hands of concentrated wealth. Indeed, for the past several centuries, economic muscle has been the dominant power center in our societies, so democratization of this sphere of human life would probably have a lot of positive "externalities" for the rest of our lives.

The answer to the current conditions of ecological deterioration, ruling class power and financial instability seems to be more economic democracy, where working people have more influence over what happens in the economy. This may sound a little familiar, because "worker control of the means of production" is the old radical ideal of a democratically run economy. In the socialist magazine *Monthly Review* in 1949, Albert Einstein suggested that

> The economic anarchy of capitalist society as it exists today is, in my opinion, the real source of the evil ... Insofar as the labor contract is "free," what the worker receives is determined not by the real value of the goods he produces ... Private capital tends to become concentrated in few hands, partly because of competition among the capitalists, and partly because technological development and the increasing division of labor encourage the formation of large units of production at the expense of smaller ones. The result of these developments is an oligarchy of private capital the enormous power of which cannot be effectively checked even by a democratically organized political society. This is true since the members of legislative bodies are selected by political parties, largely financed or otherwise influenced by private capitalists ... Moreover, under existing conditions, private capitalists inevitably control, directly or indirectly, the main sources of information (press, radio, education). It is thus extremely difficult, and indeed in most cases quite impossible, for the individual citizen to come to objective conclusions and to make intelligent use of his political rights.[10]

Einstein was calling for democratic control of the economy. Without any say in the investment decisions that determine what the economy of tomorrow will be like, the last 30 years have taught Americans that they are considered disposable as a workforce, and the lesson has indeed been learned by many Americans—in a 2009 Rasmussen poll, barely half (53 percent) of Americans backed capitalism, with large fractions supporting radical restructuring of the economic system.[11] Additionally, a Pew Research Center survey found "about two-thirds of the public (66%) believes there are 'very strong' or 'strong' conflicts between the rich and the poor," meaning that "the public's evaluations of divisions within American society, conflicts between rich and poor now rank ahead of three other potential sources of group tension—between immigrants and the native born; between black and whites; and between young and old."[12] The polling agency attributes the growth in these numbers in part to the Occupy Wall Street movement.

The figures are impressive, especially considering the total lack of media support for anything other than private ownership of the economy. But whatever words are used for the democratic solution to our economic problems, Einstein's point was that we should actually work to change the system.

OCCUNOMICS

For the first time in a long while, a movement has emerged that is focused on the power of money, power concentrated in the few richest percent of US and world households. Occupy Wall Street managed to surprise everyone by breaking through the media lockout of the increasingly dire situation for most Americans (see Chapters 6 and 8). It draws its ranks from many sectors of the country, including, obviously, youth, but also large numbers of white and black veterans, out-of-work professionals, antiwar groups, environmentalists, and the labor movement.

This latter addition of labor to the OWS movement is especially promising. Labor, although seriously beaten down by the business community (see Chapter 7), is still an important presence with some significant resources, and the two tendencies of Occupation and labor have already helped one another. For example, the labor movement has benefited from and been energized by OWS and its bold tactics, but also the slim resources available to OWS have been very significantly increased by union locals that have contributed food, energy, and first aid to the demonstrators. A major instance of this was seen when New York City's billionaire and media-empire-owning Mayor Michael Bloomberg first tried to forcibly remove the Zuccotti Park demonstrators, the flagship of the Occupy movement. Several hundred union members quickly filled the area to discourage the police from evicting the demonstrators. After two months of occupation, the final eviction at 1 a.m. on November 16, 2011, is considered to have been executed in the middle of the night in part to prevent support from OWS's labor allies, asleep hours away or working third shift.[13]

Another promising aspect is the networks forming between Occupy and movements organizing low-income communities, including the many victims of the waves of foreclosures in today's housing markets. Despite the media's efforts to portray the demonstrators as privileged white kids, the movement's composition of youth, vets, and the out-of-work has been "heaven sent" to organizers of poor communities, "partly because it has done something [that] black, white, Asian and Latino [figures] in the city's grass-roots organizing community have struggled to do over the years; focus public attention on poverty and rising economic inequality."[14] A branch of the movement, Occupy the Hood, has arisen to help build coalitions among these groups. This recalls the style of activist comportment of the civil rights movement of the 1960s, when demonstrators would go out dressed seriously and often wearing their Sunday best. The idea was to encourage those currently outside the movement to take it seriously, and not to give them some reason to immediately dismiss it.

But most importantly, in a movement primarily aimed at addressing economic issues, the average activists' grasp of economics needs to be far stronger if we're hoping to convince America to organize as the 99%, rather than line up behind the billionaire-directed Tea Party. While the typical Occupier, like the typical American, definitely tends to understand the basic issues, the mainline economist will bring plausible-sounding arguments defending the 1%, so understanding is especially important in the struggle. Capitalism is a somewhat more complex subject than desegregating the South; it just requires more education and understanding. And the movement looks to remain relevant for some time, with the media conceding that "A look at the finances of those vying for the presidency shows that almost all of them rank at the very top of the country's earners. In other words, they are the 1 percent."[15] This book has tried to be a small step in the direction of preparing Americans to take over their own economic lives and run the system for their own benefit and for our species' survival.

We're far away from that goal today, but the average American's discontent with our crashing variety of capitalism makes it closer than it seems. A democratized economy would take a much more organized American public, brought together to learn from and support one another, struggling against the PR machine of money, with the ultimate goal that someday, some descendents of ours will inherit a society they actually control, which provides them with economic security and fair prosperity, and which treats nature as more than throughput.

It looks like this is the time to drag our economic system, kicking and screaming, into the twenty-first century and points beyond.

Notes

PREFACE

1. Ajay Kapur et al., "Plutonomy: Buying Luxury, Explaining Global Imbalances," Citigroup, 16 October 2005; Ajay Kapur et al., "The Global Investigator: The Plutonomy Symposium—Rising Tides Lifting Yachts," Citigroup, 29 September 2006.
2. Kapur et al., "Plutonomy."
3. "A double blow," *Economist*, 22 July 2010.

INTRODUCTION TO PART I

1. Michael Porter, "Strategy & Society: The Link Between Competitive Advantage and Corporate Social Responsibility," *Harvard Business Review*, December 2006.
2. E.K. Hunt and Ralph C. d'Arge, "On Lemmings and Other Acquisitive Animals: Propositions on Consumption," *Journal of Economic Issues*, Vol. 7, No. 2, June 1973.

CHAPTER 1

1. Brian Walker et al., "Looming Global-Scale Failures and Missing Institutions," *Science*, Vol. 325, No. 5946, 11 September 2009.
2. Scott Collins, "Biodiversity Under Climate Change," *Science*, Vol. 326, No. 5958, 4 December 2009.
3. Michael Rands et al., "Biodiversity Conservation: Challenges Beyond 2010, *Science*, Vol. 329, No. 5997, 10 September 2010.
4. Kathy Willis and Shonil Bhagwat, "Biodiversity and Climate Change," *Science*, Vol. 326, No. 5954, 6 November 2009.
5. Thomas Karl and Kevin Trenberth, "Modern Global Climate Change," *Science*, Vol. 302, No. 5651, 5 December 2003.
6. Matt Wade, "Rising sea level settles border dispute," *Sydney Morning Herald*, 25 March 2010.

 7. Elizabeth Flock, "South Pacific water shortage means some islands have only a week's worth of water left," *Washington Post*, 4 October 2011.

 8. Eli Kentisch, "Stolen E-mails Turn Up Heat on Climate Change Rhetoric," *Science*, Vol. 326, No. 5958, 4 December 2009.

 9. John Cassidy, "An Economist's Invisible Hand," *Wall Street Journal*, 28 November 2009.

10. Samuel Wasser et al., "Elephants, Ivory, and Trade," *Science*, Vol. 327, No. 5971, 12 March 2010.

11. Herold Neu, "The Crisis in Antibiotic Resistance," *Science*, Vol. 257, No. 5073, 21 August 1992.

12. Archie Clements et al., "Overcrowding and understaffing in modern health-care systems," *The Lancet—Infectious Diseases*, Vol. 8, No. 7, July 2008.

13. Martin Enserink, "Developing Countries to Get Some H1N1 Vaccine— But When?" *Science*, Vol. 326, No. 5954, 6 November 2009.

14. Betsy McKay, "Uproar as Firms Get Swine-Flu Vaccine," *Wall Street Journal*, 6 November 2009.

15. Lucy Tobin and Anna Davis, "Glaxo Charges £6 for £1 swine flu vaccine," *Evening Standard*, 22 July 2009.

16. Jeanne Whalen, "Glaxo's Big Bet on Battling Pandemics," *Wall Street Journal*, 12 October 2009.

17. Peter Waldman and Hugh Pope, "Worlds Apart: Some Muslims Fear War on Terror Is Really a War on Them," *Wall Street Journal*, 21 September 2001.

18. Peter Waldman and Hugh Pope, "The Question in the Rubble: Why Us?" *Wall Street Journal*, 14 September 2001.

19. Greg Jaffe and Neil King Jr., "Rumsfeld's Control Of Military Policy Appears To Weaken," *Wall Street Journal*, 17 April 2006.

20. Eric Schmitt, "U.S. Envoy's Cables Show Worries on Afghan Plans," *New York Times*, 25 January 2010.

CHAPTER 2

 1. Paul Krugman, "Betraying the Planet," *New York Times*, 29 June 2009; Editorial, "The House and Global Warming," *New York Times*, 26 June 2009.

 2. Phillip van Mantgem et al., "Widespread Increase of Tree Mortality Rates in the Western United States," *Science*, Vol. 323, No. 5913, 23 January 2009.

3. Anne Kelly and Michael Goulden, "Rapid shifts in plant distribution with recent climate change," *Proceedings of the National Academy of Sciences*, Vol. 105, No. 33, 19 August 2008.

4. Leif Kullman and Lisa Oberg, *Journal of Ecology*, "Post-Little Ice Age tree line rise and climate warming in the Swedish Scandes: a landscape ecological perspective," Vol. 97, No. 3, May 2009.

5. Margaret Davis and Ruth Shaw, "Range shifts and adaptive responses to quarternary climate changes," *Science*, Vol. 292, No. 5517, April 2001.

6. Susan Solomon et al., *Climate Change 2007: The Physical Science Basis*, Fourth Assessment Report of the IPCC, 2007.

7. Thomas Ledig et al., "Projections of suitable habitat for rare species under global warming scenarios," *American Journal of Botany*, Vol. 97, No. 6, April 2010.

8. Kevin Krajick, "All Downhill from here?" *Science*, Vol. 303, No. 5664, March 2004.

9. Gordon Bonan, "Forests and climate change: Forcings, feedback, and the climate benefits of forests," *Science*, Vol. 320, No. 5882, June 2008.

10. R.J. Scholes and I.R. Noble, "Storing carbon on land," *Science*, Vol. 294, No. 5544, November 2001; Bruce Hungate et al., "Nitrogen and climate change," *Science*, Vol. 302, No. 5650, November 2003.

11. Steven Mufson, "Obama Praises Climate Bill's Progress but Opposes Its Tariffs," *Washington Post*, 29 June 2009.

12. Ibid.

13. Greg Hitt and Stephen Power, "House Passes Climate Bill," *Wall Street Journal*, 27 June 2009.

14. Carl Hulse and David Herszenhorn, "Democrats Call Off Climate Bill Effort," *New York Times*, 22 July 2010.

15. Ian Austen, "GM and Canadian Union Reach a Deal," *New York Times*, 28 September 2005.

16. Anthony Leiserowitz et al., *Climate change in the American Mind: Public support for climate & energy policies in June 2010*. Yale University and George Mason University. New Haven, CT: Yale Project on Climate Change Communication, 2010.

CHAPTER 3

1. "Changing Oceans" issue, *Science*, Vol. 328, No. 5985, 18 June 2010.

2. Richard Kerr, "Ocean Acidification Unprecedented, Unsettling," *Science*, Vol. 328, No. 5985, 18 June 2010; John Pandolfi et al., "Projecting Coral Reef Futures Under Climate Change and Ocean Acidification," *Science*, Vol. 333, No. 6041, 22 July 2010.

3. David Malakoff, "A Push For Quieter Ships," *Science*, Vol. 328, No. 5985, 18 June 2010.

4. Jocelyn Kaiser, "The Dirt On Ocean Garbage Patches," *Science*, Vol. 328, No. 5985, 18 June 2010.

5. Ibid.

6. Scott Doney, "The Growing Human Footprint on Coastal and Open-Ocean Biogeochemistry," *Science*, Vol. 328, No. 5985, 18 June 2010.

7. Ibid.

8. Robert Nicholls and Anny Cazenave, "Sea-Level Rise and Its Impact on Coastal Zones," *Science*, Vol. 328, No. 5985, 18 June 2010.

9. Douglas Fox, "Could East Antarctica Be Headed for Big Melt?" *Science*, Vol. 328, No. 5986, 25 June 2010.

10. Stephen Power, "BP Cites Crucial 'Mistake,'" *Wall Street Journal*, 25 May 2010.

11. Ben Casselman and Russel Gold, "BP Decisions Set Stage for Disaster," *Wall Street Journal*, 27 May 2010.

12. John Broder, "BP Shortcuts Led to Gulf Oil Spill, Report Says," *New York Times*, 14 September 2011.

13. Russell Gold, Ben Casselman and Maurice Tamman, "BP Revised Permits Before Blast," *Wall Street Journal*, 30 May 2010.

14. Stephen Power, "Off-Shore Oil Regulators Are Ordered To Cut Their Oft-Deep Industry Ties," *Wall Street Journal*, 1 September 2010.

15. Gold, Casselman and Tamman, "BP Revised permits Before Blast."

16. Lauren Schenkman, "After Outcry, Oil Data Inches Into the Open," *Science*, Vol. 239, No. 5994, 20 August 2010.

17. Lauren Schenkman, "The Case of the Missing $470 Million," *Science*, Vol. 329, No. 5994, 20 August 2010.

18. Mark Schrope, "Oil-spill Research Funds Begin to Flow," *Nature News*, 1 September 2011.

19. Chuck Hopkinson, *Outcome/Guidance from Georgia Sea Grant Program: Current Status of BP Oil Spill*, Georgia Sea Grant, 17 August 2010.

20. Timothy Crone and Maya Tolstoy, "Magnitude of the 2010 Gulf Oil Leak," *Science*, Vol. 330, No. 6004, 29 October 2010.

21. Richard Kerr, "A Lot of Oil on the Loose, Not So Much to Be Found," *Science*, Vol. 329, No. 5993, 13 August 2010; Richard Kerr and Erik Stokstad, "Government Chided for Poor Planning and Communication," *Science*, Vol. 330, No. 6002, 15 October 2010.

22. Eli Kintisch, "Audacious Decision in Crisis Gets Cautious Praise," *Science*, Vol. 329, No. 5993, 13 August 2010.

23. Sara Reardon, "Ten Months After *Deepwater Horizon*, Picking Up the Remnants of Health Data," *Science*, Vol. 331, No. 6022, 11 March 2011.

24. David Valentine et al., "Propane Respiration Jump-Starts Microbial Response to a Deep Oil Spill," *Science*, Vol. 330, No. 6001, 8 October 2010.

25. Richard Camilli et al., "Tracking Hydrocarbon Plume Transport and Biodegradation at *Deepwater Horizon*," *Science*, Vol. 330, No. 6001, 8 October 2010; Terry Hazen et al., "Deep-Sea Oil Plume Enriches Indigenous Oil-Degrading Bacteria," *Science*, Vol. 330, No. 6001, 8 October 2010.

26. Camilli et al., "Tracking Hydrocarbon Plume Transport."

27. Steve Newborn, *Oil Found Deep in Gulf Is Toxic to Tiny Marine Life*, University of Southern Florida, 17 August 2010 <http://www.wusf. usf.edu/news/2010/08/17/oil_found_deep_in_gulf_is_toxic_to_tiny_ marine_life>.

28. Jad Mouawad and Barry Meier, "Risk-Taking Rises as Oil Rigs in Gulf Drill Deeper," *New York Times*, 29 August 2010.

29. Katarzyna Klimasinska and Brian Swint, "BP Gulf Drilling Plan Criticized by Environmentalists, Lawmakers," *Bloomberg Businessweek*, 26 September 2011.

30. Joe Carroll, "US Says Sunken Transocean Rig May Be Source of Oil Sheen," *BusinessWeek*, 27 September 2011.

CHAPTER 4

1. Dan Fagin, "China's Children Of Smoke," *Scientific American*, 14 July 2008.

2. Joseph Needham and Wang Ling, *Science and Civilization in China*, Vol. 3, Cambridge: Cambridge University Press, 1959, p. 171.

3. V. Ramanathan et al., "Atmospheric Brown Clouds: Regional Assessment Report With Focus on Asia," UN Environment Programme, 2008.

4. Ibid., p. 10.

5. Ibid., pp. 3, 16.

6. S. Solomon et al. (eds), Contribution of Working Group 1 to the Fourth Assessment Report of the Intergovernmental Panel on Climate Change, *Climate Change 2007: The Physical Science Basis*, Cambridge and New York: Cambridge University Press, 2007.

7. V. Ramanathan, , "Warming trends in Asia amplified by brown cloud solar absorption," *Nature*, 2 August 2007.

8. Lester Brown, "Melting Mountain Glaciers Will Shrink Grain Harvests in China and India," Earth Policy Institute, 20 March 2008.
9. Ramanathan et al., "Atmospheric Brown Clouds," pp. 34–5.
10. Dan Fagin, "China's Children Of Smoke," *Scientific American*, 14 July 2008.
11. Hajime Akimoto, "Global Air Quality and Pollution," *Science*, Vol. 302, No. 5651, December 2003.
12. V. Ramanathan, "Indian Ocean Experiment: An integrated analysis of the climate forcing and effects of the great Indo-Asian haze," *Journal of Geophysical Research*, Vol. 106, No. 2001, 27 November 2001.
13. Orjan Gustafsson et al., "Brown Clouds Over Asia: Biomass or Fossil Fuel Combustion?" *Science*, Vol. 323, No. 5913, 23 January 2009; T.V. Padma, "Biomss-burning 'behind Asian brown clouds,'" *Guardian*, 27 January 2009.
14. "The smoke in Asia's eyes," *The Economist*, 4 October 1997.
15. L.Y. Chan et al., "A Case Study on the Biomass Burning in Southeast Asia and Enhancement of Tropospheric Ozone over Hong Kong," *Geophysical Research Letters*, Vol. 27, No. 10, 15 May 2000.
16. "Pollution. An Asian pea-souper," *The Economist*, 27 September 1997.
17. Peter Waldman, "Southeast Asian Smog Is Tied to Politics—Jakarta's Business Concession Fueled Rash of Fires," *Wall Street Journal*, 30 September 1997.
18. "Indonesia shudders," *Economist*, 9 May 1998.
19. Sander Theones, "Optimistic Targets Market Expectations for a Surprisingly Quick Economic Turnaround," *Financial Times*, 14 May 1999; "Stuck in a haze," *Economist*, 14 October 2006.
20. C. Venkataraman et al., "Residential Biofuels in South Asia: Carbonaceous Aerosol Emissions and Climate Impacts," *Science*, Vol. 307, No. 5714, 4 March 2005.
21. Elisabeth Rosenthal, "Third-World Stove Soot Is Target in Climate Fight," *New York Times*, 16 April 2009.
22. Togar Napitupulu, "Biogas: Helping Poor Farmers Help the Planet and Themselves," *CAPSA* Flash, Vol. 6, No. 3, March 2008.
23. Hamish McDonald, "India—Healthy Recovery," *Far Eastern Economic Review*, Vol. 155, No. 44, 5 November 1992.
24. World Wire, "India raises fuel prices," *Wall Street Journal*, 17 September 1992; World Wire, "India raises fuel prices," 2 February 1994; Jackie Range and Elffie Chew, "India, Malaysia Trim Fuel Subsidies," *Wall Street Journal*, 5 June 2008.
25. Hajime Akimoto, "Global Air Quality and Pollution," *Science*, Vol. 302, No. 5651, December 2003.
26. David Biello, "Can Coal and Clean Air Coexist in China?" *Scientific American*, 4 August 2008.

27. "A large black cloud," *Economist*, 13 March 2008.

28. Tao Wang and Jim Watson, "Who Owns China's Carbon Emissions?" Tyndall Centre Briefing Note No. 23, October 2007.

29. Christopher Weber et al., "The Contribution of Chinese Exports to Climate Change," IIOMME paper, 9 July 2008.

30. Tao Wang and Jim Watson, "China's Energy Transition," Sussex Energy Group, SPRU, and Tyndall Centre, April 2009.

31. David Biello, "Can Coal and Clean Air Coexist in China?" *Scientific American*, 4 August 2008.

32. Vaclav Smil, "Poor Visibility on China's Air Pollution," *Far Eastern Economic Review*, Vol. 170, No. 10, December 2007.

33. Chris Haslam, "Disney in Hong Kong," *Times* of London, 18 September 2005.

34. Victor Mallet, "Pollution Haze Clouds Disney's Hong Kong Hopes," *Financial Times*, 20 April 2005; Erika Kinetz, "Briefcase: Where's Mickey? Hidden in the Smog," *International Herald Tribune*, 7 May 2005.

35. Steve Knipp, "Hong Kong Fades Under China's Smog," *Christian Science Monitor*, 13 December 2004.

36. Victor Mallet, "Pollution Haze Clouds Disney's Hong Kong Hopes," *Financial Times*, 20 April 2005.

37. Kenji Hall, "China's Commuter Olympics," *BusinessWeek*, 12 Februrary 2008.

38. Taryana Gershkovich and Catherine Arnst, "Beijing's Olympic Smog: How Bad Will It Be?" *BusinessWeek*, 1 August 2008.

39. Andrew Jacobs, "UN Reports Pollution Threat in Asia," *New York Times*, 14 November 2008.

40. Juliet Macur, "Review of Air Quality Are Mixed, and So Is Attendance," *New York Times*, 9 August 2008.

41. Elisabeth Rosenthal, "Third-World Stove Soot Is Target In Climate Fight, *New York Times*, 15 April 2009; Nicholas Kristof, "Asian Pollution Is Widening Its Deadly Reach," *New York Times*, 29 November 1997.

42. Sonia Kolesnikov-Jessup, "Asian Catalyst Spurs Oil's Renewed Advance," *New York Times*, 19 October 2009; David Streitfeld, "Fields of Grain and Losses," *New York Times*, 21 November 2008.

43. Hajime Akimoto, "Global Air Quality and Pollution," *Science*, Vol. 302, No. 5651, December 2003; David Biello, "Can Coal and Clean Air Coexist in China?" *Scientific American*, 4 August 2008; Kenneth Wilkening et al., "Trans-Pacific Air Pollution," *Science*, Vol. 290, No. 5489, 6 October 2000.

44. O.L. Hadley et al., "Trans-Pacific transport of black carbon and fine aerosols (D<2.5 μm) into North America," *Journal of Geophysical Research*, Vol. 112, 14 March 2007.

CHAPTER 5

1. Anthony Barnosky et al., "Has the Earth's sixth mass extinction already arrived?" *Nature*, Vol. 471, No. 7336, March 2011.
2. Ibid.
3. Stuart Butchart et al., "Global Biodiversity: Indicators of Recent Declines," *Science*, Vol. 328, No. 5982, May 2010.
4. J.A. Thomas et al., "Comparative Losses of British Butterflies, Birds, and Plants and the Global Extinction Crisis," *Science*, Vol. 303, No. 5665, March 2004.
5. Donella Meadows et al., *Limits To Growth*, White River Junction, VT: Chelsea Green Publishing Co, 2004, pp. xvii, 223, 281.
6. Franz Broswimmer, *Ecocide*, London: Pluto Press, 2002, pp. 44–5.
7. Ibid, p. 58.
8. For example, at <http://www.trialwiki.com/mcgee-v-general-motors/the-plaintiffs-case-for-liability/ivey-memo/>.

CHAPTER 6

1. 2007 Economic Census, data for the last 15 years available at <http://www.census.gov/econ/concentration.html>.
2. Robert Frank, "The Wealth Report: The Hedonism Index," *Wall Street Journal*, 20 April 2007.
3. George Will, "A Lexus In Every Garage," *Washington Post*, 11 October 2007.
4. Rob Cox and Aliza Rosenbaum, "The Beneficiaries of the Downturn," *New York Times*, 29 December 2008.
5. Brian Stelter, "Camps Are Cleared, but '99 Percent' Still Occupies the Lexicon," *New York Times*, 30 November 2011.
6. Ibid.
7. Greg Jaffe and Neil King Jr, "Rumsfeld's Control Of Military Policy Appears To Weaken," *Wall Street Journal*, 17 April 2006.
8. Christopher Dickey and Evan Thomas, "How Saddam Happened," *Newsweek*, 13 September 2002.
9. Edward Bernays, *Public Relations*, Norman, OK: University of Oklahoma Press, 1952, p. 78.
10. Edward Bernays, "Manipulating Public Opinion: The Why and the How," *American Journal of Sociology*, Vol. 33, No. 6, May 1928.
11. Louise Story, "Home Equity Frenzy Was a Bank Ad Come True," *New York Times*, 14 August 2008.
12. Ibid.
13. Ibid.

INTRODUCTION TO PART II

1. Mark Whitehouse, "Number of the Week: Workers Not Benefiting From Productivity Gains," *Wall Street Journal*, 5 March 2011.
2. Serena Ng and Cari Tuna, "Big Firms Are Quick To Collect, Slow To Pay," *Wall Street Journal*, 31 August 2009.

CHAPTER 7

1. Fiona Harvey, "*Financial Times*, US Cities Among Most Divided On Rich-Poor Lines," *Financial Times*, 23 October 2008.
2. Robert Frank, "Why the Rich Like to Eat Gold," *Wall Street Journal*, 16 January 2009.
3. "European Luxury Goods Groups Defy Downturn," *New York Times*, 29 August 2008.
4. Daniel Thomas, "World's Rich Shrug Off Credit Crunch," *Financial Times*, 20 April 2008.
5. Peter Bernstein and Annalyn Swan, *All the Money In the World*, New York: Knopf, 2007; David Glenn, "Father and Son Play Matchmakers to the Rich," *Financial Times*, 22 September 2008.
6. Jeff Mills, "Berth Pangs Of the Super Rich," *Financial Times*, 23 September 2008.
7. David Kaplan, "The Yachting Class Sails Along," *Fortune*, 13 April 2009.
8. Chrystia Freeland, "Bosses' Greed Releases Class Politics Genie," *Financial Times*, 25 September 2008.
9. Economic Policy Institute, *The State of Working America 2008/09*, Washington, DC: Economic Policy Institute, 2009.
10. Shawn Tully, "Fortune 500: Profits Bounce Back," *Fortune*, 15 April 2010.
11. Telis Demos, "Trainspotting," *Fortune*, 8 February 2010.
12. "Holding Hands," *Economist*, 27 March 1993.
13. Aaron Bernstein, "Can This Man Save Labor?" *BusinessWeek*, 13 September 2004.
14. David Kirkpatrick, "In a Message to Democrats, Wall St. Sends Cash to GOP," *New York Times*, 7 February 2010.
15. Adam Liptak, "1 in 100 US Adults Behind Bars, New Study Says," *New York Times*, 28 February 2008.

CHAPTER 8

1. Bureau of Labor Statistics, *Job Openings and Labor Turnover*, 8 November 2011.

2. Nina Munk, "Greenwich's Outrageous Fortune," *Vanity Fair*, July 2006.

3. Louis Uchitelle, "Unions Yield on Wage Scales to Preserve Jobs," *New York Times*, 19 November 2010.

4. Louis Uchitelle, "Glass-making Thrives Offshore, But Is Declining in U.S." *New York Times*, 18 January 2010.

5. Krishna Guha, Edward Luce and Andrew Ward, "Anxious Middle," *Financial Times*, 2 November 2006.

6. Kate Bronfenbrenner and Stephanie Luce, "Offshoring: The Evolving Profile of Corporate Global Restructuring," *Multinational Monitor*, Vol. 25, No. 12, December 2004.

7. Keith Bradsher, "Demonstrators in Hong Kong March to Seek Free Elections," *New York Times*, 2 January 2004.

8. International Monetary Fund, "The Fund's Role Regarding Cross-Border Capital Flows," 15 November 2010.

9. Board of Governors of the Federal Reserve System, Survey of Consumer Finances, February 2009.

10. Rachel Donadio, "Worried Greeks Fear Collapse of Middle Class Welfare State," *New York Times*, 24 September 2011.

11. Landon Thomas, "As Greece Turns Leftward, Its Tycoons Stay in Background," *New York Times*, 23 May 2012.

12. Landon Thomas, "Next Times, Greece May Need New Tactics," *New York Times*, 9 March 2012.

13. Jack Ewing, "In Greek Debt Deal, Clear benefits for the Banks," *New York Times*, 25 July 2011.

14. James Kanter, "Europe Agrees to Bailout Fund for Euro of Over $1 Trillion," *New York Times*, 30 March 2012.

15. Kerin Hope, "Grim Effects of Austerity Show on Greek Streets," *Financial Times*, 17 February 2012.

16. Katie Benner, "Pimco's Power Play," *Fortune*, 30 March 2009.

17. Timothy Canova, "The Transformation of U.S. Banking and Finance," *Brooklyn Law Review*, Vol. 60, No. 4, 1995.

18. Dexter Roberts, "Waking Up to Their Rights," *BusinessWeek*, 22 August 2005.

19. Rachel Donadio and Niki Kitsantonis, "Thousands in Greece Protest Austerity Bill," *New York Times*, 19 October 2011.

20. Cara Buckley, "After Losing Footholds, Movement Faces Test," *New York Times*, 15 November 2011.

21. Cara Buckley and Rachel Donadio, "Buoyed by Wall St. Protests, Rallies Sweep the Globe," *New York Times*, 15 October 2011.

22. Al Baker and Joseph Goldstein, "After an Earlier Misstep, a Minutely Planned Raid," *New York Times*, November 15, 2011.

23. Esme Deprez, "Wall Street Occupiers Depend on Kindness of Strangers for Personal Hygeine," Bloomberg, October 10, 2011.

24. Sharon Otterman, "Even in Churches, Wall Street Protestors Can't Escape Watch of Police," *New York Times*, November 17, 2011.

25. The report can presently be downloaded at <http://upwithchrishayes.msnbc.msn.com/_news/2011/11/19/8896362-exclusive-lobbying-firms-memo-spells-out-plan-to-undermine-occupy-wall-street-video>.

26. Nicolai Ouroussoff, "New Look for Mecca: Gargantuan and Gaudy," *New York Times*, 29 December 2010.

CHAPTER 9

1. Eric Foner, *A Short History of Reconstruction*, New York: Harper & Row, 1990, p. 246.

2. David Stowell, *Streets, Railroads, and the Great Strike of 1877*, Chicago, IL: University of Chicago Press, p. 74.

3. Jeremy Brecher, *Strike!*, Boston, MA: South End Press, 1997, pp. 18–21, 35.

4. David Riehle, "1934 brought three successive Teamsters strikes," *Minneapolis Labor Review*, 24 May 2007.

5. Howard Zinn, *A People's History of the United States*, New York: HarperCollins, 2003, pp. 355–7; "Hold Rockefeller At Fault In Strike," *New York Times*, 28 August 1915.

6. Peter Whoriskey, "Under Restructuring, GM to Build More Cars Overseas," *Washington Post*, 8 May 2009.

CHAPTER 10

1. Robert Fisk, *The Great War For Civilization*, New York: First Vintage Books, 2007, p. 758.

2. Ibid., p. 841.

3. Mark Landler et al., "Diplomatic Scramble As Ally Is Pushed to the Exit," *New York Times*, 1 February 2011.

4. Helene Cooper, "With Egypt, Diplomatic Words Often Fail," *New York Times*, 29 January 2011.

5. Mina Kimes, "America's Hottest Export: Weapons," *Fortune*, 24 February 2011.

6. Scott Shane, "Western Companies See Prospects for Business in Libya," *New York Times*, 28 October 2011.

7. Hernando de Soto, "Egypt's Economic Apartheid," *Wall Street Journal*, 3 February 2011.
8. Joshua Stacher, "Egypt Without Mubarak," *Middle East Report*, 7 April 2011.
9. David Kirkpatrick and Liam Stack, "Violence Erupts in Cairo, Even as Military Cedes Ground," *New York Times*, 19 November 2011.
10. David Kirkpatrick, "Egypt's Cabinet Offers to Resign As Protests Rage," *New York Times*, 22 November 2011.
11. Charles Levinson et al., "Egypt's Activists Unite Against Military," *Wall Street Journal*, 26-7 November 2011.
12. David Kirkpatrick, "Egypt Military Council Partly Curbs State of Emergency Law," *New York Times*, 24 January 2012.
13. Monica Davey and Steven Greenhouse, "Angry Demonstrations in Wisconsin As Cuts Loom," *New York Times*, 16 February 2011.
14. Steven Greenhouse, "Strained States Turning to Laws to Curb Labor Unions," *New York Times*, 3 January 2011.
15. Michael Cooper and Megan Thee-Brenan, "Majority in Poll Back Employees in Public-Sector Unions," *New York Times*, 28 February 2011.
16. "Bahrain Taps ex-Miami Chief John Timoney for Police Training," *Miami Herald*, 2 December 2011.
17. Andy Kroll, "Eating Egyptian Pizza in Wisconsin," *Asia Times*, 4 March 2011.

CHAPTER 11

1. Timothy Aeppel, "Pittsburgh Steels Itself For G-20 Protests," *Wall Street Journal*, 11 September 2009.
2. "Obama's New Conference at the G-20," *New York Times*, 25 September 2009.
3. Jackie Calmes, "Geithner Outlines Future for TARP," *New York Times*, 9 December 2009.
4. "Banks With Political Ties Got Bailouts" *New York Times Dealbook*, 22 December 2009.
5. Mark Landler, "US Treasury chief says banks must deploy new capital," *New York Times*, 14 October 2008.
6. Patrick Jenkins and Brooke Masters, "Dividend and bonus rules face reform," *Financial Times*, 17 December 2009.
7. Paul Street, "There Is No Peace Dividend," *Z Magazine*, January 2009.
8. Jonathan Weisman and Elizabeth Williamson, "Trade Moves Up White House Agenda," *Wall Street Journal*, 14 November 2010.

9. Julianna Goldman, Hans Nichols, Mark Drajem, and Lizzie O'Leary, "Obama Wants a Détente with Business," *BusinessWeek*, 6 October 2010.

10. Jane Sasseen, "The Changes Business Wants From Obama," *BusinessWeek*, 5 November 2008; Kate Anderson Brower, "Big Business Takes on Obama," *Bloomberg BusinessWeek*, 21 July 2010.

11. Jane Sasseen, "Obama's Business Report Card," *BusinessWeek*, 29 April 2009.

12. "Price may be high for spurning tough economic reforms," *Financial Times*, 24 June 1999.

13. Peter Fritsch, "Brazil Promises Severe Steps to Win IMF Aid," *Wall Street Journal*, 28 October 1998.

14. Thomas Vogel and Pamela Druckerman, "Ecuador Nears Agreement With IMF," *Wall Street Journal*, 30 August 1999.

15. Nicholas Kristoff anad Sheryl Wu Dunn, "Of World Markets, None an Island," *New York Times*, 17 February 1999.

16. Michael Phillips, "IMF Weary of Criticism," *Wall Street Journal*, 22 September 2000.

17. "All the world's a stage as fear grows," *Financial Times*, 26 October 2008.

18. "Road from Cancun leads to Brussels," *Financial Times*, 16 September 2003.

19. John Miller, "Blame Goes Global at WTO," *Wall Street Journal*, 3 December 2009.

20. David Wessel, "New Rules Have Potential to Alter Path of Global Trade," *Wall Street Journal*, 14 May 2009.

21. Peter Brown, "Obama: Washington Liberal, Copenhagen Conservative," *Wall Street Journal*, 16 December 2009.

22. See Open Secrets, "2008 Presidential Election Contributions by Sector" <http://www.opensecrets.org/pres08/sectorall.php?cycle=2008>.

23. James Kanter, "EU Blames Others for 'Great Failure' on Climate," *New York Times*, 23 December 2009.

24. Darrell Kaufman et al., "Recent Warming Reverses Long-Term Arctic Cooling," *Science*, Vol. 325, No. 5945, 4 September 2009.

25. Steffie Woolhandler, Terry Campbell, and David Himmelstein, "Costs of Health Care Administration in the United States and Canada," *New England Journal of Medicine*, Vol. 349, 2003.

26. Lee Walczak and Richard Dunham, "I Want My Safety Net," *BusinessWeek*, 16 May 2005.

27. Chad Terhune and Keith Epstein, "The Health Insurers Have Already Won," *Bloomberg BusinessWeek*, 6 August 2009.

28. Transcript available at <http://www.whitehouse.gov/the_press_office/ Remarks-by-the-President-in-Rio-Rancho-Town-Hall-on-Credit-Card-Reform/>.
29. Peter Wallstein, "Democrats' Blues Grow Deeper in New Poll," *Wall Street Journal*, 17 December 2009.
30. Doug Henwood, "Jonesing for a Slump," *Left Business Observer*, July 2010.
31. Robert Brenner, "The Economics of Global Turbulence," *New Left Review*, No. 229, May/June 1998.

CHAPTER 12

1. "Partial Reversal," *Wall Street Journal*, 19 April 2007; "Roberts Rules," *Wall Street Journal*, 26 June 2007.
2. Nick Timiraos, "Roberts Court Unites on Business," *Wall Street Journal*, 30 June 2007.
3. Robert Barnes, "Court Defies Pro-Business Label," *Washington Post*, 8 March 2009.
4. Patti Waldmeier, "Trade Group Backs Supreme Court Nominee," *Financial Times*, 11 August 2005.
5. "The Supreme Court Has Been Bad For Business," *Financial Times*, 29 June 2006.
6. Michael Orey, "The Supreme Court: Open For Business," *BusinessWeek*, 9 July 2007.
7. Robert Barnes and Carrie Johnson, "Pro-Business Decision Hews To Patten of Roberts Court," *Washington Post*, 22 June 2007.
8. Linda Greenhouse, "Analysis: Roberts Supreme Court Is A Conservative's Dream," *New York Times*, 1 July 2007.
9. "Supreme Court Backs US States' Tax Breaks," *Financial Times*, 16 May 2006.
10. "Roberts Rules," *Wall Street Journal*, 26 June 2007.
11. Center For Responsive Politics, "2008 Overview" <http://www.opensecrets.org/overview/blio.php>.
12. Linda Greenhouse and David Kirkpatrick, "Justices Loosen Ad Restrictions In Campaign Finance Law," *New York Times*, 6 June 2007.
13. Richard Hasen, "Beyond Incoherence: The Roberts Court's Deregulatory Turn in FEC vs. Wisconsin Right to Life," *Minnesota Law Review*, Vol. 92, p. 1064, April 2008.
14. Jess Bravin, "Court Kills Limits on Corporate Politicking," *Wall Street Journal*, 22 January 2010.

15. The Center for Responsive Politics, "Business-Labor-Ideology Split in PAC & Individual Donations to Candidates and Parties" <http://www.opensecrets.org/overview/blio.php>.

16. Adam Liptak, "Supreme Court Strikes Down 'Millionaire's Amendment,'" *New York Times*, 27 June 2008.

17. Jess Bravin, "High Court Split Over Case on Judicial Ethics," *Wall Street Journal*, 3 March 2009.

18. Patti Waldmeir, "Court Weighs Up Value Of Price-Fixing Against Discounts," *Financial Times*, 27 March 2007.

19. Joseph Pereira, "Why Some Toys Don't Get Discounted," *Wall Street Journal*, 24 December 2008.

20. Christopher Maag, "Supreme Court Decision On Exxon Valdez Damages A Blow To Alaskans," *New York Times*, 26 June 2008.

21. Chris Bryant, "Court Narrows US Money Laundering Law," *Financial Times*, 3 June 2008.

22. Patti Waldmeir, "Supreme Court May Limit Class Action Lawsuits By Investors," *Financial Times*, 19 January 2006.

23. Robert Barnes and Carrie Johnson, "Pro-Business Decision Hews To Pattern of Roberts Court," *Washington Post*, 22 June 2007.

24. Linda Greenhouse, "Analysis: Roberts Supreme Court Is A Conservative's Dream," *New York Times*, 1 July 2007.

25. Jess Bravin and Ann Zimmerman, "Justices Curb Class Actions," *Wall Street Journal*, 21 June 2011.

26. Jess Bravin, "High Court Gives Business New Shield," *Wall Street Journal*, 28 April 2011; Adam Liptak, "Supreme Court Allows Contracts That Prohibit Class-Action Arbitration," *New York Times*, 27 April 2011.

27. Robert Barnes, "Court Defies Pro-Business Label," *Washington Post*, 8 March 2009. Congress has since changed the law, undermining the court's decision; this will probably not be the only such episode.

28. Andrew Jack, "Drugs Groups Fear Rash of Label Litigation," *Financial Times*, 5 March 2009.

29. Robert Barnes, "Court Defies Pro-Business Label," *Washington Post*, 8 March 2009.

30. Ibid.

31. Adam Liptak, "Makers Win Two Supreme Court Decisions," *New York Times*, 23 June 2011.

32. Nathan Koppel, "The Coming SCOTUS Term: What's In It For Business?" *Wall Street Journal*, 29 September 2011.

33. Adam Liptak, "Supreme Court to Hear 2 Human Rights Cases," *New York Times*, 17 October 2011; Mark Sherman, "Court to Hear Bid to Sue Shell for Nigerian Abuses," *New York Times*, 17 October 2011.

34. "Supreme Success," *The Economist*, 7 July 2007.

35. Nick Timiraos, "Roberts Court Unites on Business," *Wall Street Journal,* 30 June 2007.

36. Adam Liptak, "Justices Offer Receptive Ear to Business Interests," *New York Times*, 18 December 2010.

CHAPTER 13

1. Economic Policy Institute, *The State of Working America 2008/2009*, 2009, pp. 125, 336; Conor Dougherty, "High-Degree Professionals Show Power," *Wall Street Journal*, 10 September 2008.

2. Bureau of Labor Statistics, *Multiple Jobholding during the 2000s,* July 2010; Bureau of Labor Statistics, *Twenty-first Century Moonlighters*, September 2002.

3. Kris Maher, "More People Pushed Into Part-Time Work Force," *Wall Street Journal*, 8 March 2008.

4. Christopher Swann, "Taking a Break From Taking Holidays," *Financial Times*, 22 August 2005.

5. Economic Policy Institute, *The State of Working America 2008/2009*, p. 91.

6. Abraham Mosisa and Steven Hipple, "Trends In Labor Force Participation In the United States," *Monthly Labor Review*, Vol. 129, No. 10, October 2006, p. 37.

7. "Got the time?" *Economist*, 26 June 1999.

8. Dalton Conley, "Network Nation," *New York Times*, 22 June 2008.

9. Judith Warner, "The Full-Time Blues," *New York Times*, 24 July 2007.

10. Juliet Schor, *The Overworked American*, New York: HarperCollins, 1991.

11. Sylvia Ann Hewlett and Carolyn Buck Luce, "Extreme Jobs: The Dangerous Allure of the 70-Hour Workweek," *Harvard Business Review*, December 2006.

12. Mosisa and Hipple, "Trends In Labor Force Participation In the United States," p. 49.

13. David Wessel, "Moving Up: Challenges to the American Dream," *Wall Street Journal*, 13 May 2005.

14. Dirk Krueger and Fabrizio Perri, "Does Income Inequality Lead To Consumption Inequality? Evidence and Theory," *Review of Economic Studies*, Vol. 73, No. 1, January 2006.

15. Peter Kilborn, "Falling Wages and Troubled Lives: Town Stumbles as Economy Shifts," *New York Times*, 17 June 2002.

16. Phil Izzo, "Bleak News For Americans' Income," *Wall Street Journal*, 14 October 2011.

INTRODUCTION TO PART III

1. John Eatwell and Lance Taylor, *Global Finance At Risk*, Cambridge: Polity Press, 2000, pp. 17–18.

CHAPTER 14

1. Louise Story, "Banks Fear Next Move by Shorts," *New York Times*, 15 September 2008.
2. John Eatwell and Lance Taylor, *Global Finance At Risk*, Cambridge: Polity Press, 2000, pp. 17–18.
3. John Plender, "Watchdogs Must Not Kick Banks When They Are Down," *Financial Times*, 4 February 2009.
4. John Plender, "Capitalism In Convulsion," *Financial Times*, 20 September 2008.
5. Janis Sarra, *Credit Derivatives, Market Design, Creating Fairness and Stability*, Network for Sustainable Financial Markets, January 2009.
6. Carmen Reinhart and Kenneth Rogoff, *This Time Is Different: Eight Centuries of Financial Folly*, Princeton, NJ: Princeton University Press, 2009, p. 155, original emphasis.
7. John Plender, "Dissent at the Bubble Spotters' Convention: Speculating on Speculation," *Financial Times*, 22 April 2002; Floyd Norris, "After the Bubble: Are Rates Low Enough?" *New York Times*, 16 April 2002.
8. Robert Brenner, *The Boom and the Bubble*, London: Verso 2002.
9. Plender, "Dissent at the Bubble Spotters' Convention."
10. Krishna Guha, "Troubled by bubbles," *Financial Times*, 16 May 2008.
11. Stephen Roach, "America's ominous housing bubble," *Financial Times*, 10 December 2004.
12. Charles Kindleberger and Robert Aliber, *Manias, Panics, and Crashes*, Hoboken, NJ: John Wiley & Sons, 2005, pp. 38–40.

CHAPTER 15

1. Judith Samuelson and Lynn Stout, "Are Executives Paid too Much?" *Wall Street Journal*, 26 February 2009.
2. Tom Braithwaite, "Geithner Presses Congress for Action on Reform," *Financial Times*, 23 September 2009.
3. Phillip Zweig, "Intrastate Mergers Between Banking Giants Might Not Be Out of the Question Anymore," *Wall Street Journal*, 25 March 1986.

4. Bruce Knecht, "Chemical Banking Plans Acquisition of Margaretten," *Wall Street Journal*, 13 May 1994; Eric Weiner, "Banks Will Post Good Quarterly Results," *Wall Street Journal*, 10 January 1997.
5. Gabriella Stern, "Four Big Regionals To Consolidate Bank Operations," *Wall Street Journal*, 22 July 1992.
6. "Pressure for Change Grows," *Financial Times*, 27 September 1996.
7. Tracy Corrigan and John Authers, "Citigroup To Take $900 Million Charge: Cost-cutting Program to Result in Loss of 10,400 Jobs," *Financial Times*, 16 December 1998.
8. Eleanor Laise, "Mutual-Fund Mergers Jump Sharply," *Wall Street Journal*, 9 March 2006.
9. "Pressure for Change Grows," *Financial Times*, 27 September 1996.
10. Bernard Shull, "Banking, Commerce and Competition Under the Gramm-Leach-Bliley Act," *The Antitrust Bulletin*, Vol. 47, No. 1, Spring 2002; David Humphrey, "Why Do Estimates of Bank Scale Economies Differ?" *Economic Review*, Federal Reserve Bank of Richmond, Vol. 76, No. 5, September/October 1990, note 4.
11. Michael Mandel and Rich Miller, "Productivity: The Real Story," *BusinessWeek*, 5 November 2001.
12. John Yang, "Fed Votes to Give 7 Bank Holding Firms Additional Power in Securities Sector," *Wall Street Journal*, 16 July 1987.
13. "Banking Behemoths—What Happens Next: Many Companies Like to Shop Around for Their Providers of Financial Services," *Wall Street Journal*, 14 September 2000.
14. Carrick Mollenkamp and Paul Beckett, "Diverse Business Portfolios Boost Banks' Bottom Lines," *Wall Street Journal*, 17 July 2001.
15. Steven Piloff, "Does the Presence of Big Banks Influence Competition in Local Markets?" *Journal of Financial Services Research*, Vol. 15, No. 3, May 1999.
16. "Credit-Card Wars," *Wall Street Journal*, 29 March 2008.
17. Barbara Pacheco and Richard Sullivan, "Interchange Fees in Credit and Debit Card Markets: What Role for Public Authorities," *Economic Review* of the Federal Reserve Bank of Kansas City, January–March 2006.
18. Jonathan Orszag, "Credit Where It's Due," *Wall Street Journal*, 12 January 2006.
19. Keith Bradsher, "In One Pocket, Out the Other," *New York Times*, 25 November 2009.
20. Sarena Ng and Cari Tuna, "Big Firms Are Quick To Collect, Slow to Pay," *Wall Street Journal*, 31 August 2009.
21. Ibid.
22. Center For Public Integrity, "Finance/Insurance/Real Estate: Long-Term Contribution Trends" <http://www.opensecrets.org>.

23. Dean Baker, "Banks Own the US Government," *Guardian*, 30 June 2009.

24. Anita Raghavan and Mitchell Pacelle, "To the Rescue? A Hedge Fund Falters, So the Fed Persuades Big Banks to Ante Up," *Wall Street Journal*, 24 September 1998.

25. Theo Francis, "Will Bank Rescues Mean Fewer Banks?" *BusinessWeek*, 25 November 2008.

26. Joe Nocera, "So When Will Banks Give Loans?" *New York Times*, 25 October 2008.

27. Dan Fitzpatrick and Robin Sidel, "A City Feels the Squeeze In the Age of Mega-Banks," *Wall Street Journal*, 20 July 2010.

CHAPTER 16

1. Bradley Keoun, "Bank Profits Are Worse Than They Look," *Bloomberg Businessweek*, 22 July 2010; Eric Dash, "JPMorgan Chase Exceeds Forecasts," *New York Times*, 15 July 2010.

2. Suzanne Kapner, "Citi Shines, But Investors Shrug," *Wall Street Journal*, 18 October 2011.

3. Matthias Rieker and Marshall Eckblad, "Banks Generate Profits, but Struggle to Lend," *Wall Street Journal*, 22 July 2010.

4. Eric Dash, "Federal Report Faults Banks on Huge Bonuses," *New York Times*, 22 July 2010; "Bankers' Pay," *New York Times*, 27 July 2010.

5. Carrick Mollenkamp and Lingling Wei, "To Fix Sour Property Deals, Lenders 'Extend and Pretend,'" *Wall Street Journal*, 7 July 2010.

6. David Streitfeld, "Mortgage Data Leaves Bankers Uncertain of Trend," *New York Times*, 19 May 2010.

7. Mollenkamp and Wei, "To Fix Sour Property Deals."

8. Floyd Norris, "Banks Stuck With Bill for Bad Loans," *New York Times*, 19 August 2010.

9. Manuel Adelino et al., *Why Don't Lenders Renegotiate More Home Mortgages? Redefaults, Self-Curse and Securitization*, NBER (National Bureau of Economic Research), July 2009.

10. Jack Ewing, "Crisis Awaits World's Banks as Trillions Come Due," *New York Times*, 11 July 2010.

11. David Reilly, "Euro Pain Could Blow Back on Big US Banks," *Wall Street Journal*, 15 May 2010; Ian Talley, "IMF Warns EU Debt Crisis Could Hit US Banks, Cause Funding Strains," *Wall Street Journal*, 24 January 2012; Min Zeng, "Fund Managers Aren't Showing Much Faith In Euro-Zone Debt," *Wall Street Journal*, 30 March 2012.

12. "Why Small Banks Are Big Losers in Bailout," *Wall Street Journal*, 14 July 2010.

13. Ibid.
14. Center for Responsive Politics, "Finance, Insurance and Real Estate," Sector Profile, Annual Lobbying Totals <http://www.opensecrets.org/lobby/indus.php?id=F&year=2010>.
15. Randall Smith and Aaron Lucchetti, "Biggest Banks Manage to Dodge Some Bullets," *Wall Street Journal*, 26 June 2010; Eric Dash and Nelson Schwartz, "Banks Seek to Keep Profits as New Oversight Rules Loom," *New York Times*, 15 July 2010.
16. Eric Lichtblau, "Ex-Regulators Get Set to Lobby on New Financial Rules," *New York Times*, 27 July 2010.
17. Ben Protess, "Wall Street Lobbyists Aim to 'Reform the Reform,'" *New York Times DealBook*, 14 July 2011.
18. Aaron Luchetti and Jenny Strasburg, "What's a 'Prop' Trader Now?" *Wall Street Journal*, 6 July 2010; Nelson Schwartz and Eric Dash, "Despite Reform, Banks Have Room for Risky Deals," *New York Times*, 25 August 2010.
19. Damian Paletta, "Late Change Sparks Outcry Over Finance-Overhaul Bill," *Wall Street Journal*, 2 July 2010.
20. Peter Eavis, "A Bank Overhaul Too Weak to Hail," *Wall Street Journal*, 26 June 2010; "Killing Them Softly," *Economist*, 26 August 2010.
21. Damian Paletta and David Enrich, "Banks Gain in Rules Debate," *Wall Street Journal*, 15 July 2010.
22. Eric Dash, "Higher Reserves Proposed for 'Too Big to Fail' Banks," *New York Times* 25 June 2011.
23. Jack Ewing, "Few Signs of United Approach to Financial Regulation," *New York Times DealBook*, 27 January 2011.
24. Damian Paletta and David Enrich, "Risks Rulebook Is Nearly Done," *Wall Street Journal*, 27 July 2010.
25. Damien Paletta, "Banks Get New Restraints," *Wall Street Journal*, 13 September 2010.
26. Paletta and Enrich, "Banks Gain in Rules Debate."

CHAPTER 17

1. Peter Goodman, "Policy Options Dwindle as Economic Fears Grow," *New York Times*, 28 August 2010.
2. Sewell Chan and Jo Craven McGinty, "Fed Papers Show Breadth of Emergency Measures," *New York Times*, 1 December 2010.
3. Sewell Chan and Ben Protess, "Cross Section of Rich Invested With the Fed," *New York Times*, 2 December 2010.
4. Javier David, "Euro, Dollar Look To Central Banks," *Wall Street Journal*, 31 October 2011.

5. Christine Hauser, "A Bond Rush as Treasury Prices Fall," *New York Times*, 8 December 2010; Mark Gongloff, "Bond Market Defies Fed," *Wall Street Journal*, 16 November 2010.

6. Brian Blackstone, "Central Banks Pour Dollars Into Europe," *Wall Street Journal*, 16 September 2011.

7. Michael Derby, "Treasury Fall Poses Long-Term Dilemma for Fed Balance Sheet," *Wall Street Journal*, 10 December 2011.

8. Jon Hilsenrath, "Fed Chief Gets a Likely Backer," *Wall Street Journal*, 10 January 2011; "Fed's Fisher: Bond Buying Likely to Run Its Course," *Wall Street Journal*, 10 January 2011; Luca Di Leo, "Yellen Staunchly Defends Fed's Bond Program," *Wall Street Journal*, 8 January 2011.

9. Sewell Chan, "Fed's Contrarian Has a Wary Eye on the Past," *New York Times*, 13 December 2010.

10. Jon Hilsenrath, "Fed Fires $600 Billion Stimulus Shot," *Wall Street Journal*, 4 November 2010.

11. Binyamin Applebaum, "Mortgage Securities It Holds Pose Sticky Problem for Fed," *New York Times*, 22 July 2010.

12. Sewell Chan, "Fed Pays a Record $78.4 Billion to Treasury, *New York Times*, 10 January 2011; Agnes Crane and Robert Cyran, "Rising Interest Rates and the Fed's Red Ink," *New York Times*, 15 December 2010.

13. Crane and Cyran, "Rising Interest Rates and the Fed's Red Ink."

14. Binyamin Appelbaum, "Stimulus by Fed Is Disappointing, Economists Say," *New York Times*, 24 April 2011.

CHAPTER 18

1. Jayati Ghosh, James Heintz, and Robert Pollin, *Speculation on Commodities Futures Markets and Destabilization Of Global Food Prices: Exploring the Connections*, Political Economy Research Institute, Working Paper Series No. 269, October 2011; Jayati Ghosh, *Commodity Speculation and the Food Crisis*, World Development Movement, October 2010.

2. Food and Agriculture Organization of the United Nations, *Price Surges in Food Markets*, New York and Geneva, June 2010.

3. Ibid.

4. United Nations Conference On Trade and Development, *The Global Economic Crisis: Systemic Failures and Multilateral Remedies*, New York and Geneva, 2009, p. 25.

5. Ibid., p. 26.

6. Ibid., p. 29.

7. Ibid., p. 31.

8. Ed Wallace, "Blame High Oil Prices on Speculators and Bernanke," *Bloomberg Businessweek*, 19 April 2011.

9. Cited in Brewster Keen, *Invisible Giant*, 2nd edn, London: Pluto Press, 2002, p. 85.

10. H. Charles Godfray et al., "Food Security: The Challenge of Feeding 9 Billion People," *Science*, Vol. 327, No. 5967, 12 February 2010.

11. Ibid.

12. Asjylyn Loder and Silla Brush, "CFTC Votes 3-2 to Approve Limits on Commodity Speculation," *Bloomberg Businessweek*, 18 October 2011.

13. Ben Protess, "Wall St. Groups Sue Regulator to Challenge New Trading Rule," *New York Times DealBook*, 2 December 2011.

CONCLUSION

1. Peter Coy, "Hey, Economics Geniuses! What Happened?" *Bloomberg BusinessWeek*, 16 April 2009.

2. Edward Herman, *Triumph of the Market*, Boston, MA: South End Press, 1995.

3. Alan Blinder et al., *Asking About Prices*, New York: Russell Sage Foundation, 1998.

4. Ibid., p. 102.

5. Wilford Eiteman and Glen Guthrie, "The Shape of the Average Cost Curve," *American Economic Review*, Vol. 42, December 1952.

6. 2007 Economic Census, for last 15 years available at <http://www.census.gov/econ/concentration.html>.

7. Michael Cooper, "US Infrastructure Is in Dire Straits, Report Says," *New York Times*, 28 January 2009.

8. Ben Casselman and Justin Lahart, "Companies Shun Investment, Hoard Cash," *Wall Street Journal*, 17 September 2011.

9. Mike Dorning and Catherine Dodge, "Americans Want Government to Spend For Jobs, Send Bill to Rich," *Bloomberg*, 9 December 2009; Rich Miller, "Wall Street Fix Seen Ineffectual by Four of Five in U.S." *Bloomberg*, 13 July 2010; Aaron Bernstein, "Can This Man Save Labor?" *Businessweek*, 13 September 2004; Juliet Eilperin and Jon Cohen, "Support for federal backing of renewables slips, driven by GOP skepticism," *Washington Post*, 10 November 2011.

10. Albert Einstein, "Why Socialism?" *Monthly Review*, May 1949.

11. Available at <http://www.rasmussenreports.com/public_content/politics/general_politics/april_2009/just_53_say_capitalism_better_than_socialism>; <http://www.people-press.org/2011/12/28/little-change-in-publics-response-to-capitalism-socialism/12-28-11-2/>.

12. Available at <http://www.pewsocialtrends.org/2012/01/11/rising-share-of-americans-see-conflict-between-rich-and-poor>.
13. Steven Greenhouse, "Occupy Movement Inspires Unions to Embrace Bold Tactics," *New York Times*, 8 November 2011.
14. Don Terry, "Occupy Chicago Inspires Some South Side Groups," *New York Times*, 5 November 2011.
15. Shaila Dewan, "Presidential Candidates? Few Are the 99 Percent," *New York Times*, 28 October 2011.

Index